The $5 Dinner Mom
Cookbook

The $5 Dinner Mom Cookbook

200 RECIPES FOR QUICK, DELICIOUS, AND

NOURISHING MEALS THAT ARE EASY

ON THE BUDGET AND A SNAP TO PREPARE

ERIN CHASE

ST. MARTIN'S GRIFFIN ⚜ NEW YORK

THE $5 DINNER MOM COOKBOOK. Copyright © 2009 by Erin Chase. All rights reserved.
Printed in the United States of America. For information, address St. Martin's Press,
175 Fifth Avenue, New York, N.Y. 10010.

www.stmartins.com

Photos courtesy of the author

Book design by Jessica Shatan Heslin/Studio Shatan, Inc.

Library of Congress Cataloging-in-Publication Data

Chase, Erin (Erin E.)
    The $5 dinner mom cookbook : 200 recipes for quick, delicious, and nourishing
meals that are easy on the budget and a snap to prepare / Erin Chase. — 1st ed.
        p. cm.
    ISBN 978-0-312-60733-3
    1. Low budget cookery. 2. Consumer education—United States. I. Title. II. Title: The five
dollar dinner mom cookbook.
    TX652.C4847 2009
    641.5'52—dc22

                                                                    2009039990

First Edition: January 2010

10 9 8 7 6 5 4 3 2

To the Official $5 Dinner Taste-Test Team:
Steve, Ryan, and Charlie

CONTENTS

ACKNOWLEDGMENTS

First, I'd like to thank my family and friends for their help, inspiration, and support since the start of this grand adventure. To my dear friends, who offered to care for the boys on days when I needed some peace and quiet to work. To Grandma, for allowing the boys to attend "Camp Grandma" while I put the finishing touches on the manuscript. To my sister, for keeping me up to date on all the latest and greatest outside of the blogging- and book-writing world. To my dad, for all your practical and professional insight in helping turn my passion into a business. And to my mom, for all your advice, editorial assistance, and encouragement through each step in making this cookbook a reality.

Second, this would not have been possible if not for my blogging buddies. When I started the $5 Dinners Web site, I had no idea of its potential and what it would become. Many of my blogging buddies stepped in to offer advice, encouragement, and practical knowledge that helped the site grow to what it is today. And let's not forget the #bigdealmoms, who kept me sane, made me laugh, and got me out of the house. You are each near and dear to my heart.

I am forever grateful for my literary agent, Alison Picard, who connected me with the amazing folks at St. Martin's Press. And to my editor, Michael Flamini, for his insight, wisdom, and encouragement during each phase of the book-writing process. I appreciate the work of my entire team at St. Martin's Press for throwing themselves behind this book.

And lastly, my deepest gratitude to my wonderful, and *not at all picky eating* husband, Steve. Thank you for eating my meals and for supporting me on this wild and exciting adventure. And to my precious little boys, for being the integral part of the $5 Dinner Taste-Test Team. I'm so grateful for your love of broccoli "trees" and sweet potatoes. I love you each dearly.

INTRODUCTION

Is it really possible to feed a family of four for just $5 . . . for the entire meal? In August of 2008, I challenged myself to do just that. And not only would these meals cost $5, they would be made with the highest quality and most wholesome ingredients that I could find. To be honest, I wasn't sure how many meals I could come up with. But once I had all my strategies in place and I got into a groove, this challenge proved to be easier than I thought.

I have always been "frugal minded." In high school, I wrote a feature article for the school newspaper on where to find the cheapest lunch for those students allowed to leave campus during the lunch hour. I drove a great distance from the school just for the $3.99 all-you-can-eat Chinese buffet, barely making it back in time for the start of calculus class. I remember rushing to Fuddruckers and buying a bun for just $.37 and loading it up with lettuce, tomatoes, and pickles from the veggie bar. Lunch for $.37. Not free, but close to it! (Please note that Fuddruckers no longer offers this fine "bun for lunch" meal. We did have permission from the manager to do this, but they did change their policies. Who knows, maybe it was my article and the fact that 308 students showed up that week for a nearly free lunch that caused the policy change!)

Let's fast forward a few years into adulthood.

My young adult grocery shopping days were spent in the Dominican Republic. There were no coupons, no sales, no advertisements, and few choices at the grocery store. There were just one brand of canned tomatoes, two brands of orange juice, and maybe three brands of deli cheese to choose from. I had no need to pay attention to what I was buying or how much it cost because of the limited options. There were no chains to compete against one another in our little town, and prices were completely dependent on the American dollar. A few American brand products existed in my Dominican grocery store, but my "frugal mindedness" prevented me from spending $5 on a box of American brand granola bars or $6 on a 14-ounce box of Special K with Red Berries. I would not pay that much on a regular basis, even for my favorites. So I was left with no granola bars, generic cornflakes, and "just getting whatever I needed and wanted for groceries."

After six years in the Dominican Republic and six years of "just getting what I needed and wanted," I returned to the United States and was overwhelmed just walking into the grocery store. For months, I experienced reverse culture shock! Standing in the toothpaste aisle, with nearly a hundred choices, I was simply in shock. For six years I had just bought the one brand of toothpaste from the Dominican grocery store. *What was going on? One hundred choices.*

And then I found myself in front of the chocolate chips. *Oh boy! Are you kidding?* I had not seen chocolate chips in my grocery store in the Dominican Republic, but there I stood. Dumbfounded. Milk chocolate, mini chocolate chips, Andes mint chips, toffee chips, chunk chocolate, white chocolate, and so on. I believe I did not move for eight minutes. I stood completely overwhelmed and had *no idea* which bag to choose. I was not used to this many choices, and did not know how to respond.

The grocery store culture shock began to fade over the next year and a half, but I still found myself "just getting groceries." I would go into the store, get whatever I thought I needed and wanted, and head home to upload my loot. I would put things away, only to discover that I already had that item in my cupboard or in the fridge.

The $.37 "bun for lunch" voice in the back of my head told me I was doing something wrong. *But what? I was after all, "just getting groceries." What else was I supposed to be doing?*

I did not know . . . until I had a startling revelation in July of 2008.

Remember that summer of 2008 . . . when the gasoline prices shot through the roof and the entire nation was paying at least $4 a gallon for gas. I stood at the gas pump every two weeks or so, and pumped $70 worth of gas into my Nissan Maxima. $70! That was painful! Even more painful when I thought about my husband pumping the same amount of gas into his car every five or six days. Do the math and that's about $500 a month. We did not drive excessively and did not take road trips. This was just everyday driving around town. Something had to be done . . . or we were going to find ourselves in a heap of debt.

We had already made the decision that I would stay at home with the kids while they were little. Although this decision was best for our family and our kids, it did put a strain on our finances. My husband picked up a second job delivering pizzas a few nights a week to make ends meet during this tough time.

I vividly remember sitting down with my husband to review our budget each month that summer. We went through every item of the budget discussing what could be done, and where we could cut back. There was no changing the mortgage payment, as we were locked in at the lowest thirty-year fixed-interest rate (at the time). There was no cutting back on entertainment costs, as we did not have cable and rented free movies from the local library. And we had the simplest and cheapest of all cell phone plans. Plus, we could not lower the prices at the gas pump nor could we part with our health and mortgage insurance policies.

The one line in the budget that could be reduced was the *grocery* line. *$500. That seemed like a lot. Surely I could get that down. Surely we did not need to be spending that much money each month at the grocery store.* That's what ran through my mind as we crunched numbers and worked up a plan to keep our budget *in the black.*

During this difficult time, with the gas prices sky-high and my husband working two jobs, I took on the challenge of reducing our grocery spending. This was the only way to keep our finances healthy and stay out of debt. After one of our budget talks, it occurred to me that this would be my way of contributing to the family's income. My mission was now clear.

It became my "job" to create and execute a plan in which I spent less of my husband's hard-earned money. I considered the amount saved each week at the store to be like my earnings. That summer, I implemented a number of strategies to help me save more money at the grocery store. I found great pleasure and felt fulfilled spending less at the store, putting coupons to use, and having a plan for dinner each week.

After putting these strategies into practice for a few weeks, I shared with my husband the prices of each ingredient and the total cost for the entire meal. *Honey, I found these pork chops with a "Manager's Special" sticker for only $2.02, plus these peaches were just $.39/pound, and rice is only about $.20 a cup. Can you believe this dinner only cost $3.85?* He could not believe it, but he indulged me anyway.

Following this delicious meal, while doing the dishes and cleaning up the kitchen, I thought . . . *I wonder if I could make more meals that cost less than $5. Surely spaghetti costs less than $5, if I made my own sauce and found ground beef on sale. And I know chicken breasts have a great sale price, so chicken and rice would be easy to make under $5. Was this really possible? Could I really do it?*

My $5 Dinner Challenge brought new clarity to my mission. The way I was going to keep reducing our grocery budget was to make $5 dinners every night! As I got started, I realized that I wanted to share what I had learned and the recipes I was making with others. The Web site, $5 Dinners (www.5dollardinners.com), was born out of my passion to encourage and inspire others to do the same. And from the Web site, the cookbook was born.

In this cookbook, I will teach you about Strategic Grocery Shopping (pg. 1), Strategic Couponing (pg. 16), and Strategic Meal Planning (pg. 33). Also included are 200 recipes, complete with cost breakdowns and frugal facts. Please note these recipes are written for a family with 2 adults and 2 children, but most of the recipes will feed 4 adults. Larger families and/or families with teenagers will need to double or triple the recipes, depending on family size and the number of bottomless stomach pits at the table.

The prices associated with each ingredient are more or less standard throughout the book. Some prices may vary, especially on fresh produce, as produce prices fluctuate widely throughout the seasons. Prices are accurate and reflect the lowest sale prices that I paid for the products during the years 2008 and 2009. I live in the Midwest, where prices tend to be lower than other parts of the country. Please do not expect to find these exact prices in your stores. I will, however, teach you how to be on the lookout for rock-bottom prices on your favorite products from your grocery store.

I hope you catch on to my vision and the concept behind making $5 Dinners. Make it a priority to feed your family healthy, well-balanced meals for less! Let's get started, shall we?

The $5 Dinner Mom
Cookbook

ONE

Strategic Grocery Shopping

Here is where I'll share how I went from "just getting groceries" and spending more than $500 a month to really saving money on my groceries and spending less than $300 a month. The strategies outlined in the following chapters all play an important role in making the most out of each trip to the grocery store and, of course, they are essential to making $5 Dinners.

Before I get into the temptations and obstacles that are thrown my way every time I go to the store, I'd like to share with you what kind of shopper I used to be, and what kind of shopper I am now.

Shopper Profiles

I used to be the kind of shopper who just went to the store and did all that I could to keep the children entertained and happy. I paid little attention to what I added to the cart. I just wanted to make sure there would be enough food to last until the next week, when we'd load into the car and do it all over again. I was happy to see the sale tags on some of the products that I purchased each week, but did not seek out sale items or use coupons.

Although I wouldn't call myself an "Impulse Shopper," I certainly wasn't being smart in my grocery spending. I knew that I could do better. I wanted to become a "Savvy Shopper."

I wrote up a little quiz that will help you determine what kind of shopper you are. It's a quick ten questions that will help you think about your grocery shopping and spending habits.

"WHAT KIND OF SHOPPER ARE YOU" QUIZ

Answer the following questions to determine what kind of shopper you are:

1. When it comes to the grocery store circular, I . . .
   a. Don't know where to find it or when it comes out.
   b. Toss it out with the rest of the newspaper ads.
   c. Review it each week to see what is on sale at my grocery store.

2. In my family, the grocery budget is . . .
   a. A free-for-all. No care or attention is paid to how much is spent at the store.
   b. Loose. But I know I'm spending too much money each week.
   c. Tight. I know exactly how much I have to spend each week.

3. When I go through the grocery store, I . . .
   a. Grab what I think I need or might use and get out of there as fast as I can.
   b. Have a list, but still find myself buying eight items not found on my list, as I just can't help but grab a box of donuts and bag of chocolate.
   c. Have a list, a stack of coupons, and only get what I need each week.

4. I use coupons . . .
   a. Never. I don't have time or energy to devote to couponing.
   b. Sometimes. I use them for a few products on my grocery list.
   c. Always. I plan how I will use my coupons, and try to use them only when the product is already on sale.

5. I am willing to sacrifice quality and taste to save money.
    a. True. I simply can't afford the highest-quality items in the store.
    b. False. I would rather pay a little more for higher-quality ingredients.
    c. False. I still buy the same great quality products, but only when they are on sale.

6. The thought of taking my children with me to the grocery store makes me want to . . .
    a. Shrug. Doesn't bother me at all to bring the kids along.
    b. Pout. I wish I didn't have to take them with me, but I don't have a choice.
    c. Cringe. I would *never* take my kids with me to the grocery store. They always make me spend more money than I want to.

7. When I see a fantastic sale price for my favorite product, I . . .
    a. Don't seem to notice that it's on sale.
    b. Grab several boxes and add them to my cart.
    c. Will hunt down coupons so that I can replenish my stockpile.

8. Meal planning is something that . . .
    a. I've never heard of or thought of doing.
    b. Happens on occasion, but doesn't seem to be a consistency in my house.
    c. Occurs every week in my kitchen.

9. If I see a product on "super sale" at a grocery store where I don't typically shop, I . . .
    a. Never think to compare prices at other stores.
    b. Am glad that I have an appointment near that store later in the week, so I can stop in to buy it.
    c. Would drive out of my way just to get the great deal because I need to get more of that product.

10. The cashier hands me my receipt and says, "Thanks for shopping with us today, your total savings were . . ." What is the percentage of savings?
    a. 0%
    b. 25%
    c. 60%

Total # As _____
Total # Bs _____
Total # Cs _____

QUIZ RESULTS

If you answered mostly As, then you are an **"Impulse Shopper."**
If you answered mostly Bs, then you are a **"Decent Shopper."**
If you answered mostly Cs, then you are one **"Savvy Shopper."**

My Quiz Results: Before the summer of 2008, I would have classified myself somewhere between an "Impulse Shopper" and a "Decent Shopper." Since discovering and implementing the following strategies and learning to be more disciplined while in the store, I declare myself a "Savvy Shopper."

Temptations and Obstacles in the Grocery Store

A savvy shopper understands the temptations and obstacles within the grocery store, and comes armed and ready to fight. I had to learn about the many stumbling blocks found through the aisles of the grocery store. I had to learn to spot a real deal and a fake deal. And I had to learn the common marketing tactics that manufacturers and grocery stores use to get consumers to buy more products. Let me share an overview.

First, I want to share a little about what I call, "Sensory Overload—Grocery-Store Style." At first I misclassified this as "reverse grocery store culture shock." After so many years shopping in Dominican Republic grocery stores, I was not used to the culture of the American grocery stores. Upon re-entry into the American culture, I found myself in "reverse culture shock," both in life and when in the grocery store. My first few trips to the grocery store in the United States were overwhelming. Not just the one-hundred choices of toothpaste, but the sights and smells that floated through the air. It was almost too much for my "third-world brain" to take in.

It took me many months to realize that this sensory overload was not going anywhere. I had grown accustomed to the number of choices in the store and the reverse culture shock had worn off. But the sensory overload remained. Have you ever noticed how intense and bold the sights and smells are when you walk into the grocery store?

In the summer months, I can hear the flowers in a store's entryway shouting, *"Buy Me. No, pick me. Hey, look at my pretty petals."* And then I walk through the doors, right past the ginormous table of pies and cookies. *Geesh!* I don't know how much more of this I can take. Next, I stroll right on past the floral department, admiring what could be that week's centerpiece on my dining room table, and head through the produce department picking up bags and bags of fresh produce, only to find myself next to the bakery. I can smell it from the potatoes. It just has that powerful luring effect. The donuts and cookie cakes cry out for my attention as I speed on by. *It's tempting, it really is!*

I manage to make it to the other end of the store, only to find that the in-store homemade potato chip–making machine is in full gear, cranking out the most delicious and fresh-tasting chips known to man. Or at least known to me. Knowing that they were made right there from real potatoes somehow makes them healthier. But it's the smell that gets me every time. The smell of fresh fried potato chips . . . mmmmm.

I've had enough of these fabulous sights and smells. *I have got to get out of here before I run back for that floral centerpiece, a dozen donuts, and seven bags of homemade potato chips.* I remind myself that I only have $60 cash and I don't have enough for such luxuries. I've almost made it!

Finally, it's time to check out. Whether I just popped into the store for bananas, eggs, and milk, or I have a cart full of groceries, the final battle takes place in the checkout line. This one is the toughest for me to fight because I'm a sucker for celebrity gossip and chocolate. I'm losing the battle before I even walk into the line. *Focus. Focus. Don't read the headlines. Get your coupons ready. Do something other than stare at the chocolate bars or pick up that magazine. But come on, I just want to know what's happening with Brad and Angelina this week!* Thankfully there is no line and I don't have to stand waiting and fighting the chocolate and gossip temptations.

GROCERY STORE MARKETING STRATEGIES

Now that I've walked you through the grocery store from my vantage point, let's talk specifics as far as grocery store marketing tactics. There are some other important marketing strategies that grocery stores use to better display and market the products for sale. A major marketing strategy used by grocery stores is the endcap. The endcap is the set of shelves at the end of the aisle used to display popular items that are on sale that week. The purpose of the endcap is to allow the customer to grab the sale item while they walk down the main aisle without having to walk all the way through the middle aisles looking for the item. But I have discovered that the prices on the endcap products are not always the best price for that product. It may be on sale, but there may be other cheaper options down the aisle. The store wants you to buy the more expensive product, even if the product is technically on sale. The products on endcaps are attractive, but might not be the best bargain.

A second strategy that grocery stores utilize is strategically placing specialty items in the middle of the aisle so that customers have to walk past other commonly purchased items to find the specialty item. I will use the example of the coffee in my grocery store. The coffee is located in the middle/back of the "drink" aisle. On the way to grab a bag of coffee, customers must go past the bottled water, juices, and chocolate syrup. On the way back out of the "drink" aisle, many customers' carts will have a case or two of bottled water, a jug of fruit juice, and a bottle of chocolate syrup. Even though they intended on grabbing one bag of coffee, they ended up with water and acai berry juice to go with their chocolatey mocha for breakfast.

A third marketing tool that manufacturers utilize is the "eye-level" strategy. Companies pay a premium to get their products displayed at "eye level" so that customers will see them first and add them to their cart. The problem for the customer is that the premium that the companies pay is reflected in a higher price for the product. When looking for the better deal, look high and low for similar products that cost less.

A fourth, and very potent marketing tool for any grocery store is the "location tool." Location, location, location. What are the three most common items that people run into the store to grab? Bananas, milk, and eggs. And where are these products located? In my grocery store, they are located in three opposite corners of the store. That is not random. The purpose of this is to get customers to walk through the entire store for their three items. Inevitably, the customer will pick up two to nine other items along the way that they don't need. Think about that next time you have to run into the store for bananas, eggs, and milk.

The store did its job. It enticed me into purchasing more than I intended to. But I did my job as well. I did not fall for such temptations and I stuck to my budget and my list. With a little practice and discipline, I have learned not to succumb to these strategies. The temptations and obstacles will always be there, but as long as I remember to stick to my list, I won't come up short on change at the cash register.

Victory!

How to Get the Most for your Time and Money at the Store

So I figured out how to resist the temptations and obstacles while browsing through the aisles, but it came time for me to put my own consumer strategies into play. I needed to figure out how to get in and out of the store as fast as possible, spending the least amount of money. I needed a plan.

STORE CIRCULARS

Store circulars are released each week, letting shoppers know what is on sale in the store that week. Each store arranges their circulars in a different way, but one feature is consistent across the board for all grocery stores; the products with the best sale prices will be on the front page of the circular. These products are called "loss leaders." A loss leader is a product that is on sale at such a low price that the grocery store will take a loss on the sale. By advertising popular products for at-cost or below-cost prices, grocery stores can entice consumers to come into their store. The word "leader" in the phrase indicates that once the consumer is in the store to get the great deal, they will *be led* to purchase other groceries, which will in turn make up for the profit loss on the loss-leader product.

Prices in the store circular, and especially on loss-leader products, are often listed as follows:

1 DOZEN EGGS, 10/$10, OR 10 FOR $10

This does *not* mean that I have to purchase ten dozen eggs to get this great price of $1/dozen. This is a gimmick that stores use to encourage consumers to buy more than what they really need of products that are on sale. I would just buy one or two dozen at this price to last for a week or two. I have spoken with many consumers who assumed that ten dozen had to be purchased to "get the deal."

Loss leaders can certainly be alluring. It would take an amazing bargain to get me to drive out of my way to get a product from somewhere other than my normal grocery store. It happens on occasion, but I am sure to *only* buy that one product that drew me into the store. I will not be tempted by other deals I might spot in the other store. I am there for one reason and one reason only. That specific loss-leader product.

Once I decide which loss leaders are worth buying each week, I continue looking through the circular circling items that I need to buy for the week. I will look at the different cuts of meat that are on sale and decide if I should write a meal using that meat into my weekly meal plan, or if I should buy a few extra packages and "stock-pile" them in the freezer. Once the best deals have been marked, they are added to my grocery list.

When it comes time for matching coupons with sale prices, store circulars are crucial. After I've circled all the products that I'm *interested* in purchasing, whether because of the sale price or the need for the product, I go back through the circular to look for coupon matches. By using coupons when the product is on sale, I can maximize my savings in the store. (More on this in chapter 2.)

Another way to use the store circular is to track sale prices and keep a record of them in a price book. I like to call this list my "never-pay-more-than" list. I created this list over time, and make updates to it when necessary. I began keeping track of the prices of my favorite meat cuts and fruits and vegetables, since their sale prices can fluctuate throughout the seasons and sale cycles. Paying attention to these prices allowed me to come up with a sale price that "was worth paying." Some sale prices are just pennies or dimes below the original retail price. While this does help save here and there, it doesn't typically make a large impact in the savings percent-age. My "never-pay-more-than" list helps me keep track of my favorite products and when they go on sale for 40 to 50 percent off their original price.

Here are a few examples from my "never pay more than" list. Please note these prices are sale prices with coupon matchup, if applicable.

- Fresh strawberries, blueberries, raspberries - $1.50 a pint or quart

- Frozen vegetable bags (16 ounces) - $.88

- 10-pound bag of potatoes - $2.99

- Sweet potatoes - $.88/pound

- Canned tomatoes (15 ounces) - $.59

- Olive oil (25.5 ounces) - $5.99

- Diapers - $8.99/Jumbo pack

- Antibacterial hand soap - $.30/bottle

- Shampoo - $1/bottle

- Toothpaste - Free! By matching a $1 coupon with a $1 sale price, toothpaste can often be purchased for free.

I also add to my "never-pay-more-than" list after shopping trips. Because what is in the store circular is only about one-third of what is actually on sale in the store, I often find other great deals that I didn't know about going into the store. I will quickly jot down the price (if I don't buy it and have record on my receipt) and add it to my "never-pay-more-than" list when I get home.

By analyzing and planning my grocery trip with the store circular, I can save both time spent in the store, as well as money in my pocket. But, there are a few other essential tools I use to make it out of the store "under budget."

MAKING THE GROCERY LIST

Each week I create a shopping list. I need a list for two reasons, the first being that I will forget something that I need if it's not written down (yet, strangely my brain remembers the prices on products!). The second is that I want to buy only what *I need* for that week. My budget doesn't allow for impulses and randomly adding products to my cart. I have learned that having a list is essential for saving money at the grocery store.

I make my grocery list based on sales in the store circular, my weekly menu plan, and what I already have stored in the cupboards, refrigerator, and freezer. My list always includes milk, yogurt, eggs, apple juice, fruits, and vegetables. After those few items, the list varies week by week, depending on the sales and my menu plan.

Making a list and sticking to it will also prevent those quick trips into the grocery store for a single ingredient that inevitably turns into a mini shopping spree. Occasionally I will come up short an ingredient, but I like to think of it as "part of the fun." It gives me an opportunity to be creative with ingredient substitutions while cooking.

If I don't have taco seasoning mix, I can substitute it with spices like ground cumin, chili powder, garlic powder, and onion powder. I often find myself out of butter on a night when I'm making mashed potatoes. I have discovered that olive oil is a lovely, and healthier, substitute for the butter. When I'm out of BBQ sauce or Sloppy Joe sauce, I can make my own using ketchup or tomato sauce, mustard, brown sugar, and a few spices. By utilizing what I already have on hand, I can save myself those few extra dollars each time I "need" to run back to the store for just one ingredient.

CASH AND A CALCULATOR

The question remains . . . how do I actually stay within my budget? What practical tools do I use to accomplish this task? I've got my grocery list and my stack of coupons, but there are two items that help me stay accountable to my budget each week.

1. A calculator

2. Cash

Yep, that's right. I carry a calculator and cash only. No "plastic" allowed in the grocery store. I used to be able to keep a running total in my head as I went through the store, but I have found that a calculator is much more effective and less stressful. Because I have a finite amount of money in my pocket, I can't go over budget. I have to keep track of how much I will be spending. My state does not have a sales tax on food, so I typically can run right up to my total budget without worrying about going over because of sales tax.

I even did a little plastic-versus-cash experiment. My credit card offered five times the "points" for purchases made at the grocery store. I thought, *What if I make use of my credit card to buy a $300 gift card to my grocery store to use each month? That way I have a "finite" amount of money to spend at the store, plus I got five times the "points" on my credit card.*

I tried this method for two months. I did not go over budget and spend more than my gift card during either month. But I did find that my "plastic" mentality still existed each week. *Well, I could just get a few more things and just spend less next week.* Or, *I really should get an extra bag of flour, even though it's not on my list, because I know we'll need it. It's okay if I go over my $60 for this week.*

That plastic mentality left me with just $25 to spend the last week of the month, during both months. That really wasn't enough, but I was left to plan meals based on what I had on hand from previous shopping trips. It left little room for "stockpiling" sale items those weeks because I had not been disciplined enough in previous weeks.

After my experiment, I settled on cash and a calculator. I could *not* show up at the cashier with $82 worth of products and only $60 in my pocket. Using cash forced me to be disciplined in my spending and challenged me to be more creative with my meal plans.

Now, when I go to the grocery store, I carry only what will fit in my pockets plus my coupon binder. I typically have my list with the coupons that I already pulled out, a pencil, my cash, and my car keys with the store loyalty card. Oh, and my trusty little calculator. (Wouldn't my calculus teacher be proud!)

PRODUCT MARKDOWNS

I have asked at one time or another every department manager about product markdowns. Dairy, meat, produce, deli, bakery . . . they all know me! And no, they don't run and hide when they see me coming. I like to ask about product markdowns.

- Is there a certain day of the week that your department marks down products for quicker sale?

- Is there a time of the day that is better for getting the best selection of marked down products?

- Where can I find marked down products? Is there a specific location in the department to find these markdowns?

My store has this bright red sticker that says, MANAGER'S SPECIAL. This sticker is added to products that are marked down so they can be sold before they "expire." The stickers are also used on products that have not sold fast enough in the store.

I have found these stickers on everything from baking powder to milk to bags of snap peas and coleslaw. I find them regularly on bakery items and fresh meat products. My grocery store even has a section in the meat department devoted to the packages that have been marked down, as well as a shelf at the back of the store with markdowns on non-perishable items. I scan through the marked down products to see if there is anything I can squeeze into my budget. If I have coupons in my binder for these products, it's a double bonus.

Another product to look for with markdown stickers is milk. *Seriously?* Yes, seriously. I have seen half gallons of milk priced as low as $.25. Milk can be found on markdown and used up right away. It can be used to make homemade yogurt, a large batch of homemade waffles for the freezer, a pot of creamy soup, or homemade basic white sauce.

When looking for markdowns, I always check the quality of the product, as well as the original price. Occasionally markdown prices are just dimes less than the original retail price. Although every penny counts, it's sometimes not worth purchasing if I know I can't use or freeze the product right away, or if it will push me over my weekly budget.

ANATOMY OF THE SHELF TAG—UNIT PRICING AND SALE DATES

Paying close attention to prices is essential to saving money. When making bulk purchases and buying products that I know we will use up quickly, I carefully check the unit prices on the different-size containers or bags of the same product. The shelf tag typically lists a unit price, per ounce or per individual item, depending on the product. I like to buy "in bulk" products like laundry detergent, dish soap, dishwasher soap, bags of rice and pasta, as well as certain condiments, and olive oil. I always choose the size with the lowest unit price, which is typically the largest package for that product. I am careful to check the unit prices on sale items, because sometimes a medium-size package that is on sale is much cheaper than the larger "bulk" package. Checking unit prices helps me stretch my dollars as far as possible.

My grocery store also has a "sale expire" feature listed on the sale tag. Not only is the sale tag brightly colored and flashy, it also lists how long the product will be on sale. There is a "sale expires" date on the sale tag. This comes in handy on weeks when I just don't think I can squeeze that particular product in and stay under budget. Knowing that the product will be on sale for another two weeks, I can add it to next week's list without stressing that I "missed a good deal" on a great product. I know of two other grocery stores in my area that have sale dates on their tags. I suggest asking the customer service desk if your store has a similar feature.

MULTIPLE STORE SHOPPING

Like I mentioned before, I typically don't shop at more than one grocery store in the same week for one reason: proximity. I live very close to the grocery store in my neighborhood and all the other grocery stores are at least 15 minutes away. There is a shopping center about fifteen minutes away from my house that has four (yes, four!) grocery stores all in a row. That is a bargain shopper's dream. To be honest, I'm a little jealous of my friends who live close to this grocery store "central."

But would I really save money by going into more than one store each week? Knowing myself and my propensity to stick to my grocery list, yes, it would be worth going into more than one store. If you are not inclined to stick to your list, then shopping at multiple stores might not be such a great money-saving strategy.

Let me share a practical real life scenario using this shopping center with four grocery stores in my town. The center includes two regular grocery stores, one discount grocery store, and a "big box" grocery store. A discount grocery store is defined as a store that sells only generic or store brand products. A "big box" grocery store sells both groceries and all types of other household goods, clothing, and toys.

Here is a potential weekly shopping list and sale prices for each store.

Store A
2 acorn squash ($.69)
4 pounds bananas ($.25/lb.)
1 watermelon ($2.50)
4 canned tomatoes ($.59 each)

Store B
Peaches ($1.48 for 2 pounds)
3 half-gallons milk ($.75 each)
2 loaves bread ($1.25 each after coupon)
BBQ sauce (free after coupon)
5 yogurts ($.33 each)

Store C
Sweet potatoes ($.49/lb.)
4 packages (about 6 pounds) boneless, skinless chicken breast ($1.66/lb.)
One 6-ounce package deli meat ($1.50 after coupon)
4 Rice Krispies cereal ($1/box after coupon)

Store D
2 packages (about 3 pounds) ground chuck ($1.79/lb.)
4 broccoli ($.88/bunch)
12-ounce sour cream (free after coupon)
4 bags shredded cheese ($1.50 each)

Total Spent at all 4 stores: **$44.97**

This is a typical grocery list for me. A few of the items are "stockpile" items like the cereal, chicken breasts, ground chuck, broccoli, shredded cheese, and canned tomatoes. I will stash them away in the freezer or cupboard for use in future meals. I will also use other items that I purchased in previous weeks when making meals that week.

Because these stores are so close together, and because I would not be shopping with my children, I can run in and out quickly, getting just the few items from each store. If I had simply gone to my regular grocery store for the same items, I might have spent $15 to 20 more for this exact same list, as not all the products would be on sale.

For now, I will stick with my strategies at my neighborhood grocery store and save myself the 30 minutes driving time, as well as gas mileage . . . and dream of other grocery stores moving into my area.

DECIDING ON A WEEKLY GROCERY BUDGET

When coming up with an amount of money for the grocery budget, I encourage others to track spending for a few weeks, or even months. Then apply several of the strategies discussed here to see how much you can lower your grocery bill. With a little practice and tracking the savings, a "doable figure" for the weekly grocery budget will become evident.

When I first started on this journey to saving money at the grocery store, I averaged about $125 to 150 a week. Once I started paying closer attention and put these strategies into play, my grocery bill came down every week. After a few weeks, I noticed that my weekly total at the grocery store averaged around $60. Some weeks I spent a little more than $60, and other weeks I spent less. That figure became my weekly spending goal.

I have made exceptions to this figure, depending on life's seasons. For example, during the first trimester of my third pregnancy, I raised my weekly goal to $80. And for two or three weeks, I spent $100 for the week's worth of groceries. It was all I could do to simply get myself through the store, thanks to the fatigue and nausea. Couponing and bargain shopping were put on hold, until I came through that short season. After a few weeks of giving myself a break, I was back to my $60 a week budget. Exceptions must be made during times like these.

So what happened to that $65 to $80 a week savings? For the first few months, that savings was simply keeping our budget in the black, as the gasoline prices were still sky-high. But as the gasoline prices came back down and we weren't spending $500 a month to get around town, we began allocating the savings to a vacation fund and to college funds for the kids. Knowing that we could go on vacation with a little extra breathing room was motivation enough for me to keep on saving and keep on with my savvy shopping. Whether our monthly budget is tight or not, I will continue to put these strategies to good use and stash away the money saved at the grocery store into a college fund, trust fund, or vacation savings account.

By utilizing these strategies while in the grocery store and by overcoming the many temptations and obstacles found throughout the store, I now stay comfortably within my grocery budget each week.

There are many other strategies that come into play that help me save money at the store. The next set to be discussed is the couponing strategies. Get your scissors ready, because it's time to start clipping!

TWO

Strategic Couponing

At the start of this adventure making $5 Dinners every night, I knew what coupons were and I knew that they came every Sunday in the newspaper. And that's about it. Since then, I've learned just how useful and powerful coupons really are. I quickly discovered that making dinner for my family for $5 or less and maintaining my weekly grocery budget would *not* be possible without the strategic use of coupons.

The Truth about Coupons

The basic truth is that coupons are money. A coupon is a little piece of paper with a dollar amount that will be removed from my receipt if I buy the product listed on the coupon. The more coupons I use, the more money I save.

If I were to say the word "coupon" to ten random people, I would likely get ten different responses, including the following:

"Too much work."

"I really don't understand how to use them properly."

"Too difficult to manage and keep track of."

"I never see coupons for the products I like."

"You really can't save that much money."

"I thought those were only for poor people."

I'll get to these common misconceptions in a minute. First, I want to share the truth about coupons.

Coupons are the equivalent to "free money." Coupons are issued by manufacturers and stores in the hopes that consumers will buy their product because they won't have to pay full price. Manufacturers and companies know that the common consumer and grocery shopper will more likely buy their product over a competitor's product if the consumer will spend less money by buying their product because they have a coupon.

As a smart and savvy consumer, I don't want to simply buy a product just because I have a coupon and I'll save $1. I want to be the shopper who will use my coupons as effectively as I can, and not just using them to use them on products that I don't need or want. I don't want to save just one dollar. I want to save hundreds of dollars!

COMMON COUPON MISCONCEPTIONS

I need to be honest. I had misconceptions about coupons at some point in the past, the same misconceptions listed above. But I have come full circle now and want to share why those thoughts really were misconceptions.

"Too much work."

Yes, coupons do require work. Clipping, organizing, and finding coupons requires time, energy, and focus. But once I realized that it was my "job" to spend less of my husband's hard-earned money, it was less "trouble." I looked at the amount of money that I saved as my payment to the family. Couponing expert Stephanie Nelson, author of *The Coupon Mom's Guide to Cutting Your Grocery Bill in Half,* says, "It's possible to save $50 to $100 a week with coupons by spending only 1 hour a week planning your shopping list of deals and cutting out coupons you need. That's a great hourly wage!"

"I really don't understand how to use them properly."

In the beginning of my adventure, I did not understand that the savings potential from coupons because I did not know how to use them. One very common myth about coupons is that you can only get one of that product with one coupon. For example, if I have two coupons for a loaf of bread, then only one coupon can be used to buy one loaf of bread. The truth is that two coupons can be used to buy two loaves of bread. The "limit one coupon per purchase" wording found on most coupons is misleading. The "per purchase" phrase indicates "per item." It is not possible to use two coupons for one product. If a coupon states "limit one coupon per customer," then only one coupon can be used with each purchase.

"I never see coupons for the products I like."

Do you use toothpaste, deodorant, or soap? Stephanie Nelson states, "Over half of coupons available are for nonfood items that everyone uses, like toothpaste, bath tissue, shampoo, soap, and cleaning products. Start by using coupons for basic items and start watching for more coupons you'd use after you have the coupon system down." Of course, if you are brand specific, finding coupons for your specific product might be difficult. I find that most major toothpaste, deodorant, and soap manufacturers distribute coupons on a regular basis, allowing brand-specific customers to find coupons for their favorite products.

"Too difficult to manage and keep track of."

Initially, the task of managing and organizing coupons seemed daunting, but once I figured out the system that worked for me, the savings grew exponentially—

"You really can't save that much money."

This statement is true if shoppers don't use their coupons to their fullest potential. Simply using a coupon for a product when you need it will save a few dollars here and there. Intentionally using coupons only when products are on sale and stockpiling products is where the real savings occurs.

"I thought those were only for poor people."

Guilty. This thought has flashed across my mind on occasion. *Blush!* But upon seeing in real life the potential to save real money, I realized that smart people use coupons. Annual income really has nothing to do with coupons. Coupons are coupons, and they can be used by all. Stephanie Nelson agrees, "Coupons are for the smart ones!"

FINDING COUPONS

Now that the air has been cleared about the truths and myths of couponing, it's time to look at where coupons can be found. The most common place to find coupons is the Sunday paper. Coupons come out in every Sunday paper, with the exception of holiday weekends. Coupon inserts are planned out months ahead of time and can even be previewed online. The number of coupon inserts that are released in the newspaper varies each week, ranging from just one insert to as many as five inserts. Depending on your local newspaper, coupon inserts can only be found in the papers that are delivered to homes. Certain newspapers do not put coupon inserts and store advertisements onto newsstands in gas stations and other locations. Home delivery is the easiest option for most people who clip coupons.

Another great resource for coupons is magazines. A wide range of magazines will stash coupons among their pages. The coupons in the magazines typically target the magazine's audience. Although I don't go seeking out coupons in magazines, I do know they are there and will clip them if I come across them.

My grocery store sends me "store" coupons in the mail that I can use only in their store. Their database formulates a personal set of coupons for me based on the products that I have purchased using my store loyalty card. The great part about these coupons is that nearly all of them are for products that I purchase on a regular basis. Other grocery stores offer coupons that can be printed from their Web sites. These store coupons can be for both store-brand and name-brand products. I encourage shoppers to stop at their store's customer service desks and ask if their store offers such options.

Coupons can be printed from many corners of the Internet these days. The number of online printable coupon sites has more than quadrupled in recent years. Technology, the decline in the economy, and the new mentality that couponing is "cool" have each contributed in the rise of Internet printable coupons. Today there are coupon databases where you can search for specific products and find a direct link to a coupon on a coupon Web site or on a manufacturer's Web site. There are coupon Web sites with lists of a hundred or more coupons that can be printed with just two clicks of the mouse. Most coupon Web sites allow shoppers to print two of the same coupon. (See Appendix B for complete list of online resources.)

Another resource for coupons is the company itself. I have signed up for the company mailings and e-mail newsletters for my favorite products. In most of the mailings and e-mails, the company includes a coupon as a way of saying thank you for being a loyal consumer of their products. I have also written directly to companies asking if they offer coupons by mail or e-mail. When the boys started drinking rice milk, I wrote to a rice milk company asking if they offered coupons for their rice milk because I could not find any coupons online or in the newspaper. They promptly sent me a response with several coupons included.

Several different companies are now offering electronic coupons, or "e-coupons," for those consumers who don't want to clip and organize paper coupons. E-coupons are coupons that can be loaded from a computer onto a store loyalty card. The loyalty card holds onto the e-coupon and then takes the coupon amount off of the receipt when that product is purchased.

I load my store loyalty card each week with the available coupons, and then I print out the list of the electronic coupons that I added to my card. When I am at the store, I can reference my e-coupon list. When it comes time to check out, I give the cashier my store loyalty card. The e-coupon amount is automatically deducted from my card and credited as a coupon on my receipt. Because e-coupons are considered manufacturers coupons, they are not to be used in conjunction with paper coupons from the newspaper, Internet, or other places.

So I've now got an ever-growing pile of coupons from the newspaper and the Internet, plus e-coupons loaded onto my store loyalty card . . . how do I keep them all organized so that I can use them most effectively?

ORGANIZING COUPONS

I find the most challenging part of couponing is keeping the coupons organized in such a way that I can find them quickly when I need them. I don't mind clipping them and using them, but that oh-so-important middle step has been the most difficult part for me to maintain. Because I don't always use coupons right away after clipping them, the older coupons tend to get lost behind the newer coupons. I have tried several systems to keep track of my coupons. And I'll tell you my favorite method after I share them all with you!

When I first started clipping coupons, I would file them into a small accordion-style file folder. I had several different categories and found it easy to divide the coupons up based on their category. This was the simplest way to keep the coupons organized. But, I had trouble finding the coupons that I needed, as I had to shuffle through the entire stack of "cleaning/household products" coupons to find the two coupons that I was looking for to use that week during the cleaning supply sale. This system was discrete, as my file folder fit into my purse and was hardly noticeable in my shopping cart.

After several months of using the small accordion file folder, I heard about another method for effectively managing coupons. One afternoon as I was rummaging through my coupon stacks I thought, I really should try out this "insert filing" method. The idea is to file whole coupon inserts from the newspaper in an orderly fashion in a file box. Inserts are dated and filed in order by date in which newspaper they were released. Many online resources and blogs will tell you in which newspaper insert the coupons came out. So if I needed six specific coupons for a particular trip to the store, then I would go through my whole coupon inserts, find the dated insert in which the coupon was released, and clip just the coupon that I needed. Stephanie Nelson endorses this system because "grocery deals Web sites and blogs make it easy to use coupons by referencing the date the required coupons came out, so all shoppers have to do is date their circulars and cut out the coupons they need when they need them." I can see how this would save time for some people, but it just wasn't working for me. I tried the insert filing method for about six weeks, before returning to my accordion file folder.

I seemed to manage the file folder quite well after that. Until I saw, in person, a fully stocked and functioning "coupon binder." I was visiting a friend who used a coupon binder. I sat in awe as I flipped through it. My type-A brain wanted to jump out of my skull! I had heard how wonderful these coupon binders were, how easy they were to maintain, and how easy they were to use. But I had yet to see one in real life. I was sold instantly. When I returned home, I rushed to the store to get a binder, some baseball card inserts, and page protector inserts. I was set. It took me just thirty minutes to get the binder set up and to get my coupons moved into the pages and organized by type and category.

The coupon binder allows for much greater flexibility in arranging coupons by category. I was not limited to just ten categories, like I was with my accordion file folder. I added tabs to each section and created a list of categories that I taped to the front page in the binder. My coupons are categorized as follows: organic coupons, dairy coupons, produce coupons, meat coupons, cereal coupons, snack coupons, toiletry coupons, paper products, cleaning supplies, etc. When it comes time to find my coupons, I simply flip the tab to the correct category and look on that page for the coupon I need. If I am in the store and I see a favorite product that is on sale and was not advertised in the store circular, I can quickly flip through my binder and find the coupon.

Have you figured out which method is my favorite? I love my coupon binder, and will likely stick with it for many years to come. The other systems work for others and even worked for me at one point, but now I love my coupon binder.

Now I've got all my coupons organized and ready for use, but I did have to learn the details and the "fine print" that can be found on coupons.

THE FINE PRINT OF COUPONS

The one thing I've learned about coupons is that you must read the fine print. Each time I walk up to the cash register with a stack of coupons, I hope that not one of them will "beep." This beep is the system's way of telling the cashier, "Hey, this coupon cannot be used. The wrong product or number of products was purchased." By understanding the fine print on each coupon, I avoid such embarrassing moments.

There are many types of coupons in circulation, but I wanted to summarize some of the more common coupon types based on certain phrases found on the coupon.

"$1 off any brand X"
Tip: Look for the least expensive of brand X to match with the coupon.

"$1 off when you buy 2 of product X"
Tip: Because you have to buy 2 of the same product, use this coupon only when the product is on sale to maximize savings.

"$1 off when you buy any product X of Y size or larger"
Tip: Pay attention to the sizes indicated to avoid the coupon being denied.

"$1 off when you buy 1 of product X, product Y, or product Z, including product sizes"
Tip: These coupons are typically for very specific products, so be sure to check the bar codes if in doubt.

"Buy One Get One Free coupon or Buy product X, get another product X or product Y free"
Tip: Some grocery and drugstores will allow customers to use a Buy One Get One free coupon with a Buy One Get One free sale or promotion. Products can be purchased for free in this situation.

"Free Product when you buy product X"
Tip: Don't forget to grab the product X (Not that I speak from experience, or anything!).

"Get $5 off when you buy brand X and product Y"
Tip: To get the most from this coupon, buy the least expensive of brand X and the smallest of product Y.

Because manufacturers need to make a profit on their products, they often put a picture of their most expensive product on the coupon, but the coupon states "$1.50 off *any* box of X." Stephanie Nelson reminds consumers that "coupons are interpreted based on their wording, not just the picture. So even if the coupon pictures the most expensive variety of toothpaste, if the wording says "any variety" that means you'd be smart to use the coupon on the smallest or least expensive variety to pay the lowest cost. You might even get the product free."

If I am unsure of whether I can use a coupon for a specific product, I will look at the product's bar code on the shelf tag and compare it with the bar code on the coupon. If the coupon is for a line of products, just a few of the numbers will match up. If the coupon is for a very specific product and size of that product, then the bar codes will be identical.

Some coupons have fine print that reads "redeem only by purchasing the brand sizes indicated," and other coupons will state which specific products and sizes can be purchased with that coupon. Another phrase commonly found on coupons is "consumer pays any sales tax." The consumer is responsible for paying the sales tax on the price of the product before the coupon discount. Plan accordingly if you use the cash only system when shopping.

COUPON ETIQUETTE

A common practice among active couponers is stockpiling products when they are on sale, so they don't have to pay full price in between sale cycles. (I promise, we'll get to stockpiling soon.) When products go on sale for a price that's more than 50 percent less than their normal price, there is great temptation to "clear the shelves" in the store and fill up the shelves in your house. I have heard many stories of frustrated customers heading out to the store to snag a great deal, only to find that the shelves have been cleared and the next shipment doesn't come in for three days.

Coupon etiquette frowns on "shelf clearing." *I know, I can't believe it either. Who would do that? Seriously people, it's a good deal and all, but don't be rude to the customers coming in after you.* Sadly, it happens on a regular basis. Yes, it is a pet peeve, and no, I am not a "shelf clearer."

Another person I always consider when I've got a stack of coupons is the person behind me in the checkout line. Every third time I'm checking out with my groceries, I get "the evil eye." It does take an extra minute or three for the cashier to scan and check over all the coupons. Not really long enough to deserve the "evil eye," but some people are in such a hurry these days. I typically will look back, smile and say, "Thanks for your patience. I really saved a lot of money this trip thanks to my coupons." This usually leads to a smile and question about how I do it. I prefer to turn these moments into teaching opportunities rather than having the "evil eyes" glaring at the back of my head as I roll my cart full of groceries away. Not in the mood for talking with "evil eyes," simply ignore them. Stephanie Nelson assures that "they're probably just jealous that your stack of coupons just took $100 off your grocery bill."

And let's not forget the cashier. There are several things that I do when I check out to make the process smooth and easy for the cashier. If I have a "free item" coupon, I will place that item with the coupon on top at the very front or back of my groceries on the conveyor belt. This way the cashier can quickly reference the price and write the price onto the coupon, as that type of coupon requires a price written on it for the store to redeem it from the manufacturer. I also kindly let the cashier know that I have a stack of coupons for my groceries. Typically, cashiers are impressed with the amount of savings and will ask for tips or tricks on how I make it all work. I also prefer the cashiers that are encouraging and avoid those who are less enthusiastic about coupons. Having the cashier smile about my coupon stack, as opposed to frown at me, makes the whole experience more pleasant for everyone.

I simply follow the golden rule, "Treat others as you wish to be treated." I won't frown at your coupon use, give you the "evil eye," or clear the shelves, if you won't do the same.

I do my best to be courteous in my couponing, but what happens if I run into trouble trying to use coupons at the store. *Beep!* I rarely have trouble with coupons "beeping" or getting rejected because I know the terms and "fine print" on the coupons. And also, because I know my store's coupon policies.

UNDERSTANDING STORE COUPON POLICIES

A difficult part about using coupons effectively at multiple stores is understanding (and remembering) the different coupon policies for each store. Most, if not all grocery stores, accept paper coupons, Internet printable coupons, and coupons direct from the manufacturer. Some grocery stores accept electronic coupons (e-coupons). (At the time of this writing, the e-coupon companies are expanding their reach into new markets and new stores every quarter.)

Some grocery stores will double, and even triple, the value on the face of the coupon. Doubling and tripling policies vary by store and region. My grocery store doubles coupons with a value less than $.99, up to a maximum of $1. This means that a $.40 coupon, doubles to $.80; a $.50 coupon, doubles to $1; and a $.75 coupon, doubles to $1. Coupons with a value of more than $1 will be redeemed at their face value. That is my store's doubling policy.

Stores that normally just double coupons might offer a week or weekend of triple coupon days. Typically, coupons up to $.50, and even $1, will be tripled in value. It's during these triple coupon days that many products can be "bought" for free.

Some stores allow "stacking" of store-issued coupons with manufacturer's coupons. Stacking means that both coupons issued by the store and the manufacturer may be used for the same single product. For example, I have printed off coupons for Annie's All Naturals snacks from the Target Coupon Generator. I used the Target coupons with a coupon that I had from the manufacturer to get the best and lowest price possible. Using the Target store coupon and the manufacturer's coupon, I only spent $.29 on the box of crackers. Not a bad price for a box of crackers that normally costs $2.79. Stephanie Nelson reveals this same stacking system works at Walgreens drugstores, "If you have a $1 store coupon off Colgate toothpaste from the Walgreens weekly circular and you also have a $1 Colgate toothpaste coupon from the newspaper, you can use both coupons together to get $2 off the toothpaste." If the toothpaste at Walgreens is on sale for $2, then using both coupons would allow me to get the toothpaste for free. Again, it is important to know and understand how to use coupons in the different stores.

Buy One Get One Free coupons (abbreviated BOGO) used to be a mystery to me. I understood that you buy one product you can get another free. What I did not understand was how to use them to get the most out of the coupon. Most drugstores and several grocery store chains allow BOGO coupons for products that are on sale for BOGO. Doing the math, a BOGO coupon plus a BOGO sale=2 free products. This type of BOGO deal happens only on occasion, as the manufacturers are careful when to release BOGO coupons and stores are cautious about BOGO sales when coupons are in circulation.

What happens when a store runs a great deal and hundreds of customers flock to buy that particular product and the store runs out of inventory before the end of the sale week? Most stores offer rain checks for items that are on sale and out of stock. A rain check is a slip of paper that is given by the customer service desk with the name and sale price of the item. The rain check can be redeemed at any time in the future to purchase that particular product for the specified price. I have used rain checks on occasion for some of our favorite products. I found myself in one particular situation where I had a coupon match for a particular item and the coupon was set to expire during the sale period for that item. Because I would not be back to the store until the next week to redeem my rain check, I asked the customer service if they would override my expired coupon, since I intended to use it before it expired.

They agreed and made the override for that particular coupon. Politely ask customer service what the options are if you find yourself in a similar situation. On occasion, the advertisement will specify "no rain checks" for products for which the store will not give out rain checks.

Some stores will accept competitor's coupons. I always ask the customer service desk at the grocery store what their specific policies are for each of the different possibilities listed above.

Because I typically know exactly how much money I plan to spend at the store and because I have only $60 in my pocket to spend, being overcharged for an item might push me over my budget. Many grocery store chains have a policy stating that if the customer is charged the incorrect price for the product, then they will be refunded the full value of the product. If I don't watch the prices ring up on the register, then I scan my receipt to make sure there were no errors and that I was not overcharged for an item.

I personally have not had any bad experiences with using coupons, but know many who have. If you come across a cashier who is rude about coupons, or who insists that the store will not take the coupons, please ask to speak to a manager right away. I encourage everyone to carry a copy of the store's corporate coupon policy from their Web site and show it to the cashier and/or manager, if there has been trouble using coupons in their store in the past. If they still will not accept the coupons, feel free to contact the corporate offices to let them know of the experience. Those would be the steps I would take if that were to happen to me personally.

Once I fully understood my store's coupon policy and got to know the policies of the other grocery stores in my area, I was ready to start stockpiling my favorite products.

THE DRUGSTORE GAME

Another way I have cut down on my grocery bill is by applying these same couponing principles at the national drugstore chains. Each store offers a different type of rebate or in-store coupon program that allows shoppers to maximize savings on both food and toiletry items. Combining sales with coupons and rebates allows me to get many toiletry products at the lowest possible price. Because I can get these products for less at the drugstores, I can save that money that I would have spent at the grocery store.

The Art of Stockpiling

Stockpiling is indeed an art. After watching sale cycle trends and coupon trends, experts began to notice a distinct pattern. On average, most products sales cycles run on a twelve-week basis. The sale price might be slightly different every twelve weeks, but the product is still available for a reduced price.

The basic idea of stockpiling is to purchase several bottles or boxes of the same product when it is on sale and can be matched with a coupon, so I have enough of the product to last until it goes back on sale in twelve weeks. By matching the coupon with the sale price, the product can be purchased at its lowest possible price. The key to stockpiling, and therefore saving the most money, is to wait to use your coupons until the product is on sale. Like I mentioned before, manufacturers want consumers to use coupons right away or simply when they need the product. The *challenge* lies in holding onto coupons and matching them with sale prices to then purchase the product at its very lowest price.

I used to clip coupons and use them when I needed a product, not paying attention to when the product was on sale. I didn't realize how much money I was losing, or simply not saving. It had not yet occurred to me that I should buy more than 1 product at a time and stockpile my favorite products. Remember, the purpose of stockpiling is to buy enough of the product when it is on sale and matched with a coupon to last until the next sale (which will most likely occur in twelve weeks).

Here are several real-life examples of different products and the potential savings when stockpiling is put into practice.

For example, when my favorite natural cereal bars went on sale for $2.50 a box, I used five $1.50 coupons that I had received directly from the company to buy the boxes for just $1 each. That's a 75 percent savings from the original price of $3.99/box. We ate these as special snacks and I printed more $1 coupons for the cereal bars during the "in-between sales cycle" period, and used the $1 coupons the next time the cereal bars went on sale.

In the summer of 2009, over thirty coupons were released for popular grilling products and condiments. One of the coupons was for $1 off a bottle of BBQ sauce. I printed two of these BBQ sauce coupons. The company re-released the same coupons a few weeks later, and I was able to print two more coupons. I knew that this same BBQ sauce was on sale for $1 at my grocery store. By using the $1 off coupon with the $1 sale price, I was able to get four free BBQ sauce bottles. That was enough to last the summer grilling season.

Another product that I have found easy to stockpile is cereal. Boxes of cereal can cost upwards of $4. My "never-pay-more-than" price when buying cereal is $1 per box. Typical sale price for our favorite non-sugary cereals is around $2, and just like other products, these prices come around every twelve weeks. I'm always on the lookout for the best cereal coupons for these cereals. Sometimes they come out in the newspaper, but often I find them on the Internet. When these cereal boxes go on sale for $2 and I use a coupon that doubles to $1, then I can get the cereal for $1 per box. I can print two of each coupon, and will get two boxes of cereal. Occasionally, manufacturers will release multiple coupons for different lines or brands of cereal. When this happens, I can sometimes get ten to fifteen boxes of cereal at once. I'd much rather pay a total of $15 for fifteen boxes of cereal, than $60 for those same fifteen boxes. It was scenarios such as these that opened my eyes to the potential savings when using coupons.

Sometimes with coupon matching, I just get lucky. This was the case for brand-name mustard. I used to think it was a better deal to purchase the generic or store brand. I wasn't convinced that name brands were actually the better deal. Until I happened upon this mustard deal and learned the truth firsthand. One week I came across an Internet printable coupon for $.50 off name-brand mustard. I printed two coupons. That same week I was in the grocery store and happened to notice the sale tag of that same name-brand mustard said $1. *Oh lucky day!* The two coupons I had printed were at the front of my binder, ready to be used. Because my store doubled coupons, I was able to get two free bottles of brand-name mustard. Several months later when it was time for the mustard to go on sale again, the sale price was 4/$5 (or $1.25 a bottle.) The coupons that were available at the time were $.40, or $.80 when doubled. I did buy two more bottles of mustard, but this time they were not free. I paid $.45 a bottle. Still better than the store-brand price, but not quite free! I knew that $.45 was the best price for the mustard, so I bought these two bottles to keep my stockpile from dwindling, and to keep my husband's sandwiches happy. This is a perfect real-life example of the differences in sale prices, coupons, and how shoppers might not always be able to get items for free. I'm thankful to have paid attention to the prices and coupons, as I only had to pay $.90 for four bottles of mustard that would last nine to twelve months. I'd much rather pay $.90 and add them to my pantry than $2.49 per bottle "when we ran out" and needed more. Four bottles of name-brand mustard at regular price would have cost me $9.96, but I only paid $.90, for a total savings of 90 percent.

Another product I have not paid for since starting on this adventure is toothpaste. Just about every other week, a new coupon for toothpaste is released in the newspaper inserts. We are not "brand particular," but I do prefer paste over gel. I found that the different brands of toothpaste are on different sale cycles. It seemed that every four weeks, one of the major brands of toothpaste would go on sale for $1, either at the grocery store or at one of the drugstores. Because I had cut every toothpaste coupon that I came across in the newspaper, I was always ready when toothpaste went on sale for $1. Match a $1 coupon with a $1 sale price, and the toothpaste was free.

Many grocery stores will offer "store promotions" for a product line. For example, buy ten of these participating products and get $5 off your total grocery bill that day. This translates to another $.50 in savings on each of the ten products in the promotion. My personal favorite store promotion is the cleaning supply promotion. (I have not made my own cleaning supplies at this point in my adventure, although I would like to try someday!) Every several months my grocery store offers this promotion I mentioned above for a line of cleaning products, including laundry detergent and paper products. When the store offers this promotion, the products are marked down to a sale price and shoppers can get the additional $.50 off each product. To really take advantage of this sale, I would also match up coupons for the specific products that I needed. I set out to buy only ten products from the promotion, use coupons for each product, and get the $5 off store promotion. This is a "triple whammy"—on sale, matching coupon, plus store promotion discount.

Here are four examples of what I purchased during this store promotion:

PRODUCT	ORIGINAL PRICE	SALE PRICE	COUPON	FINAL PRICE
Bleach Bottle	$1.49	$1	$.50 doubled + $.50 discount	−$.50
Kitchen Cleaner	$2.49	$1.99	$.50 doubled + $.50 discount	$.49
Laundry Detergent	$10.99	$8.99	$1 + $.50 discount	$7.49
Toilet Bowl Cleaner	$2.99	$1.99	$.50 doubled + $.50 discount	$.49
Totals	$17.96			$7.97

This store promotion allowed me to get expensive laundry detergent for a great price, and several other cleaning products for less than $.50 each. This is the power of the "triple whammy."

STOCKPILING FRESH MEATS

The first thing that I look for each week when I scan through the grocery circulars is the best prices on meats. Because fresh meats are typically the most expensive part of a $5 Dinner, I am always on the lookout for the very best prices on our favorite meat products. Just as other products in the store, meat sales cycle about every twelve weeks. I find that I save the most money by stockpiling my favorite meat cuts when they are on sale. Does this mean that we eat eight packages of ground beef in one week? No. I fill my freezer with meat when it's on sale. I have tracked these prices for months and will share the best sale prices for my grocery store for ten different cuts of meat.

MEAT CUT	SALE PRICE
Boneless, Skinless Chicken Breast	$1.77/pound
Bone-in Split Chicken Breast	$1.09/pound
Whole Chicken	$.88/pound
Boneless Pork Chops	$1.69/pound
Pork Loin	$1.69/pound
Pork Ribs	$1.39/pound
Pork Shoulder Roast	$1.99/pound
Ground Chuck, 80%	$1.79/pound
Ground Beef, 73%	$1.39/pound
Beef Roast	$1.99/pound
(These reflect the lowest sale prices from the first half of 2009.)	

I typically purchase more than one package when these meats are on sale for these prices. I might get six packages of chicken breasts when the sale price is $1.77/pound. This way I can go shopping from my freezer and make meal plans from my freezer stockpile. Because I am constantly turning over my freezer stockpile and don't let meats stay in there for more than three months, I have not had any trouble with freezer burn or changes in the quality of the meat. Vacuum-sealer systems can help with freezer burn issues, if needed.

Coupons on fresh meat products are released on occasion in the newspaper and online. Because these fresh meat coupons are rare, I am sure to use them before they expire.

STOCKPILING FRUITS AND VEGETABLES

After tracking produce prices for months, I began to notice that every few weeks there would be a fantastic sale for a particular fruit or vegetable. I could not believe my eyes the first time I saw raspberries and blueberries on sale for just $1/pint. Nor could I believe it when sweet potatoes were just $.29/pound. And I was shocked to learn that my local farmers' market has an entire section of ripe and overly ripe fruits and vegetables for 50 percent and more off their regular price. $.25 for a zucchini, that's simply too good to pass up. I did the only thing a vegetable-loving, bargain-shopping fool would do, I bought way more of these fabulous fruits and vegetables than we could eat in one week.

Although these prices did not all happen in the same week, they are real and I did buy enough to feed a small army. Yes, fruits and vegetables can be stockpiled.

Raspberries, blueberries, and other berries can be placed on a cookie sheet and put in the freezer. Once frozen, the berries can be put into freezer baggies or containers for use at a later time. Other fruits that can be frozen straightaway using this method are: bananas, mangoes, and apples (tossed with lemon juice to prevent browning). Frozen fresh fruit is best used to make smoothies or for baking, as it tend to turn "mushy" as it thaws.

Fruits can also be pureed or juiced and put into ice cube trays. The ice cubes can be added to smoothies, or used to make fruity salad dressings.

Vegetables like green peppers, onions, and zucchini can be sliced or diced and frozen without cooking. Sliced green peppers and onions can be tossed in with chicken or beef fajitas. Thawed zucchini can be thrown into a stir-fry, or used to make zucchini bread or muffins.

White potatoes and sweet potatoes can be baked, mashed, and frozen. I make an extra batch or two of mashed potatoes or sweet potatoes and freeze them in freezer baggies. All types of squash can also be baked and then frozen for use in future meals, or to add to pasta or cheese sauces.

Vegetables like broccoli, celery, eggplant, okra, peas, and many other vegetables are best frozen after blanching. Blanching is a process of partially boiling the rinsed and cut vegetable for 3 to 4 minutes, then immersing the vegetable into ice cold water for 5 minutes. The water is then drained and the vegetables are patted dry. Once blanched and dried, the vegetables can be placed in freezer ziplock bags, or vacuum-sealed and frozen for up to six to nine months.

When I found broccoli on sale for $.88/bunch, I searched through the entire section of broccoli until I found the bunch with the largest broccoli heads. The sale price was for "the bunch," and not per pound. Since this happens rarely with vegetables like broccoli or squash, finding the largest ones got me the most bang for my buck. I remember purchasing six bunches of broccoli at this great price and blanching and freezing it to use in the coming weeks.

I find stockpiling fruits and vegetables to be rewarding, as I know that I am both saving money while still using the best ingredients when feeding my family and preparing our meals.

MY PERSONAL STOCKPILE

I have found that my freezer stockpile mostly consists of fruits and vegetables, and our favorite meat cuts. My pantry is stocked with canned tomatoes, 10-pound bags of rice and pasta, baking ingredients, and boxed cereal. My storage closets are filled with shampoos, soap, and toothpaste, and other toiletry items purchased at the grocery store and drugstores. When I find that my stockpile is overflowing, I will send boxes to local shelters or ministries who are in need of soap, shampoo, and other self-care items. I also donate pantry items to the food pantry.

Coupons are a powerful money-saving tool. When used strategically, real money can be saved. I predict that I have saved thousands of dollars at the grocery store, simply by using coupons and matching them with sale prices to stockpile my favorite products.

Another useful and practical way to save money, that doesn't involve clipping and matching, is meal planning. I can't wait to share my meal-planning strategies and tips with you!

THREE

Strategic Meal Planning

There is much more that goes into meal planning than just sitting down to write out a "what's for dinner?" plan. A few things must be considered: What kinds of meals should you plan? What type of ingredients will you use for your meals? How much food do you need to prepare for your family? Should you plan snacks? What foods does your family prefer, or dislike? What about food allergies?

And what's the big hoopla about meal planning anyway? How will it help me? And what do I do to get started and make the most out of a meal plan? Well let's look at some answers to these questions. And who knows, with a little practice, you'll be a professional meal planner, saving even more money at the grocery store each week as a result!

Healthy Eating

What does a healthy diet look like? It really looks different to everyone, so I thought it important to share my definition of healthy eating.

I believe food should be prepared from its simplest form. Delicious and nutritious meals can be made with just a handful of ingredients. Convenience and pre-packaged foods do not fall under my definition of healthy foods, as most are loaded with preservatives and additives that are not beneficial to the body. I prefer fresh and frozen produce over canned fruits and vegetables. There are a handful of processed ingredients that I purchase, like canned tomatoes or tomato paste, but I carefully read labels to be sure these products contain no preservatives, additives, or added sodium. Thankfully, many manufacturers have come out with "all-natural" products that are preservative- and additive-free, and there are no-sodium and no-sugar options for many canned vegetables and fruits.

Sadly, our taste buds have been tainted by the likes of high-fructose corn syrup and MSG. Of course these ingredients make food taste oh-so-much better, but they wreak havoc in the body. My stomach turns for hours after eating foods with MSG and I crash exactly 38 minutes after eating anything with high-fructose corn syrup.

I have learned that I cannot sacrifice my health for the convenience of a pre-packaged meal. I would rather spend ten extra minutes making my own sauce from scratch than preparing a pre-packaged boxed dinner.

I admire the women of the pioneer days who had no other option but to make everything from scratch. I often wonder what it would be like to have lived in those days. Because they spent time growing their food and caring for their homes, and their husbands exerted far more energy than I can imagine catching their food or raising their meat, obesity, high cholesterol, and other food-related health isuses were nonexistent.

Because I value and appreciate a healthy diet and active lifestyle, I do my best to make simple, from scratch meals that will help our bodies feel and look great!

So where exactly do I find such foods that keep me feeling good every day?

SHOPPING ON THE EDGE

Have you ever noticed how the freshest and healthiest ingredients are found on the perimeter of the store? Produce, fresh baked bread, meats, and dairy products are all located around the edge of the store. I have yet to walk into a grocery store that is not laid out in this manner. Because fresh and natural foods are so important for maintaining a healthy diet, I find myself spending a great deal of time in the produce department looking for the best and ripest produce. I always run through the meat department scanning for great deals and those magical REDUCED FOR QUICK SALE stickers. I do as much shopping from the edge of the store as I can, with the occasional dive into the middle aisles for spices, baking products, or other nonfood items. Because, yes, toothpaste and chocolate chips are important, too!—even if there are too many choices!!!

About 60 percent of the items in my grocery cart are found on the edge of the store. There are many grocery shopping experts who can get over $100 worth of groceries for less than $3. Most of the items they are purchasing are processed foods that yield little nutrition to the diet. While I wholeheartedly endorse saving money, there is a balance that needs to be maintained. If I were to get $100 worth of groceries for $3, I would feel guilty for not buying enough fresh produce or meat for my family. Don't get me wrong, I am all for teaching people how much to stockpile and how to save as much money as possible. But I believe that we should not sacrifice our health, and the need for fresh ingredients for the sake of saving money.

Because there are not very many coupons in circulation for fresh produce, meats, and dairy products, I try to save as much money as possible on other items in the grocery store, like cleaning products or toiletries, even bread and spices, so that I will have plenty of money in my weekly grocery budget to purchase the fresh produce and meat needed for breakfast, lunch, and dinner.

Let me share a few practical examples of what I mean. If I don't have to pay for toothpaste (remember, I "buy" it free all the time), and I only have to pay $.09 for a can of shaving cream, $1 for a large bottle of cleaning solution, and just $.30 for antibacterial hand soap, then I will have more room in my budget for fresh blueberries, peaches, and asparagus. Each of those prices for the toothpaste, shaving cream, and antibacterial hand soap are real-life examples of what I look for each week at the store. By matching a coupon with a sale price, I can get a wide variety of products for just a few pennies, and even free. (see The Art of Stockpiling, page 26)

How many times have you heard someone say "it's too expensive to eat healthy foods?" Well, it simply doesn't have to be. The concept of spending as little as possible on products from the "interior" of the grocery store, allows me to purchase the products from the edge that are typically thought of as more expensive, thus not worth spending money on. Just put this concept into practice and you'll be surprised at the extra money in your grocery budget for products "from the edge of the store."

PORTION DISTORTION

There is no doubt that portion sizes in the United States and in some countries abroad have grown grossly out of control. Experts agree that portion distortion is a major factor in the rise of obesity rates in the past twenty years. What most people consider an appropriate amount of food for a meal is actually far too much.

It sickens me to see the size of the main dish served at many restaurants. A drink, an appetizer, an oversized dinner plate filled to the rim, and 3,000 calories later, I find myself asking my husband to "roll me out the door." I'm too stuffed to walk comfortably. *I knew I should have asked the waiter for a to-go box when he brought the meal out so I could split it in half right away and avoid a huge scene at the front door as my husband rolled me out!* In all seriousness, I highly recommend splitting your restaurant meal in half before you start eating it.

So what are proper portion sizes? According to the United States Department of Agriculture's Official Food Pyramid the following daily requirements are recommended for adults: 5 ounces whole grains, 2 to 3 cups of vegetables, 2 cups of fruit, 3 cups of dairy and 5 to 6 ounces of meat/protein. (Note: These are not just for a dinner meal; these recommendations are for the entire day.) For children, the Food Pyramid suggests these daily requirements (varies depending on age): 2 to 3 ounces of whole grain, 1 to 2 cups of fruit, 1 to 2 cups of vegetables, 2 to 3 cups of dairy, and 3 to 5 ounces of meat/protein.

Online resources are available where an individual can enter their age, height, weight, and activity level. The USDA and My Pyramid recommend that I consume 6 ounces of whole grains, 2½ cups of vegetables, 2 cups of fruit, 3 cups of dairy and 5½ ounces of meat/protein each day, based on the criteria mentioned above. For a dinner meal, my personal goal is 2 ounces of whole grain or starch, 1 cup of vegetables and 3 to 4 ounces of meat/protein.

For my family, I aim to make a meal with approximately 1 pound of meat/protein, about 3 cups of starch or grain, and 2 to 3 cups of vegetables. The other daily requirements are eaten for other meals and snacks. I encourage you to utilize this great online tool to determine your daily dietary needs. (see Appendix B for USDA Web site information).

When buying our dinnerware, I considered the size of the dinner plates and salad plates. If I had purchased the trendy and increasingly oversized plates, we would have gained a few too many pounds in our first few years of marriage. Knowing that plate size plays a crucial role in portion control, I opted for plates that would not be the demise of our waistlines. Also, I consider the percentages of the foods on our plates. Is there three times the rice as there are vegetables or protein on the plate? If so, then the plate is "off balance," and the proper portions and percentages need to be served. I also like to eat lunch on our smaller salad plates, as I know I will have a light afternoon snack to get me to the dinner hour. I don't like to arrive starving to the dinner table, as I know I would eat twice as much as I need. I caution against the use of large plates and advise people to look closely at the percentages of each food on their plate.

For me, another important factor in "the portion game" is knowing just how much my family eats. I find that the amount of food that I have to put on my husband's and kid's plates can vary through the different seasons and stages of life. In the summer time when the kids are playing for hours on end in the backyard, they will polish their "normal portion" in forty-five seconds and be asking for more. And it seems they do eat less in the winter months when we spend more time inside and exert less energy throughout the day. Another season that our family faces is marathon-training season. Both my husband and I have trained and run marathons and half-marathons in the past. The quantity of food needed to keep the body properly fueled for these training periods is remarkably higher than the off-season. As I write today, my husband is training to run a full marathon at the end of the summer, while I need extra calories to nourish our third little one in the womb. I have noticed a dramatic increase in the amount of food that we need to meet our needs during this time.

When making meals, all these factors need to be considered. With careful planning of each week's menu, I can accommodate these needs without sacrificing quality. While some meals will get polished off, many of the meals I prepare have leftovers; some intentionally, and others not (more on effectively using your leftovers shortly). Before we get to that, we need to establish the guidelines for a balanced meal.

BALANCED MEALS

When making $5 Dinners, I strive to balance each plate with a complete protein, a grain or starch, and a vegetable or fruit. Proteins help build strong muscles and are essential to many regulatory processes within the body; starches give my husband and the kids the energy they need to play, grow and learn; and fruits and vegetables provide a myriad of nutrients and minerals important to the overall functioning of the body. As for drinks, my husband and I prefer water and the kids drink milk and water with their dinner.

Have you ever stopped to look at the different colors of the foods on your plate? I strive to serve at least three different colors in each meal—a dinner with pork chops, sweet potatoes, and green beans, or grilled chicken with asparagus and marinated tomatoes. The more colorful the meal, the more nutrients will be found in the meal.

Because I am feeding small children who have distinct preferences for vegetables and fruits, you will find many recipes with broccoli, peas, and green beans. I am thankful that they will eat these green vegetables on their own. My hope is to teach them to eat a wide variety of fruits and vegetables as they grow older. But for now, I'm thrilled that they enjoy broccoli or "trees" as we call them.

When planning meals, I also try to serve "foods that fit." For example, a home-made pizza with fresh fruit or a side salad, or a fish fillet with a splash of lemon and broccoli. And pork with sweet potatoes, chicken with just about anything, a beef roast with potatoes, carrots, and celery. I find we enjoy meals that "fit," although it is fun to throw in a "smorgasbord" meal on occasion.

Balanced meals, made with wholesome ingredients, are essential to good health, but what to do about that afternoon tummy rumble, or those late-night chocolate cravings?

SNACKING

Those hunger pangs roll around about the same time every day, 3:30 and 9:30 P.M. *Sheesh, they are annoying and pesky!* I've learned that if I don't have a little something to munch on, I'll go on a binge at dinnertime in an attempt to appease my stomach that's been angry with me for over two hours. I believe that we should listen to our bodies and feed them healthy snacks when they ask. And by healthy snacks, I don't mean Ding Dongs and Oreos. There is a time and a place for chocolate, but I've learned for myself, that time is not 3:30 in the afternoon. I'd be tempted to eat eight Oreos for a snack, instead of saving those treats for after a meal, when I'd be more likely to just eat one or two for dessert.

My favorite healthy snacks include baby carrots, grapes, apples, an orange, fresh mango, a 100-percent fruit smoothie, applesauce, a cup of cottage cheese, a few cheese and crackers, almonds or mixed nuts, and a glass of water. But on a hor-monal day, my preferred snack is a dark chocolate-raspberry granola bar (bought on sale, with a coupon, of course!).

But, snacking on a chocolate-y granola bar sends my taste buds and chocolate cravings into a downward tailspin that is difficult to pull out of. And I know exactly why! A wise friend shared with me a phrase that stuck like superglue in the front of my mind—"*You crave what you eat.*"

Upon thinking about this new eating-craving concept and paying closer atten-tion to what I was craving each time the hunger pangs struck, I began to realize the truth to this simple statement. If I found that when I ate a chocolate-y granola bar,

I wanted to eat another one and perhaps yet another one a few hours later. And then I'd finish off the box after the kids were in bed. That's a few more calories than I'd like to have consumed that day!

After mustering up enough self-control to pass up the chocolate-y granola bars in the cupboard and snack on an apple instead, I was surprised at what I started craving. Fruit! I didn't "need" those granola bars after all! Also, I stopped tempting myself by not even buying the chocolate-y granola bars. If I didn't put them into my grocery cart, then they wouldn't find a home in my cupboards and eventually be the demise of my waistline.

Snacking is tricky business because it's important to provide your body with energy and fuel, but it is so tempting to just grab a quick sugar-laden snack. Planning our daily snacks has allowed me to provide healthier snacks and has reduced the number of sugary convenience treats that we consume.

Now for a quick look at the benefits of meal planning—and how it keeps me from dropping $35 on a meal at our "takeout" spot—that's a week's worth of meals for us!

Benefits of Meal Planning

There is nothing more frustrating than looking down at my watch, only to find that it is already 5:30. *How did that happen? No wonder the kids are whining. What time did they have that after-school snack?* Opening the fridge to find half a plate of last night's leftovers next to the chicken I forgot to marinate only adds to my frustration, as I open the drawer with the phone book. *Hi there. I'd like to place an order to go. . . . Great, we'll be there in fifteen minutes to pick it up.* Click. My next phone call is to my husband who is on his way home from work.

Honey, I forgot to marinate the chicken. Again! I know and there isn't anything else in the fridge and the kids are whining and I just couldn't figure out what to make. I called for takeout at your favorite deli. Would you mind picking it up before coming home? They said it would be ready in fifteen minutes. Thanks honey.

Disaster averted. I'll just entertain the kids for a few minutes until Daddy gets home. And then we can eat! *Or was the disaster really averted? Did we really have the money to be doing this two to three times a week? Not really, but I just didn't have it together today, so it's okay.*

But is it OK to spend money you don't have for convenience sake? No!

The benefits of meal planning are clear:

1. **Moments of sheer frustration will be avoided.** With a plan in place and a refrigerator full of groceries, I can avoid that *what's-for-dinner?* feeling and sense of frustration as I rummage through the fridge looking for something to throw together.

2. **Takeout charges on the credit card will be averted.** $28 here, $35 there. Do that just two nights a week and the monthly credit card bill will be $250 higher than it needs to be! Consider that $3,000 for the year.

3. **Healthier meals will be served.** Because I am planning a simple home-cooked meal, I can control what ingredients are used, how much salt is added to the meal, and fresh vegetables and fruits are more likely to be included. If I plan to bake chicken and boil some corn, I will be less inclined to grab convenience, pre-packaged meals for dinner.

4. **More money will be saved.** If I create a meal plan at the beginning of each week and write my shopping list based on that plan, I most likely will have all that I need to prepare each meal. There is no need for that extra trip to the grocery store mid-week for that one missing ingredient. I know myself well enough to know that I just can't go into the grocery store for just one item. It doesn't seem like enough. So I grab a few more items, and maybe even a magazine. *Another $15 down the drain, when really I only needed some onions!*

5. **Mealtime will be cherished.** Dinner is an important time to gather around the table and be together as a family. The entire family can join in the process of getting the meal onto the table. Older children can help in the preparation of the meal, while younger children set the table. With all family members working together, the meal will get on the table faster and the hungry tummies will be satisfied much sooner. Mealtime is the perfect time to find out what other meals your family would like to eat. Get them involved in the meal-planning process.

These benefits far outweigh the potential bickering in the car on the way to a restaurant where only two family members want to eat, and later the argument with my husband about the $45 credit card charge for dinner, when we could have eaten at home for $5! I'll take the hearty, home-cooked meal for $5 any night!

Now I'd like to share a little about how I started meal planning and show a few examples from the different phases of meal planning.

PHASES OF MEAL PLANNING

My first days of meal planning actually came in the Dominican Republic. Because there was no convenience food, no fast food in our town, and few restaurants that served "American style" food, I was left with just one option: Cook from scratch! *I can do that. After all, I do need to eat to survive.* So I started exploring new recipes and planning what we would eat each week.

Since moving back to the United States, meal planning has evolved from simply planning our favorite meals to planning around sales and planning around my freezer stockpile. When I first set out to save more at the grocery store, I was just a beginner at meal planning. But as I implemented the strategies outlined thus far, I found myself with a stockpile of meats in my freezer that need to be incorporated into my weekly plans. Another few more weeks at the intermediate stages of meal planning, I found myself shopping out of my freezer. I had reached professional status! Below are the specifics on my meal planning journey from beginner to professional.

BEGINNER PHASE

At the beginning, the task of meal planning seemed daunting. I needed simplicity and I needed consistency in order to not only get started, but also to keep it going. I created "theme nights" for each night of the week. I maintained the variety in each week's menu without having to think too hard about coming up with creative meals.

"THEMED WEEK" EXAMPLE

MONDAY	TUESDAY	WEDNESDAY	THURSDAY	FRIDAY	SATURDAY	SUNDAY
Fish Night	Chicken Night	Pasta Night	Crockpot Day/Night	Homemade Pizza Night	Leftovers Night	Grill in the Summer/Soup in the Winter

WEEK 1

MONDAY	TUESDAY	WEDNESDAY	THURSDAY	FRIDAY	SATURDAY	SUNDAY
Honey-Dijon Tilapia (page 197)	Asian Chicken Wraps (page 90)	Homemade Macaroni and Cheese (page 53)	Apple-Dijon Pork Roast (page 166)	Mediter-ranean Pizza (page 75)	Leftovers	Grilled Pork Chops (page 175)

WEEK 2

MONDAY	TUESDAY	WEDNESDAY	THURSDAY	FRIDAY	SATURDAY	SUNDAY
Fish Tacos 'n Chips (page 195)	Bacon-Wrapped Apple Chicken (page 92)	Spaghetti and Oven Meatballs (page 66)	Slow Cooker Steak and Potatoes (page 149)	Ultimate Veggie Pizza (page 78)	Leftovers	Creamy Potato Soup (page 228)

INTERMEDIATE PHASE

After about two months of "themed nights" and settling into the meal-planning groove, it was time to step things up to the next level and start saving even more money. I set out to plan each week's meal based on the advertisements in the store's weekly circular. I would identify two or three cuts of meat that were on sale that week and design a meal around those items. In order to keep from eating the same cut of meat four to five nights a week, I began adding in one vegetarian meal with a complete protein source, and/or a breakfast-for-dinner meal.

SAMPLE MENU 1

Below is an example of a weekly meal plan when chicken breasts were on sale for $1.77/pound (regularly $4.99/pound) and pork roast was just $1.49/pound (regularly $3.49/pound).

MONDAY	TUESDAY	WEDNESDAY	THURSDAY	FRIDAY	SATURDAY	SUNDAY
Chicken Marinara over Angel Hair (page 99)	Cheese Enchiladas (page 236)	Pork Roast with Mashed Red Potatoes (page 184)	Breakfast—Scrambled Eggs, Toast, and Fruit	Chicken and Rice Salad (page 96)	Broiled Lemon-Pepper Fish (page 199)	North Carolina Pulled Pork Sandwiches (page 179)

SAMPLE MENU 2

Below is an example of a weekly meal plan when ground meat is on sale for $1.39/lb. (regularly $2.69/pound) and country-style pork ribs are on sale for $1.29/pound (regularly $2.29/pound)

MONDAY	TUESDAY	WEDNESDAY	THURSDAY	FRIDAY	SATURDAY	SUNDAY
Beef Enchiladas (page 136)	Cuban Black Beans and Rice (page 238)	Country Ribs with Oven Fries (page 172)	Broccoli-Tuna Casserole (page 57)	Stuffed Green Peppers (page 161)	Leftovers	Pasta e Fagioli Soup (page 225)

SAMPLE MENU 3

Below is an example of a weekly meal plan when fresh salmon fillets are on sale for $4.99/pound (regularly $6.99/pound) and the family pack of stew meat is on sale for $1.49/pound (regularly $2.99/pound).

MONDAY	TUESDAY	WEDNESDAY	THURSDAY	FRIDAY	SATURDAY	SUNDAY
Broccoli-Topped Potatoes (page 234)	Honey-Mustard Salmon (page 200)	Hearty Beef Stew (page 208)	Baked Ziti (page 53)	Hawaiian Pizza (page 77)	Cranberry Pork Chops (page 171)	Steak Sauce Stew (page 227)

PROFESSIONAL PHASE

Each week that chicken breast was on sale for $1.77/pound, I would buy five to six packages so that I would not have to pay full price for the same chicken breast during an "in between sales week." When the family packs of pork chops were on sale for $1.49/lb., I would buy a pack with enough pork chops for three meals. I froze the pork chops that were not used right away for use in future meals. Each week I scanned the meat department for those magical stickers that read "Price Reduced for Quick Sale" and would buy one or two cuts if the price was right.

After a few weeks of this "bulk" shopping for protein sources, it occurred to me that I should start shopping from my freezer. I knew that what was in the freezer had been purchased at the lowest sale price, or for a reduced price. I had enough in the freezer to make up a monthly meal plan. Since I had the meat that I needed for the month in the freezer, I would not buy meat from the store unless my favorite cuts were priced at their lowest price, or the magical sticker was too low to pass up.

When it comes time for me to make a monthly menu, I browse through the freezer and cabinets, making a list of ingredients and meats that I need to use sometime that month. From the ingredient list, I will write out a month's worth of meals on a table similar to the one below.

SAMPLE MONTHLY MENU

MONDAY	TUESDAY	WEDNESDAY	THURSDAY	FRIDAY	SATURDAY	SUNDAY
Cod with Sautéed Red Potatoes (page 194)	Sweet Potato Beef Roast (page 162)	Grammy's Pasta Salad (page 54)	Twice-Baked Potatoes (page 252)	Chili-Cornbread Cups (page 146)	Leftovers	Simple Cheeseburgers (page 143)
Gnocchi and Spinach Bake (page 243)	Chicken Potato Pie (page 101)	Cowboy Beans and Rice (page 170)	Creamy Butternut Squash Soup (page 218)	Tex-Mex Chili (page 163)	Potato Spinach Bake (page 249)	Grilled Chicken with Summer Salad (page 109)
Vegetarian Chili (page 254)	Grilled BLT Sandwiches (page 174)	Shrimp Scampi (page 205)	Beef and Rice Casserole (page 139)	Ginger-Chicken Stir-fry (page 106)	Leftovers	Honey-Glazed Pork Chops (page 178)
Honey-Lime Chicken (page 110)	Breaded Cod (page 193)	Mexican Bean Soup (page 223)	Beef Curry with Raisins (page 135)	Lentil Burritos (page 246)	Creamy Tortellini (page 58)	Tuna Melts (page 204)

OTHER KEY COMPONENTS TO CONSIDER WHEN MEAL PLANNING

The most effective strategic meal planner will also think about ways to save not just money, but also time, energy, and the inevitable dishes. Using the slow cooker, cooking in batches, and actually planning how I will use my leftovers are extensions of meal planning that help stretch my grocery budget/dollars even further.

SLOW COOKER

I love my slow cooker, but not as much as others love theirs! I have learned the savings potential from using my slow cooker, but I asked my friend and slow-cooking extraordinaire, Stephanie O'Dea for her thoughts on the benefits and savings that come from using a slow cooker. Stephanie is the author of the cookbook *Make it Fast, Cook it Slow: The Big Book of Everyday Slow Cooking.* She wrote her book after resolving to use her slow cooker every day for an entire year. She accomplished her goal and is now *the* expert "slow cooker-er."

Stephanie shares: *"I like slow cooking because I can get the food started in the morning when I am still heavily caffeinated and thinking clearly. I like that I can use inexpensive cuts of meat and how they will tenderize to perfection when simmering all day in their own juice. As a newlywed, my husband and I would save money by making a pot of beans or a stew once or twice a week, and then eat leftovers for lunches or for other dinners throughout the week. We could stretch the meal by making tacos or burritos or serving the food over rice. When I became a mom, I quickly learned that it wasn't safe to be standing over the stovetop between the 4 to 6 pm "witching hour" with cranky kids hanging on my ankles. By using the slow cooker, home cooks are forced to meal plan, which ensures money savings by sticking to a shopping list, and eradicating the need for last minute takeout. The slow cooker is also forgiving to the fledgling chef—there is plenty of time to taste and tweak recipes or fix accidental flubs. I'm not the best in the kitchen, but have found slow-cooking a great way to stretch my cooking wings."*

I try to incorporate a slow cooker meal at least once a week into my meal plans; for all the same reasons that Stephanie shared above. I much prefer to let the slow cooker do all the hard work for me! Most meals just take five to ten minutes to prepare in the morning. I try to get the slow cooker meal started just after breakfast while the kids are content and playing independently in the playroom.

The slow cooker saves my time, my sanity, my dishes, and my money.

BATCH COOKING

I love cooking from scratch and preparing meals for my family each day. I love being in the kitchen and involving the kids in the cooking experience. I want to create a warm and welcoming environment in and around my kitchen. But I know there will always be "those days," when I run out of time or energy to prepare a meal from scratch. That's where batch cooking saves the day!

Batch cooking is not to be confused with freezer cooking or once-a-month cooking. The concept is similar, in that I prepare extra portions and freeze them, but I don't do all my batch cooking in one day like those who do once-a-month cooking. I love the once-a-month-cooking concept, and think it works beautifully for many families, especially busy families, and families with both parents working outside the home.

So what does batch cooking look like? Because most of the meals I prepare are made up of a protein, starch, and vegetable, I find it helpful to make larger batches of certain ingredients that take longer to cook. For example, I love preparing dried beans. I prefer using dried beans over canned beans, despite the convenience of canned beans. I quickly learned that if I cook a larger amount of dried beans, I can save time and energy in preparing future meals. Every couple of weeks I will prepare 3 to 4 cups of dried beans in a big "batch," and then will freeze the cooked beans in 1-, 2-, and 3-cup portions. When I go to make a meal that calls for beans, I know I've got a few batches to choose from in the freezer, and I don't have to wait an hour or two for them to cook on the stove.

Another ingredient that I like to cook in batches is brown rice. Brown rice takes almost an hour to cook on the stovetop, and quite frankly, I don't always have an hour to wait for the brown rice to finish cooking. By making 5 to 6 cups at a time in a large saucepan, I save myself an hour preparing the brown rice for the next four to five meals. The brown rice can be frozen in meal-size portions. I defrost the rice in the microwave and then toss it in a small saucepan with 1/4 to 1/2 cup of water to finish reheating it, all in less than ten minutes.

Every couple of months, whole chickens will go on sale for $.88/pound at my grocery store. Most whole chickens weigh around 5 pounds, so the whole chicken will cost about $4.40. I like to buy several whole chickens when they are on sale for this price and roast them. If I don't plan to cook them all right away, I will stash them in the freezer. My favorite way to roast a whole chicken is in the slow cooker. Place the chicken in the slow cooker and cook on low for 8 hours. The chicken melts off the bones when it is finished, and tastes divine. (Recipe for roasting whole chicken in the slow cooker can be found on page 46). After removing all of the chicken meat from the whole chicken, the carcass can be used to make homemade chicken stock (details found on page 273).

Each whole chicken yields approximately 6 to 8 cups of chicken meat. I typically shred the chicken meat after pulling it from the bones and freeze it in 2-cup portions to use for meals like Chicken Quesadillas with Corn and Black Bean Salsa (page 122), Easy Chicken Potpie (page 100), and Sloppy Chicken Joes (page 88). Preparing the chicken meat ahead of time saves me those precious minutes in the kitchen when it's time to throw together a quick meal later in the week or month.

While batch cooking allows me to focus my time and energy spent in the kitchen, planning how I will use my leftovers will eliminate food waste and keep my family from complaining about "that meal again."

EFFECTIVELY USING YOUR LEFTOVERS

A common complaint I have heard over and over is the distaste for leftovers. With the exception of cold pizza, I am really not a huge fan of leftovers either. I'd much rather eat food that is fresh and warm off the stove. I have discovered that if I know that I am going to have leftovers and I plan to use those leftovers for a different meal, then I am less likely to waste food and hear grumbling at the dinner table.

I often purchase pork and beef roasts that are too large for us to eat in one meal. I generally prepare them in the slow cooker so the meat will turn out soft and tender. After I have served the meat that we will eat for dinner that night, half of the roast meat will be waiting for use in another meal.

I prepare beef roasts in the slow cooker with a little water, so that I can turn the juices into homemade beef broth (details on page 274). I like to add leftover beef roast meat to stew (page 207), or use it in Cowboy's Pie (page 148). It could also be tossed into a beef stir-fry or a Beef and Lentil Bake (page 132).

I love turning leftover pork roast into BBQ Pulled Pork Sandwiches (page 187) or even North Carolina Pulled Pork Sandwiches (page 179), or Apple-Walnut Pork (page 167).

I love to explore and be creative with different foods and their flavors, textures, and smells. I find that most challenging and creative meals are those that revolve around leftovers. I don't want any food to go to waste, and I don't want to hear any complaints for the natives! Planning on how I will use my leftovers has helped me stretch the food I buy, and the dollars I spend.

Do you feel like a professional meal planner, couponer, and grocery shopper yet?

Or at least do you have a few new strategies that you can pull out to make the planning process a bit easier and less time consuming? Before we get onto the recipes, let's quickly pull all these strategies together. I'll show you what this looks like practically for me each week—the shopping, the couponing, and the meal planning.

A Practical Look

Feeling a little overwhelmed? Need a little more time to digest all the strategies outlined thus far? Let me quickly recap and show you what this looks like each week.

Every Sunday morning, the newspaper shows up in my driveway and I dash off to get it while my husband and the kids flip pancakes. I pull out the coupon inserts and the advertisements for each grocery store in my area. I read over the store circulars, circling the products with great prices, and then I clip the coupons for the products that I like (some weeks I clip three coupons, and other weeks I clip twenty-five). I sit down with my monthly meal plan and quickly scan what's in the cupboards to see what else I need for the week. I write my grocery list based on what's on sale, what I have in the pantry and freezer, and what items I can stockpile that week. I go through my coupon binder looking for coupons that I can match for products that are on sale.

While I am making my plans and writing out my grocery lists, I always run numbers and prices through my head to make sure I can keep our family's meals under $5. I try to not go over $2.50 for the main protein source, whether that is chicken, beef, or fish, as I can always get a starch and vegetables in for less than $2.50 to round out the meal to around $5.

With my grocery list and my coupon stack, I am ready to shop. With cash in my pocket, I head out to the store to get only what is on my list. As my list consists of what I need, and was made based on what I had and what was on sale, there is no need to stray from the list, and no need to fall for marketing gimmicks and tactics. Impulse buys are old news!

Occasionally I will come upon an item that is "Price Reduced for Quick Sale." Because I have my $2.50 "meal formula" in my mind, I can decide if that particular item is worth purchasing and if it will help me keep the costs of a meal under $5.

I return home with my groceries, smiling at the percentage of savings displayed at the bottom of the receipt. 60 percent! Yet, another great day "at the office."

After a year of strategic grocery shopping, couponing, and meal planning, I have become quite the confident and savvy shopper. My experience, week after week, shows that the more time and attention I spent on making my meal plan, writing a grocery list, gathering up coupons, and sticking to my grocery list, the more money I saved that week. Of course life happens, and there is a week or two here or there when I just shopped the sales and left my coupon binder at home. And that is okay. In all things, there is a balance. I did not, however, stray from my goal of spending less of my husband's hard-earned money, and I did not fail to complete my mission each week of making $5 Dinners for my family.

I encourage shoppers to take baby steps. Don't try to start all of this at once. Start with the strategies that fit your personality best. If you are a planner by nature, start with meal planning. If you are a coupon user and sale shopper, practice using your coupons more effectively by stockpiling and paying only the very lowest prices possible for your family's favorites. If you want to challenge yourself to resist the temptations in the grocery stores, plan to *walk right past* the bakery for your usual donut, despite the fried doughy sweetness that fills the air. Both your pocketbook and waistline will thank you!

Once you have mastered the first set of strategies, move onto another area until you feel comfortable with using two sets of strategies. Lastly, add the final set to your arsenal and give yourself a pat on the back each time you leave the grocery store—satisfied with your savings and your meal plan for the week.

The remainder of the book consists of recipes, written by section. Each recipe contains a frugal fact that will help you understand how the meal was priced, or suggestions for helping reduce meal costs in general. All of the recipes use the most basic and popular ingredients and are made "from scratch." I firmly believe that getting back to the basics of making homemade meals, eating together as a family, and slowing down long enough to learn about the ins and outs of each other's day will reap many positive rewards for our family. Remember, larger families and/or families with older children should consider doubling or tripling these recipes to have enough to go around.

I can't wait to share the recipes of our family's favorite $5 Dinners with you!

FOUR

Pasta and Pizza Dinners

Baked Ziti

½ spaghetti squash, halved ($1.79)
1 package (16 ounces) ziti pasta ($.97)
3 cups Homemade Basic White Sauce
  (page 276) ($.60)

salt and pepper
1½ cups mozzarella cheese,
  shredded ($1)
1 cup frozen lima beans ($.50)

Preheat the oven to 350 degrees. Cut the spaghetti squash in half lengthwise and place it cut side down in a glass baking dish. Add ¼ inch of water to the baking dish and cover it with aluminum foil. Bake in the preheated oven for 50 to 60 minutes. Remove the squash and let cool for 5 to 10 minutes before handling. Scrape out the seeds and discard, then scrape out the squash flesh. Serve as side dish, either plain with butter and salt and pepper, or with Parmesan cheese.

In a large pot cook the ziti according to the package directions.

Prepare the white sauce.

Once the sauce has reached the desired consistency, add the cooked pasta. Transfer to 9×13-inch baking dish. Sprinkle the cheese over the top. Bake in the preheated oven for 15 minutes, or until bubbly and the cheese is golden.

Cook the frozen lima beans according to the package directions. Season with salt and pepper to taste.

Serve Baked Ziti with Spaghetti Squash and Lima Beans.

Cost $4.86

FRUGAL FACT: *Spaghetti squash can be purchased at its lowest price during the fall and early winter months. It can be used as a side dish, but also in main dishes (Spaghetti Squash and Chicken Bake, page 126). Leftover spaghetti squash can be added to casseroles such as Homemade Macaroni and Cheese (page 53).*

Homemade Macaroni and Cheese

1 package (16 ounces) elbow macaroni ($.97)

3 cups Homemade Basic White Sauce (page 276) ($.60)

salt and pepper

2 cups shredded sharp Cheddar cheese ($1.50)

1 cup leftover butternut squash, cooked and mashed ($.50)

2 heads broccoli, separated into spears ($.79)

In a large pot, cook the macaroni according to the package directions. Preheat the oven to 350 degrees.

Prepare the white sauce. Once the white sauce has thickened, stir in 1 cup of the cheese and whisk until melted. Mix in the leftover cooked butternut squash, or another cooked vegetable of a similar color. Whisk the cheese sauce well. Season with salt and pepper to taste.

Add the cooked pasta to a 9×13-inch glass baking dish, pour the cheese sauce over the pasta, and stir to combine. Top with the remaining 1 cup cheese, and bake in the preheated oven for 10 to 15 minutes, or until the sauce is bubbly and the cheese has melted.

Cut the broccoli in spears and trim the stems. Steam the broccoli in a stovetop steamer for 4 to 5 minutes, or microwave it for 4 to 5 minutes in a microwave-safe bowl, covered with plastic wrap.

Serve Homemade Macaroni and Cheese and Steamed Broccoli.

Variation: Add ¾ pound of cooked ground beef to the pasta and cheese for a "Cheeseburger Mac 'n Cheese" (adds $1.25)

Cost $4.36, or $5.61 for Cheeseburger Mac 'n Cheese (see variation)

FRUGAL FACT: *Mix a vegetable of a similar color into your homemade sauces. For example, adding a little butternut squash to a cheesy sauce, or grated carrots to a tomato-based sauce, is a great way to sneak extra veggies into the meal.*

Grammy's Pasta Salad

1 package (16 ounces) shell pasta ($.97)
1 cup frozen peas ($.50)
½ cup mayonnaise ($.20)
2 tablespoons pickle relish ($.10)
2 tablespoons grated Parmesan
   cheese ($.10)

salt and pepper
1 pint cherry tomatoes ($1.50)
1 can (6 ounces) tuna, in water ($.93)
2 Granny Smith apples ($.50)

In a large pot, cook the pasta according to the package directions. Drain and rinse with cold water.

Cook the frozen peas according to the package directions.

In small bowl, combine the mayonnaise with the relish, Parmesan cheese, and salt and pepper. Set aside.

Cut the cherry tomatoes into quarters. Remove the seeds, if desired.

In a large mixing bowl, combine the cooked pasta, chopped cherry tomatoes, tuna, cooked peas, and the mayonnaise dressing. Stir all the ingredients together. Refrigerate the salad for at least 2 hours before serving.

Slice the apples just before serving.

Serve Grammy's Pasta Salad with Sliced Apples.

Variation: Substitute ½ cup of sandwich spread for the mayonnaise, Parmesan cheese, and pickle relish.

Cost $4.80

FRUGAL FACT: *Produce coupons are* rare, *so when you see them be sure to put them to good use!*

Summer Garden Pasta Salad

1 package (16 ounces) bow-tic pasta ($.97)

3 to 4 fresh tomatoes from the garden, diced (free)

2 garlic cloves, crushed ($.10)

4 fresh basil leaves from the garden, finely chopped (free)

5 tablespoons extra-virgin olive oil ($.50)

splash of white vinegar ($.02)

2 cups mozzarella cheese ($1.50)

1 zucchini ($.79)

salt and pepper

¼ cup Parmesan cheese ($.35)

In a large pot, cook the pasta according to the package directions. Drain, but do not rinse.

In a small bowl, marinate the diced tomatoes, crushed garlic, and chopped fresh basil in 4 tablespoons of the extra-virgin olive oil and the white vinegar.

In a large bowl, toss the cooked pasta with the marinated tomatoes. Quickly add the mozzarella cheese while the pasta is still warm, and allow the cheese to melt.

Slice the zucchini into ⅛-inch rounds. In a small skillet, sauté the zucchini in the remaining olive oil for 3 to 4 minutes. Season with salt and pepper, turn the zucchini, and sauté for another 3 to 4 minutes. The zucchini can also be steamed in the microwave by placing the zucchini rounds in a microwave-safe dish with ½ cup of water, and cooking on high for 4 to 5 minutes, or until all the zucchini are translucent. Sprinkle ¼ cup shredded or grated Parmesan cheese over the warm zucchini.

Serve Summer Garden Pasta Salad and Sautéed Zucchini.

Cost $4.23

FRUGAL FACT: *Gardening is a fantastic and frugal way to add great vegetables and great taste to your summertime meals. Tomatoes and fresh herbs can easily be grown in large planters or pots on the patio. Prepare this meal using your tomato and basil harvest.*

Beef Goulash

¾ pound ground beef ($1.12)

½ cup water or homemade Beef Broth (page 274) (free)

4 carrots, peeled and julienned ($.40)

1 can (15 ounces) crushed or diced tomatoes with their juices ($.59)

1 teaspoon paprika ($.10)

¼ teaspoon ground cloves ($.05)

salt and pepper

1 teaspoon brown sugar or honey ($.05)

2 tablespoons flour ($.05)

¼ cup sour cream ($.12)

1 package (16 ounces) elbow macaroni ($.97)

2 cups frozen corn ($1)

In a skillet, brown the ground beef and drain the excess fat. Return the beef to the skillet.

To the cooked beef, add the water or homemade beef broth, the carrots, and the canned tomatoes. Season with the paprika, cloves, salt, and pepper, and the brown sugar or honey. Bring to a rolling boil. Reduce the heat to a simmer.

Meanwhile, in small bowl, whisk the flour and ¼ cup water to form a thin paste. Add the paste to the bubbling beef sauce and whisk well. Simmer about 10 minutes, or until the carrots are cooked through. Add the sour cream and simmer another 5 minutes to reduce and thicken the sauce.

In a large pot, cook the pasta according to the package directions.

Cook the frozen corn kernels according to the package directions. Season with salt and pepper to taste.

Serve Beef Goulash over Pasta with Corn.

Cost $4.45

FRUGAL FACT: *Use a $1 off coupon when sour cream is on sale for $1 or $1.50! Get 12 to 16 ounces of sour cream for just $.50, or even free!*

Broccoli-Tuna Casserole

1 package (16 ounces) penne pasta ($.97)

3 cups Homemade Basic White Sauce (page 276) ($.60)

salt and pepper

1 cup frozen broccoli ($.50)

1 can (6 ounces) tuna, in water ($.65)

1 tomato ($.50)

½ head romaine lettuce ($.75)

1 cup homemade Basic Vinaigrette dressing (page 280) ($.50)

In a large pot, cook the pasta according to the package directions. Add the frozen broccoli to the pasta water and cook, along with the pasta, for 4 to 5 minutes. Drain the pasta and broccoli and return it to the pot.

In a small saucepan, prepare the white sauce.

Add the tuna to the sauce and stir to combine.

Add the tuna sauce to the pasta and broccoli in the pot. Stir and let simmer until the sauce has reached the desired consistency.

Dice the tomato. Chop the romaine lettuce with a plastic lettuce knife to prevent browning.

Make the vinaigrette dressing. Just before serving, toss with the romaine salad.

Serve Broccoli-Tuna Casserole with Romaine Salad.

Cost $4.47

FRUGAL TIP: *Making your own white sauce and salad dressing is not only more frugal, it is healthier. You can control the amount of salt in the sauce and dressing, and there are no preservatives when they are homemade.*

Creamy Tortellini

1 pound asparagus ($.99)
2 tablespoons extra-virgin olive oil ($.20)
1 package (16 ounces) tortellini ($1.79)

5 slices turkey bacon ($.75)
3 cups of Homemade Basic White Sauce (page 276) ($.60)
1 cup frozen peas ($.50)
salt and pepper

Drizzle the extra-virgin olive oil over asparagus and let it marinate while you prepare the rest of the meal.

In a large pot, cook the tortellini according to the package directions.

In a large skillet, cook the bacon over medium-high heat until crisp. Set aside to drain on paper towels. Pour off most of the bacon fat from the skillet, saving a little to use for making the white sauce.

Prepare the white sauce.

Add the frozen peas, tortellini, and bacon to the white sauce. Stir to combine and simmer 8 to 10 minutes until the peas have softened and the sauce has reached the desired consistency.

In a skillet, sauté the asparagus in the olive oil it marinated in for 4 to 5 minutes until tender-crisp. It will turn bright green when it is ready. Season with salt and pepper to taste.

Serve Creamy Tortellini and Sautéed Asparagus.

Cost $4.88

FRUGAL FACT: *My "never-pay-more-than price" for turkey bacon is $2.50/package. When on sale for this price, buy a few packages. Divide each package in half or fourths and freeze in smaller freezer ziplock bags. Bacon freezes and thaws well.*

Fettuccine Alfredo

2 sweet potatoes ($.79)
1 package (16 ounces) fettuccine
 ($.97)
2 boneless, skinless chicken breasts,
 thinly sliced ($1.66)

3 cups Homemade Basic White Sauce
 (page 276) ($.60)
¼ cup Parmesan cheese ($.25)
1 cup frozen peas ($.50)

Preheat the oven to 350 degrees. Make a few slits in the sweet potatoes using a small sharp knife. Put the sweet potatoes in a baking dish with ¼ inch of water and cover with aluminum foil. Bake in the preheated oven for 1 hour. Remove from the oven and let cool about 10 minutes. Peel off the skins and mash the pulp.

Meanwhile in a large pot, cook the fettuccine according to the package directions. Drain.

In a skillet, prepare the white sauce. Once the sauce has thickened, add ¼- to ½-cup Parmesan cheese and whisk until it melts into the sauce. Once the sauce has thickened, add the chicken, cover, and cook for 8 to 10 minutes, or until the chicken pieces have cooked through. Stir frequently.

Cook the frozen peas according to the package directions.

Add the cooked fettuccine and peas to the skillet with the chicken and white sauce. Toss to combine.

Serve Fettuccine Alfredo and Mashed Sweet Potatoes.

Cost $4.97

FRUGAL FACT: *Frozen vegetables can be purchased for as little as $.65/16-ounce bag. Be sure to grab a few extra bags when at this great price.*

Greek Pasta Salad

1 package (16 ounces) fusilli pasta ($.97)
½ pound cherry tomatoes ($.75)
¼ pound kalamata olives with Greek seasonings ($1.20)
2 to 3 ounces crumbled feta cheese ($.75)

½ cup homemade Greek Salad Dressing (page 281) ($.35)
butter ($.25)
Honey Wheat Rolls (page 260) ($.50)

Make the dough for the homemade rolls in a bread machine or in a mixing bowl.

In a large pot, cook the pasta according to the package directions. Drain and rinse the pasta with cold water.

Quarter the cherry tomatoes and chop the olives. (Olives with Greek seasonings can be found in the "olive bar" at the grocery store.)

Prepare the salad dressing.

In a large bowl, combine the cooked pasta, cherry tomatoes, chopped olives, feta cheese, and salad dressing. Mix well.

Finish making the rolls as directed in the recipe.

Serve the Greek Pasta Salad with warm Honey Wheat Rolls and butter.

Cost $4.77

FRUGAL FACT: *Making your own bread can save you over half of what you'd pay in the store, plus you can eat the rolls when they are hot and fresh out of the oven.*

Roasted Bell Pepper Rotini

½ package (8 ounces) rotini pasta ($.48)
1 red bell pepper ($.89)
2 boneless, skinless chicken breasts
  ($1.66)
1 teaspoon olive oil ($.03)

½ cup homemade Basic Vinaigrette
  (page 280) ($.50)
½ cup mozzarella cheese, cubed
  ($.38)
4 ears corn ($1)

In a large pot, cook the pasta according to the package directions. Preheat the oven to 450 degrees.

Remove the stem and seeds from the bell pepper. Cut the bell pepper in half lengthwise. Place in baking dish or bread pan and roast in the preheated oven for 10 to 15 minutes. Let cool. Slice or dice the roasted pepper.

Dice the chicken breasts and sauté in a small skillet with the oil for 8 to 10 minutes, or until the chicken pieces are no longer pink in the middle. The cooking time will vary depending on thickness of the diced chicken.

In a small bowl, prepare the vinaigrette.

In a large bowl, toss the pasta, chicken, diced roasted pepper, and cheese with the vinaigrette dressing.

Remove the husks and silk from the ears of corn and boil the corn in large pot of water for 4 to 5 minutes, or place the ears of corn in a microwave-safe baking dish, cover with plastic wrap, and microwave for 7 to 9 minutes.

Serve Roasted Pepper Rotini with Corn on the Cob.

Cost $4.94

FRUGAL FACT: *Fantastic corn prices can be found during the early and late summer months. Best prices: 5 ears/$1 or 6 ears/$1*

Southwest Chicken Pasta Salad

½ cup dried black beans ($.20)
1 package (16 ounces) rotini pasta ($.97)
2 to 3 tablespoons extra-virgin olive oil ($.20)
1 cup water or homemade Chicken Stock (page 273)
splash of vinegar ($.01)
3 to 4 garlic cloves crushed ($.15)
2 boneless, skinless chicken breasts, diced ($1.66)
1 can (12 ounces) diced tomatoes with green chilies ($.37)
¼ cup fresh cilantro for garnish ($.25)
4 ears corn ($1)

Soak the dried black beans overnight or bring to a boil in a generous amount of water and let soak for at least 2 hours in the hot water. Drain and rinse. Add the soaked beans to a medium saucepan with at least 2 inches of water covering them. Bring to a boil. Cover, reduce the heat to medium, and cook for 1½ hours, or until the beans are soft.

In a large pot, cook the pasta according to the package directions. Drain the pasta.

In large skillet, add the olive oil, water or broth, vinegar, crushed garlic cloves, diced chicken, cooked black beans, and diced tomatoes with green chilies. Stir the ingredients together and cook over medium heat for 8 to 10 minutes, or until the chicken is cooked through.

In a large bowl, combine the cooked pasta with the chicken mixture. Stir to combine.

Chop the cilantro and sprinkle it over the pasta salad. Serve the salad warm or cold.

Remove the husks and silk from the ears of corn and boil the corn in a large pot of water for 4 to 5 minutes, or place corn ears in a microwave-safe glass baking dish, cover with plastic wrap, and microwave for 7 to 9 minutes.

Serve Southwest Chicken Pasta Salad with Corn on the Cob.

Cost $4.81

FRUGAL FACT: *Substitute 1 can of black beans with no sodium if in a time crunch.*

Spaghetti

2 to 3 cups Homemade Spaghetti
   Sauce (page 275) ($.80)
1 package (16 ounces) whole wheat
   spaghetti ($1.39)
¾ pound ground beef ($1.12)

½ cup shredded carrots ($.10)
2 cups frozen green beans ($1)
1 cup frozen corn kernels ($.50)
salt and pepper

Make the spaghetti sauce. Simmer the sauce while the pasta and ground beef are cooking.

In a large pot, cook the pasta according to the package directions.

In a skillet, brown the ground beef and drain the excess fat. Add the beef to the spaghetti sauce. Add the shredded carrots and simmer for 10 to 15 minutes, or until the carrots have cooked into the sauce.

Cook the frozen green beans according to the package directions. Cook the frozen corn according to the package directions. Season with salt and pepper to taste.

Drain the pasta and combine with the sauce. Serve Spaghetti with Homemade Sauce, Green Beans, and Corn.

Cost $4.91

FRUGAL FACT: *Spaghetti is always a frugal favorite! Adding shredded carrots or other leftover vegetables is a great way to sneak in a few extra nutrients into the meal!*

Slow Cooker Meatballs with Spaghetti

2 cups Homemade Spaghetti Sauce
   (page 275) ($.80)
¾ pound ground beef ($1.12)
½ cup bread crumbs ($.25)
1 egg ($.10)
1 teaspoon garlic powder ($.05)

1 teaspoon dried Italian seasoning
   ($.05)
salt and pepper
1 package (16 ounces) spaghetti ($.97)
2 cups frozen mixed vegetables ($1)

Prepare the spaghetti sauce.

In a large mixing bowl, combine the ground meat, bread crumbs, egg, and seasonings with your hands. If you don't wish to use your hands to combine the mixture, put the ingredients in a large plastic ziplock bag, close it, and combine.

Form the meat mixture into 1-inch meatballs, using your hands or an ice cream scoop. Place the meatballs in the bottom of the slow cooker insert. Pour the spaghetti sauce over the meatballs. Set the slow cooker on high, and cook the meatballs and sauce for 4 hours.

In a large pot, cook the pasta according to the package directions. Drain the pasta.

Cook the frozen mixed vegetables according to the package directions.

Serve Spaghetti with Slow Cooker Meatballs and Mixed Veggies!

Cost $4.34

FRUGAL FACT: *Make a large batch of Homemade Spaghetti Sauce. Divide it into 2-cup (meal-size) portions and freeze in freezer-safe plastic containers or freezer ziplock bag.*

Spaghetti and Oven Meatballs

2 cups Homemade Spaghetti Sauce
(page 275) ($.80)
1 pound ground beef ($1.49)
½ cup bread crumbs ($.20)
1 teaspoon garlic powder ($.05)
1 teaspoon Italian seasoning ($.05)
¼ cup Parmesan cheese ($.25)

1 egg ($.10)
2 tablespoons extra-virgin olive oil
($.20)
1 package (16 ounces) spaghetti ($.97)
2 heads broccoli ($.79)

Prepare the spaghetti sauce.

In a large mixing bowl, combine the ground meat, bread crumbs, garlic powder, Italian seasoning, Parmesan cheese, and egg with your hands. If you don't wish to use your hands to combine the mixture, put the ingredients in a large plastic ziplock bag, close, and combine.

Form the meat mixture into 1-inch balls, using your hands or an ice cream scoop.

Preheat the oven to 350 degrees. In a large skillet, add extra-virgin olive oil and place over medium to medium-high heat. Place the meatballs in the skillet, and brown for 1 minute on each side. Transfer the meatballs to a glass baking dish.

Once all the meatballs are browned, place them in the baking dish, in the preheated oven and bake for 15 to 20 minutes, or until each meatball is cooked through. The cooking time may vary depending on the thickness of the meatballs.

Transfer the meatballs to a serving platter and pour the homemade spaghetti sauce over the top.

In a large pot, cook the spaghetti according to the package directions. Drain the pasta.

Separate the broccoli into spears and steam in stovetop steamer for 5 minutes.

Serve Spaghetti with Oven Meatballs and Steamed Broccoli.

Cost $4.90

FRUGAL FACT: *If you purchase a "family size" package of ground beef at the store, divide the beef into 1-pound (meal-size) portions. With one of the 1-pound portions, make the meatballs. You can use them immediately or for a meal in the next few days or freeze them. To freeze, place on a cookie sheet that will fit into your freezer compartment. Once frozen, transfer the meatballs to a freezer ziplock bag or a freezer-safe container.*

Summer Pasta Salad

1 package (16 ounces) bow-tie or rotini pasta ($.97)

1 large boneless, skinless chicken breast, or 1 to 2 cups leftover, cooked, diced chicken ($.83)

1 teaspoon extra-virgin oil ($.03)

1 cucumber, peeled and diced ($.50)

1 cup shredded cheddar or mozzarella cheese ($.75)

1 can (15 ounces) Italian-style diced tomatoes ($.59)

½ cup homemade Basic Vinaigrette (pg 280) ($.40)

¼ watermelon ($.75)

In a large pot, cook the pasta according to the package directions. Drain and rinse with cold water.

Dice the chicken breasts and sauté in small skillet for 8 to 10 minutes, or until the chicken pieces are no longer pink in the middle. The cooking time will vary depending on the thickness of the diced chicken.

Slice the cucumber lengthwise. Remove the seeds with a spoon and discard. Dice the cucumbers.

Prepare the vinaigrette.

In a large serving bowl, toss the pasta with the chicken (or leftover chicken), diced cucumbers, cheese, diced tomatoes, and vinaigrette dressing.

Slice or dice the watermelon.

Serve Summer Pasta Salad and Fresh Watermelon.

Cost $4.82

FRUGAL FACT: *Using 1 to 2 cups leftover chicken from a previous meal or from preparing a whole chicken (see page 46), will lower the costs for this meal.*

Taco Macaroni and Cheese

1 package (16 ounces) elbow macaroni ($.97)
½ pound ground beef ($.75)
½ onion, chopped ($.20)
2 garlic cloves, crushed ($.10)
1 can (6 ounces) tomato sauce ($.33)
1 can (12 ounces) diced tomatoes with green chilies ($.37)
¼ cup milk ($.03)
½ teaspoon chopped fresh cilantro ($.05)
½ to 1 teaspoon cayenne pepper ($.05)
1 teaspoon ground cumin ($.05)
1 cup shredded Cheddar cheese ($.85)
½ cantaloupe ($.75)

In a large pot, cook the macaroni according to the pasta package directions. Drain and set aside.

In a large skillet, brown the ground beef with the chopped onion and crushed garlic and drain excess fat. Return the ground beef and onion mixture to the skillet, and add the tomato sauce, diced tomatoes with green chilies, and milk. Stir in the cilantro, cayenne, and ground cumin, and simmer about 10 minutes, allowing the sauce to form and the flavors to mingle. Add the cooked elbow macaroni to the sauce and mix to combine. Sprinkle the cheese over the top of the mixture while still warm in the skillet, and allow the cheese to melt.

Slice the cantaloupe—adding a sweet fruit to this meal helps balance the zesty and spicy pasta!

Serve Taco Macaroni and Cheese and Fresh Cantaloupe.

Cost $4.87

FRUGAL FACT: *Brown a 1½-pound package of ground beef with onion and plan to use it in two meals that week. Planning to split the package and use it twice will keep you from cooking too much and wasting leftovers. For example, plan to make this meal on Monday night using half of the beef from the package, and the other half on Thursday night when you make Green Pepper Soup (page 221).*

Pasta with Broccoli and Chicken

2 boneless, skinless chicken breasts
($1.66)
⅓ cup plus 1 teaspoon olive oil ($.50)
salt and pepper
2 garlic cloves, crushed ($.10)
½ teaspoon crushed red pepper flakes
($.03) (optional)

¼ cup bread crumbs ($.25)
2 heads broccoli ($.79)
1 package (16 ounces) shell pasta
($.97)
½ cup grated Parmesan cheese ($.50)

Pound the chicken breasts between two sheets of wax paper to a thickness of ⅓ inch. Rub both sides of the chicken breasts with 1 teaspoon of the olive oil and season them with salt and pepper.

In a skillet, sauté the chicken breasts for 6 to 8 minutes on each side, or until the chicken is cooked through. The cooking time will vary depending on the thickness of the chicken breasts. Remove from the skillet and let cool. When cool, dice the chicken and set it aside.

Peel and thinly slice the garlic cloves. Place them in a shallow saucepan with the ⅓ cup of olive oil and heat gently until the garlic takes on a golden color. Add crushed red pepper flakes for a bit of zing (optional). Remove from the heat and set aside, uncovered.

In the same skillet that you used to sauté the chicken, toast the bread crumbs until brown and set aside.

Remove the stems from the broccoli and separate into florets. Cook the broccoli florets in boiling salted water until they turn bright green. Drain and set aside.

In large pot, cook the pasta according to the package directions. Drain, reserving ⅓ cup of the cooking water. Return the pasta and reserved water to the pot.

Toss the broccoli and chicken with the cooked pasta. Pour the heated oil with the garlic cloves and optional red pepper flakes over the pasta and toss. Finally, toss with the grated Parmesan and toasted bread crumbs.

Cost $4.80

FRUGAL FACT: *Because there are rarely coupons for pasta, be sure to get a few extra boxes when it's on sale. Store-brand pastas are typically better for the budget!*

Fettuccine with Peas and Ham

8 tablespoons (1 stick) butter ($.80)
¾ cup grated Parmesan cheese ($.75)
1 cup heavy cream, or whole milk ($.10)
2 cups frozen peas ($.75)

⅓ pound smoked ham, diced finely ($1.60)
1 package (16 ounces) fettuccine ($.97)
salt and freshly ground black pepper

Combine the stick of butter less 1 tablespoon, the cheese, and the heavy cream in a food processor and process until smooth. Set aside.

Cook the peas as directed on the package. Drain and set aside.

Melt the remaining 1 tablespoon of butter in a skillet, then add the diced ham, and brown. Set aside.

In a large pot, cook the fettuccine according to the package directions. Drain, reserving ⅓ cup of the cooking water.

Immediately put the drained fettuccine and the reserved ⅓ cup pasta water in a large bowl and quickly scoop the butter-cheese-cream mixture onto the top of the hot pasta and toss to coat the strands. Then add the peas and diced ham and toss again. Top with freshly ground black pepper.

Serve the Fettuccine with Peas and Ham.

Cost $4.97

FRUGAL FACT: *Buy ham from the deli when it is on sale for less than $5/pound. Plan at least two meals that week using ham, as to not let it go to waste.*

Rotelle Pasta with Eggplant

1 large eggplant ($1.49)
kosher salt
¼ cup canola oil ($.10)
3 tablespoons olive oil ($.30)
2 garlic cloves, crushed ($.10)
1 can (28 ounces) crushed Italian
   tomatoes ($.79)
1 can (6 ounces) tomato paste ($.19)

1½ cups water
¼ cup fresh basil leaves, washed and
   dried ($.15)
1 package (16 ounces) rotelle (wagon
   wheel) pasta ($.97)
½ cup grated Parmesan or pecorino
   romano cheese ($.50)

Wash the eggplant. Trim off the ends and, leaving the skin intact, dice the eggplant into ½-inch cubes. Put the cubes in a colander and salt liberally. Allow the eggplant to drain in the sink for about 1 hour to remove the bitter juices. Rinse the eggplant and pat dry thoroughly on paper towels.

Heat the canola oil in a pan and brown the eggplant well on all sides. Drain on paper towels and set aside.

Pour the olive oil into a large saucepan. Add the crushed garlic, crushed tomatoes, tomato paste, and water. Cook over medium heat for about 20 minutes. Remove from the heat. Tear the basil leaves roughly, and stir them into the sauce.

In a large pot, cook the pasta according to the package directions. Drain, reserving ⅓ cup of the cooking water.

Pour the drained pasta and the reserved pasta water back into the pot. Add the eggplant and toss to combine.

Add 3 to 3½ cups of the tomato sauce to the pasta and toss well. (Reserve about 1 cup of the sauce to use when reheating leftovers.)

Sprinkle the pasta with grated Parmesan cheese.

Serve Rotelle Pasta with Eggplant.

Cost $4.59

FRUGAL FACT: *Eggplant is often on sale for $1.50 to $2 per eggplant. Remember to choose the largest eggplant when it's a "per eggplant" sale to get the most for your money. Consider growing eggplant in a clay pot on your patio.*

Mediterranean Pizza

homemade Whole Wheat Pizza
Dough (page 83) ($1)
1 cup Homemade Pizza Sauce
(page 85) ($.41)
2 plum tomatoes, thinly sliced ($.58)

1 can (6 ounces) sliced black olives
($.75)
2 cups shredded mozzarella cheese
($1.50)
2 apples, sliced ($.50)

Prepare the whole wheat pizza dough. Preheat the oven to 350 degrees. Roll out the dough and bake the crust for 8 minutes. Remove the crust from the oven.

Spread homemade pizza sauce over the partially cooked crust. Distribute the thinly sliced tomatoes and sliced black olives over the top. Sprinkle with the shredded mozzarella cheese.

Bake the full pizza another 8 to 10 minutes, or until all the cheese has melted.

Slice the Mediterranean Pizza and serve with Sliced Apples.

Cost $4.74

FRUGAL FACT: *Grow your own tomatoes for a more frugal pizza. Or look for sale prices around $.50 to $.60/pound for plum (also called Roma) tomatoes.*

Grilled Zucchini and Chicken Pizza

homemade Whole Wheat Pizza Dough
(page 83) ($1)
1 cup Homemade Pizza Sauce
(page 85) ($.41)
1 zucchini ($.79)
1 tablespoon olive oil ($.10)

1 large boneless, skinless chicken
breast ($.83)
salt and pepper
1½ cups shredded mozzarella cheese
($1.13)
1 cup baby carrots ($.49)

Prepare the whole wheat pizza dough. Preheat the oven to 350 degrees. Roll out the dough and bake the crust for 8 minutes. Remove the crust from the oven.

Cut the zucchini lengthwise into ½-inch-thick slices. Brush the slices with some of the olive oil. Grill the zucchini for about 4 minutes, flip, and grill another 3 to 4 minutes.

Brush the remaining olive oil over the chicken breast and sprinkle with salt and pepper. Grill the chicken breast about 8 minutes on each side, or until it is cooked through.

Cut the grilled zucchini into pizza-size pieces, and thinly slice chicken into 2-inch strips. Set aside.

Spread the pizza sauce over the partially cooked dough. Top with the shredded mozzarella cheese, then the zucchini pieces and chicken strips.

Bake the full pizza for another 8 to 10 minutes.

Slice the Grilled Zucchini and Chicken Pizza and serve with Baby Carrots.

Cost $4.75

FRUGAL FACT: *Use zucchini from your garden on this delicious pizza!*

Hawaiian Pizza

homemade Whole Wheat Pizza
Dough (page 83) ($1)
1 cup Homemade Pizza Sauce
(page 85) ($.41)
4 ounces thinly sliced ham ($1.09)

1 can (6 ounces) crushed pineapple,
well drained ($.44)
2 cups mozzarella cheese ($1.50)
¼ cantaloupe ($.50)

Prepare the whole wheat pizza dough. Preheat the oven to 350 degrees. Roll out the dough and bake the crust for 8 minutes. Remove the crust from the oven.

Spread the homemade pizza sauce over the partially baked dough. Top with the shredded mozzarella cheese. Arrange the sliced ham and crushed pineapple over the cheese.

Bake the full pizza another 8 to 10 minutes, or until all the cheese has melted.

Slice the cantaloupe into wedges.

Slice the Hawaiian Pizza and serve with Cantaloupe Wedges.

Cost $4.94

FRUGAL FACT: *Cantaloupe prices fluctuate throughout the year. Some weeks over $4 per melon, and other weeks they may sell for just $1.*

Ultimate Veggie Pizza

homemade Whole Wheat Pizza
   Dough (page 83) ($1)
½ cup Basic Vinaigrette (page 280)
   ($.50)
1 small red onion ($.15)
1 green bell pepper ($.68)

1 small yellow squash ($.69)
2 tablespoons extra-virgin olive oil
   ($.20)
salt and pepper
2 cups shredded mozzarella cheese
   ($1.50)

Prepare the whole wheat pizza dough. Preheat the oven to 350 degrees. Roll out the dough and bake the crust for 8 minutes. Remove the crust from the oven.

Thinly slice red onion, bell pepper, and yellow squash. Put the sliced vegetables in a large bowl and toss with the olive oil. Season with salt and pepper.

Spread the vinaigrette over the partially baked dough. Top with the shredded mozzarella cheese. Arrange the sliced vegetables over the cheese.

Bake the full pizza another 8 to 10 minutes.

Slice the Ultimate Veggie Pizza and serve.

Cost $4.72

FRUGAL FACT: *A fantastic pizza to make in mid to late summer when fresh vegetable prices are at their lowest.*

Pizza Boats

6 homemade Hamburger Buns or
  Rolls (page 266) ($.55)
1 cup Homemade Pizza Sauce
  (page 85) ($.42)
2 cups shredded mozzarella cheese
  ($1.50)

15 to 20 pepperoni slices ($.50)
4 carrots ($.40)
2 peaches, sliced ($.75)

Prepare the dough for the homemade hamburger buns in a bread machine or in mixing bowl.

Finish preparing the bread as directed in the recipe.

Preheat the oven to 350 degrees. Place the cooled, sliced buns open side up. Spread a spoonful of the pizza sauce on top. Sprinkle with the shredded cheese and top with the pepperoni. Bake the pizza boats for 10 to 15 minutes, or until the cheese melts and the pepperoni are crispy.

Peel and cut the carrots into sticks, and slice the peaches.

Serve the Pizza Boats with Carrot Sticks and Sliced Peaches.

Cost $4.12

FRUGAL FACT: *Look for sale prices around $.50/pound for peaches during the summer months.*

Pizza Wraps

6 tortillas ($.77)
½ jar (about 1 cup) store-bought or
    leftover homemade pizza sauce or
    spaghetti sauce ($.50)
15 to 20 pepperoni slices ($.50)

1 green bell pepper, thinly sliced ($.68)
2 cups shredded mozzarella cheese
    ($1.50)
3 carrots ($.30)
¼ watermelon ($.75)

Preheat the oven to 350 degrees. On a clean work surface, lay out the tortillas flat. Spread 2 to 3 tablespoons of sauce on each tortilla. Layer each with 1 to 2 rows of pepperoni and bell pepper slices. Sprinkle with the shredded cheese.

Roll up the tortillas and place snugly into 8×8 baking dish. Bake in the preheated oven for 8 to 10 minutes, or until the cheese melts.

Peel and cut the carrots into sticks.

Cut the watermelon into slices, or dice into bite-size pieces.

Serve Pizza Wraps with Carrots and Watermelon.

Cost $5.00

FRUGAL FACT: *Homemade pizza sauce (page 85) or spaghetti sauce (page 275) can be made in a large batch and frozen in freezer ziplock bags or freezer-safe plastic containers.*

Deep Dish Pizza Potpie

1 tablespoon olive oil ($.10)

1 pound Italian sausage, cut into 1-inch chunks ($1.33)

1 garlic clove, peeled and finely chopped ($.05)

1 teaspoon dried oregano ($.05)

½ large onion, sliced into strips ($.15)

1 green bell pepper, stemmed, seeded, and sliced into strips ($.68)

1 can (28 ounces) diced tomatoes, drained ($.79)

1 cup ricotta cheese ($.57)

2 eggs ($.20)

½ cup grated Parmesan cheese ($.50)

1 cup homemade Whole Wheat Pizza Dough (page 83) ($1)

Prepare dough for whole wheat pizza crust in bread machine or in mixing bowl.

Heat the olive oil in a skillet, and add the sausage chunks. Sauté for 7 to 9 minutes, or until all the sausage pieces are cooked through. Transfer the sausage to paper towels to drain.

In the same skillet, sauté the garlic and oregano until the garlic softens. Add the sliced onion and bell peppers. Sauté until the bell peppers wilt and the onions turn opaque. Add the diced tomatoes and browned sausage and simmer over low heat for 20 to 30 minutes.

In a small mixing bowl, whisk the ricotta cheese with the eggs and Parmesan.

Preheat the oven to 375 degrees. Pour half the sausage filling in a 9 × 13-inch glass baking dish. Cover with dollops of the ricotta mixture, smoothing it out with a spatula to make an even layer of cheese. Cover the ricotta with the remaining sausage mixture.

On a lightly floured work surface, roll out the pizza dough into a 10 × 14-inch rectangle. With floured fingers, carefully place the dough over the baking dish, allowing 1 to 2 inches to flop over the edge of the dish. Press the dough firmly along the edge of the dish to seal in the sausage and cheese layers. Cut 3 to 4 slits in the top of the dough with a small sharp knife to allow the steam to escape.

Bake the potpie in the preheated oven for 50 to 60 minutes, or until the crust is lightly browned and the filling is bubbling. Remove and let cool for about 10 minutes before serving.

Serve Pizza Potpie to your family or company.

Cost $5.42

FRUGAL FACT: *Coupons for fresh sausage are released in the newspaper on a regular basis. Pair the coupon with a sale price for the best deal on the sausage.*

A TWO-MEAL BONUS RECIPE: *Even though this final pizza recipe costs more than my $5.00 limit, I've included it here because it's delicious and easily feeds our family for two meals, taking it well below my $5.00 per meal limit. I also wanted to include it because everyone likes a delicious and economical dish you can serve to company!*

Whole Wheat Pizza Dough

1 cup lukewarm water
1 tablespoon extra-virgin olive oil
($.10)
1 cup whole wheat flour ($.25)
2 cups white flour ($.28)
1 packet active dry yeast ($.25)

1 tablespoon sugar ($.04)
1 teaspoon Italian seasoning ($.05)
2 tablespoons Parmesan cheese ($.10)
1 teaspoon salt
Olive oil and garlic salt (optional)

BY HAND DIRECTIONS

In a mixing bowl, combine the lukewarm water and 1 cup of the white flour. Add the yeast, sugar, salt, and oil. Whisk together to make a "spongy" dough. Let sit for 10 to 15 minutes.

Add the remaining 2 cups of flour to the sponge and stir with a wooden spoon. When the dough becomes thick enough, knead it by hand for 6 to 8 minutes on a floured surface or in a floured bowl, until it reaches the consistency of soft baby skin. Knead seasonings and Parmesan cheese into the dough. Place in a floured or greased bowl and let rise for 45 minutes to 1 hour.

Once the dough has risen and doubled in size, the dough is ready to be formed. Place the dough on a lightly floured work surface. Sprinkle flour over the dough and on the rolling pin. Roll out the dough to the desired size.

Brush the edges of the dough with olive oil and sprinkle with garlic salt, if desired.

Bake the crust for 8 minutes, remove from oven and load with toppings. Bake the full pizza another 8 to 10 minutes. Slice and serve.

BREAD MACHINE DIRECTIONS

Add the water and olive oil to the bread machine bowl. Add the whole wheat and white flours. With a spoon, create a well in the flour for the yeast. Add the yeast into the well, being careful to not let the yeast touch any water.

Add the sugar, Italian seasoning, Parmesan cheese, and salt.

Set to the dough cycle on the bread machine.

Once the dough has formed in the bread machine, carefully remove it and place it on a lightly floured counter. Sprinkle flour over the dough and on the rolling pin. Roll out the dough to the desired size.

This recipe will make two 8-inch thin-crust pizzas, four 4-inch-deep-dish pizza crusts, or one 16-inch thick-crust pizza.

Brush the edges of the dough with olive oil and sprinkle with garlic salt, if desired.

Bake the crust for 8 minutes, remove from oven, and load with the toppings. Bake the full pizza another 8 to 10 minutes. Slice and serve.

Cost $1.00

FRUGAL FACT: *Involve young children in the pizza dough–making process. It might be messy, but will create warm memories in both yours and your children's minds!*

Homemade Pizza Sauce

1 can (15 ounces) tomato sauce ($.59)
1 teaspoon dried oregano ($.05)
1 teaspoon dried basil ($.05)
1 teaspoon garlic powder ($.05)

1 teaspoon onion powder ($.05)
2 teaspoons extra-virgin olive
   oil ($.05)

In a small saucepan or skillet, whisk the tomato sauce with the spices and olive oil. Simmer for 6 to 8 minutes.

This recipe makes 2 cups of pizza sauce.

Cost $.84

FIVE

Chicken and Turkey Meals

Sloppy Chicken Joes

1½-pound package boneless, skinless chicken breasts ($2.52)

1 can (15 ounces) tomato sauce ($.59)

2 teaspoons apple cider vinegar ($.05)

1 tablespoon prepared mustard ($.05)

3 tablespoons brown sugar ($.10)

½ teaspoon salt

½ teaspoon black pepper

1 teaspoon crushed red pepper flakes (optional)

4 to 6 homemade Hamburger Buns (page 266) ($.55)

¼ watermelon ($.75)

2 apples ($.25)

Prepare the dough for the homemade hamburger buns in a bread machine or in mixing bowl.

Finish preparing the buns as directed in the recipe.

Dice the chicken breasts into ½-inch pieces.

In a large skillet, whisk together the tomato sauce, vinegar, mustard, brown sugar, salt, and pepper. Add the diced chicken breast, cover, and cook over medium heat for 8 to 10 minutes, or until the chicken pieces are cooked through.

Slice the watermelon and apples.

Serve Sloppy Chicken Joes with Watermelon and Sliced Apples.

Cost $4.86

FRUGAL FACT: *Substitute one 15-ounce can of store-bought Sloppy Joe sauce for the tomato sauce, vinegar, mustard, brown sugar, salt, and pepper. Substitute 1 to 2 cups of leftover shredded chicken meat for the chicken breasts.*

Almost Cobb Salad

1 cup shredded, cooked leftover
   chicken ($.75)
1 head lettuce ($.88)
1 tomato, diced ($.50)
2 hard-boiled eggs ($.20)
½ cup mild Cheddar cheese, shredded
   ($.37)

1 cucumber, peeled and diced ($.50)
homemade Honey-Mustard Salad
   Dressing (page 281) ($1)
homemade Cloverleaf Dinner Rolls
   (page 258) ($.49)

Prepare the dough for the rolls in bread machine or in mixing bowl.

Cut the lettuce with a plastic lettuce knife to prevent browning. Dice the tomatoes, cucumber, and hard-boiled eggs. Toss with the lettuce, shredded leftover chicken, cheese, and the homemade honey-mustard dressing.

Finish preparing the bread as directed in the recipe.

Serve Almost Cobb Salad with homemade Cloverleaf Dinner Rolls.

Cost $4.69

FRUGAL FACT: *Save $1 on this meal by getting the tomato or cucumber from your garden.*

Asian Chicken Wraps

3 boneless, skinless chicken breasts ($2.52)

2 tablespoons store-bought teriyaki sauce ($.20)

1 teaspoon soy sauce ($.05)

3 carrots, peeled and julienned ($.30)

1 handful chopped romaine lettuce ($.10)

¼ cup peanuts, finely chopped ($.25)

4 to 6 burrito-size flour tortillas ($.59)

1 bag (12 ounces) snow peas ($.99)

salt and pepper

In a bowl, marinate the chicken breasts in the teriyaki and soy sauces for at least 30 minutes in the refrigerator.

In a skillet, sauté the chicken with the marinade, 6 to 8 minutes on each side, or until it is no longer pink in the middle. The cooking time will vary depending on thickness of the chicken breast. Slice the cooked chicken into ½-inch-thick strips.

Julienne or shred the carrot sticks and chop the romaine lettuce.

Rinse the snow peas and pat dry. Place them in a saucepan with about ½ inch of water. Bring to a boil, then reduce the heat and simmer for 1 to 2 minutes. Season the steamed snow peas with a pinch or two of salt and pepper.

Assemble the wraps using the chicken strips, julienned carrots, chopped lettuce, chopped peanuts, and tortillas.

Serve Asian Chicken Wraps with Steamed Snow Peas.

Cost $5.00

FRUGAL FACT: *Keep an eye out for bags of "specialty" vegetables like snow peas and sugar snap peas that have been reduced for quick sale.*

Autumn Chicken

1 cup apple juice ($.30)
6 bone-in chicken thighs ($2.19)
salt and pepper
½ onion, quartered ($.15)
2 large Macintosh apples, sliced ($1.14)

3 tablespoons lemon juice ($.15)
1 teaspoon ground cinnamon ($.05)
1 cup white rice ($.20)
2 heads broccoli ($.79)

Pour the apple juice into the insert of the slow cooker. Place the chicken thighs in the juice and sprinkle with salt and pepper. Place the onion quarters around the chicken.

Slice the apples and toss with the lemon juice and cinnamon in a mixing bowl. Place the apples on top of chicken in the slow cooker. Set the slow cooker on low and cook for 8 hours. Once cooked, remove the chicken and serve topped with the apple slices.

In a medium saucepan, bring 2½ cups of water to boil, add the rice, and bring back to a boil. Reduce the heat, cover, and simmer for 20 minutes. Fluff the rice with a fork before serving.

Cut the broccoli into spears and trim the stems. Steam the broccoli in stovetop steamer for 4 to 5 minutes, or microwave for 4 to 5 minutes in a microwave-safe bowl, covered with plastic wrap.

Serve Autumn Chicken with Rice and Steamed Broccoli.

Cost: $4.97

FRUGAL FACT: *Best sale prices for broccoli can be as low as $.88/bunch. Look for a bunch with 4 large broccoli heads.*

Bacon-Wrapped Apple Chicken

½ cup store-bought BBQ sauce ($.25)
1 Granny Smith apple, peeled and
grated ($.25)
1 tablespoon lemon juice ($.05)
3 boneless, skinless chicken breasts
($2.52)

3 slices bacon, cut in half crosswise
($.38)
2 sweet potatoes ($.99)
1 cup frozen green beans ($.50)

In a small bowl, combine the BBQ sauce with the grated apple and lemon juice.

Place the chicken breast in slow cooker, pour the BBQ-apple mixture over the chicken. Wrap 3 pieces of bacon over each sauced chicken breast. Set the slow cooker on low and cook for 8 hours.

Preheat the oven to 350 degrees. Make a few slits in the sweet potatoes using a small sharp knife. Put the sweet potatoes in a baking dish with ¼ inch of water and cover with aluminum foil. Bake the sweet potatoes in the preheated oven for 1 hour. Remove from the oven and let cool about 10 minutes. Peel off the skins and mash the pulp.

Cook the frozen green beans according to the package directions.

Serve Bacon-Wrapped Apple Chicken with Mashed Sweet Potatoes and Green Beans.

Cost $4.96

FRUGAL FACT: *Because the protein portion of this meal is more expensive, consider using vegetables that you have stockpiled and frozen.*

Baked Chicken and Acorn Squash

½ cup orange juice ($.10)
2 bone-in, split chicken breasts ($1.79)
1 teaspoon dried or fresh rosemary
   ($.05)
1 teaspoon garlic powder ($.05)
½ teaspoon salt

½ teaspoon black pepper
1 acorn squash ($1.17)
2 teaspoons brown sugar ($.05)
1 cup brown rice ($.40)
2 heads broccoli ($.79)

Pour ¼ cup of orange juice into the bottom of 9×13-inch baking dish. Place the chicken breasts in the baking dish and pour the remaining ¼ cup of orange juice over the chicken. Sprinkle the rosemary, garlic powder, and salt and pepper over the chicken.

Preheat the oven to 350 degrees. Put the acorn squash in microwave for 3 to 4 minutes to loosen the skin so it is easier to remove. Let cool a few minutes before slicing off the skin. Scrape out and discard the seeds, and cut the squash flesh into 1-inch cubes. Put the cubes into the baking dish around the chicken. Sprinkle the brown sugar over the squash cubes.

Bake the chicken and squash in the preheated oven for 1 hour, or until the juices of the chicken breasts run clear.

In a medium saucepan, bring 2½ cups of water to a boil, add the brown rice, and bring back to a boil. Reduce the heat, cover, and simmer for 40 to 50 minutes. Fluff the rice with a fork before serving.

Cut the broccoli in spears and trim the stems. Steam the broccoli in a stovetop steamer for 4 to 5 minutes, or microwave for 4 to 5 minutes in a microwave-safe bowl, covered with plastic wrap.

Serve Baked Chicken and Acorn Squash with Brown Rice and Steamed Broccoli.

Cost $4.44

FRUGAL FACT: *Bone-in split chicken breasts often run $.50 to $1/pound less than boneless, skinless chicken breasts, plus the bones can be used to make Homemade Chicken Stock (page 273).*

Bourbon Chicken

6 bone-in, chicken thighs ($2.19)
½ cup store-bought bourbon-flavored
 marinade ($.50)
1 cup brown rice ($.40)

2 small yellow summer squash ($1.29)
¼ cup grated Parmesan cheese
 ($.25)

Marinate the chicken thighs in store-bought marinade in a ziplock bag, for at least 30 minutes in the refrigerator. Preheat the oven to 350 degrees. Bake the thighs with the marinade in a 9 × 13-inch-glass baking dish for 45 to 55 minutes, or until the chicken is no longer pink in the middle.

In a medium saucepan, bring 2½ cups of water to a boil, add the brown rice, and bring back to a boil. Reduce the heat, cover, and simmer for 40 to 50 minutes. Fluff the rice with a fork before serving.

Preheat the oven to 350 degrees. Cut the summer squash in half lengthwise and place cut side down in a glass baking dish. Add ¼ inch of water to the baking dish and cover with aluminum foil. Bake in the preheated oven for 50 to 60 minutes. Remove the squash from the oven and let cool for 5 to 10 minutes before handling. Scrape out and discard the seeds, then scrape out the squash flesh. Drain the squash and sprinkle with Parmesan just before serving.

Serve Bourbon Chicken with Brown Rice and Steamed Summer Squash.

Cost $4.63

FRUGAL FACT: *If you are in a pinch and wish to use a store-bought marinade, keep an eye out for coupons and match with sales around Memorial Day and the Fourth of July.*

Chicken and Red Bean Burritos

½ cup dried red kidney beans ($.20)
2 cups shredded, leftover cooked
    chicken ($1.50)
½ cup white rice ($.10)
1 can (15 ounces) diced tomatoes,
    drained ($.59)

1 teaspoon chili powder ($.05)
1 teaspoon ground cumin ($.05)
½ cup shredded Cheddar cheese ($.42)
8 whole wheat burrito-size tortillas
    ($1.29)
2 heads broccoli ($.79)

Soak the dried red kidney beans overnight or bring to a boil in a generous amount of water, remove from the heat and let soak for at least 2 hours in the hot water. Drain and rinse the beans. Add the beans to a medium saucepan with at least 2 inches of water covering them. Bring to a boil. Cover, reduce the heat to medium, and cook for 1½ hours, or until the beans are soft.

In a medium saucepan, bring 1¼ cups of water to a boil, add the white rice and bring back to a boil. Reduce the heat, cover, and simmer for 20 minutes. Fluff the rice with a fork. Add the shredded chicken, cooked beans, and diced tomatoes to the saucepan with the cooked rice.

Preheat the oven to 350 degrees. On a clean work surface, lay out the tortillas flat. Spoon the rice mixture onto the tortillas. Sprinkle each with a handful of shredded Cheddar cheese and roll up. Place the burritos in 8×8-inch baking dish and bake in the preheated oven for 10 minutes, or until the cheese has melted.

Cut the broccoli into spears and trim the stems. Steam the broccoli in a stovetop steamer for 4 to 5 minutes, or microwave for 4 to 5 minutes in a microwave-safe bowl, covered with plastic wrap.

Serve Chicken and Rice Burritos with Steamed Broccoli.

Cost $4.99

FRUGAL FACT: *When broccoli is on sale, buy a few extra bunches and blanch and freeze the broccoli. Blanch by boiling broccoli for 1 to 2 minutes in large saucepan with water. Remove the broccoli from the saucepan with slotted spoon and place into large bowl filled with half ice and half water. Drain. Once blanched and cooled, the broccoli can be safely frozen in freezer ziplock bags.*

Chicken and Rice Salad

2 cups brown rice ($.80)
3 boneless, skinless chicken breasts
    ($2.52)
2 teaspoons extra-virgin olive oil
    ($.10)
1 teaspoon garlic powder ($.02)

salt and pepper
1 cup frozen pineapple ($.50)
1 cup chopped or sliced almonds
    ($.50)
½ cup apple juice ($.15)
2 heads broccoli ($.79)

In a medium saucepan, bring 5 cups of water to a boil, add the brown rice, and bring back to a boil. Reduce the heat, cover, and simmer for 40 to 50 minutes. Fluff the rice with a fork.

Heat the olive oil in a medium skillet, add the chicken breasts, and sprinkle the garlic powder, salt, and pepper over the top. Sauté the chicken for 6 to 8 minutes on each side, or until no longer pink in the middle. The cooking time may vary depending on the thickness of each chicken breast. Remove the chicken from the skillet and cut into bite-size pieces.

In a large bowl, combine the cooked brown rice, apple juice, diced chicken, diced pineapple, and almonds. Refrigerate the salad for at least 2 hours, if you prefer it chilled.

Cut the broccoli into spears and trim the stems. Steam the broccoli in a stovetop steamer for 4 to 5 minutes, or microwave for 4 to 5 minutes in a microwave-safe bowl, covered with plastic wrap.

Serve warm or chilled Chicken and Rice Salad with Steamed Broccoli.

Cost $4.89

FRUGAL FACT: *Look out for coupons from the nut companies and frozen fruit companies. Without using coupons for the almonds and pineapples, this meal would have been more than $5.*

Chicken and Cornbread Dumplings

3 boneless, skinless chicken breasts, diced ($2.52)
1 bag (16 ounces) frozen mixed vegetables ($1)
3 cups Homemade Basic White Sauce (page 276) ($.60)
½ cup flour ($.10)
½ cup yellow cornmeal ($.10)
2 tablespoons sugar ($.05)
2 teaspoons baking powder ($.05)
½ teaspoon salt
½ cup milk ($.04)
1 egg ($.11)
1 head broccoli ($.40)

Dice the chicken breasts and place in the insert of a slow cooker. Pour the frozen veggies over the chicken, and then pour the homemade white sauce over the chicken and veggies. Add ½ to 1 cup of water to completely cover the chicken.

In a mixing bowl, combine the flour, yellow cornmeal, sugar, baking powder, and salt. Whisk in the milk and egg to form a batter.

Pour the cornbread batter over the chicken and sauce in the slow cooker. Set the slow cooker on low, and cook for 8 hours.

Cut the broccoli into spears and trim the stems. Steam the broccoli in a stovetop steamer for 4 to 5 minutes, or microwave for 4 to 5 minutes in a microwave-safe bowl, covered with plastic wrap.

Serve Chicken and Cornbread Dumplings with Steamed Broccoli.

Cost $4.92

FRUGAL FACT: *It is more frugal to make your own mixes, such as for cornbread, but sometimes frugality means saving time as well. Premade cornbread mixes can be purchased for sale prices as low as $.35, for a mix that makes 6 muffins. Substitute 2 boxes of premade muffin mix for this recipe if you are trying to save a little extra time.*

Slow Cooker Chicken Fajitas

2 large boneless, skinless chicken
  breasts ($1.66)
1 can (15 ounces) diced tomatoes and
  green chilies ($.37)
1 green bell pepper, sliced ($.68)
½ onion, sliced ($.15)

1 teaspoon ground cumin ($.05)
1 cup brown rice ($.40)
1 cup homemade Guacamole
  (page 279) ($.80)
6 to 8 whole wheat or corn tortillas
  ($.79)

Marinate the chicken in the diced tomatoes with green chilies for at least 30 minutes in the refrigerator (or see Frugal Fact for another option). Once marinated, place chicken breasts with the marinade juices into the insert of a slow cooker. Add the sliced bell peppers and sliced onions around the chicken. Set the slow cooker on high, and cook for 6 hours.

Prepare the homemade guacamole.

In a medium saucepan, bring 2½ cups of water to a boil, add the brown rice, and bring back to a boil. Reduce the heat, cover, and simmer for 40 to 50 minutes. Fluff the rice with a fork before serving.

Wrap the tortillas in paper towels and warm in the microwave for 2 to 3 minutes, or until the tortillas in the middle of the stack are warm. Prepare the fajitas by adding chicken, bell peppers, onions, and guacamole to each warm tortilla.

Serve Slow Cooker Chicken Fajitas with Homemade Guacamole and Rice.

Cost $4.80

FRUGAL FACT: *If you plan to freeze chicken breasts in individual portions after buying a large family pack, consider adding the diced tomatoes and green chilies before freezing. As the chicken thaws, it will marinate in the sauce.*

Chicken Marinara over Angel Hair

4 bone-in chicken thighs ($2.25)
1 teaspoon olive oil ($.05)
2 cups Homemade Spaghetti Sauce
  (page 275) ($.60)

1 package (16 ounces) angel hair
  pasta ($.97)
2 heads broccoli ($.39)
½ cup Parmesan cheese ($.50)

In a medium skillet, heat the oil, add the chicken thighs, and sauté until browned.

Without removing the thighs from the pan, add ¼ cup of water to deglaze the pan, scraping up all the browned bits.

Add the spaghetti sauce, stir well, and simmer, covered, for about 30 minutes until the thighs are cooked and tender.

When the thighs are cooked, remove them from the sauce, transfer to a plate, and cool slightly. When cool enough to handle, remove the skin and bones. Shred the thigh meat and return it to the sauce.

Cook the angel hair pasta according to the package directions.

Cut the broccoli into spears and trim the stems. Steam the broccoli in a stovetop steamer for 4 to 5 minutes, or microwave for 4 to 5 minutes in a microwave-safe bowl, covered with plastic wrap.

Drain the angel hair pasta, place on a serving platter, and top with the chicken and sauce. Sprinkle with the Parmesan cheese.

Serve Chicken Marinara over Angel Hair with Steamed Broccoli.

Cost $4.76

FRUGAL FACT: *Purchase 5-pound or larger "bulk" bags of pasta that have a lower per unit price than 1- or 2-pound bags.*

Easy Chicken Potpie

3 cups Homemade Cream of Chicken White Sauce (see variation page 276) ($.50)

2 diced chicken breasts or 2 cups leftover shredded cooked chicken ($1.66)

½ onion, chopped ($.15)

2 potatoes, peeled and diced ($.30)

1½ cups frozen peas and carrots ($.75)

½ teaspoon dried thyme ($.05)

¼ cup butter ($.40)

¾ cup white flour ($.15)

1½ teaspoons baking powder ($.05)

1 cup milk ($.10)

2 heads broccoli ($.79)

Prepare the homemade "cream of chicken" white sauce.

Combine sauce, raw diced chicken or shredded leftover chicken, chopped onions, diced potatoes, and frozen peas and carrots in a 10-inch-deep glass pie dish. Mix well.

Preheat the oven to 350 degrees. In a small mixing bowl, melt the butter. Stir in flour, baking powder, and milk. Whisk until it forms a thin batter. Pour the batter over the chicken and sauce in the pie dish; the batter will thicken as it bakes.

Bake the potpie for 45 to 55 minutes, or until the chicken pieces have cooked through and the sauce is bubbly.

Remove stems and separate the broccoli into florets. Steam the florets in a stovetop steamer for 4 to 5 minutes, or microwave for 4 to 5 minutes in a microwave-safe bowl, covered with plastic wrap.

Serve Chicken Potpie with Steamed Broccoli.

Cost $4.90

FRUGAL FACT: *Substitute shredded turkey meat in place of the chicken—another way to use up post-holiday turkey meat.*

Chicken Potato Pie

2 boneless, skinless chicken breasts ($1.66)

2 to 3 teaspoons extra-virgin olive oil ($.10)

1 to 2 tablespoons prepared mustard ($.05)

1 teaspoon garlic powder ($.01)

salt and pepper

1 bag (16 ounces) frozen mixed vegetables ($.99)

6 large white potatoes ($.80)

½ to 1 cup milk ($.08)

1 tablespoon butter ($.10)

2 ears of corn, broken in half ($.50)

Dice the chicken breasts. In a medium skillet, heat the olive oil. Add the diced chicken and the mustard. Sprinkle the garlic powder, salt, and pepper over the top. Sauté the diced chicken for 6 to 8 minutes, until cooked through. The cooking time may vary depending on the thickness of the chicken.

Cook the frozen vegetables according to the package directions. Drain and pat dry with paper towels. Add to the skillet with the cooked chicken and stir thoroughly to combine.

Peel and quarter the potatoes and boil in the medium saucepan for 10 minutes, or until tender. Drain and return to the saucepan. Mash the potatoes with ½ cup of milk, the butter, and salt and pepper to taste. Add up to ½ cup more of milk to reach the desired consistency. Because the mashed potatoes will act like a "bowl for the chicken," the consistency should be thick.

Place a portion of mashed potatoes on each serving plate and make a well in the center. Fill with the chicken and veggie mixture. Rinse the saucepan and reuse to boil the corn.

Remove the husks and silk from the corn and then snap the ears of corn in half. Boil in a large pot of boiling water for 4 to 5 minutes.

Serve Chicken Potato Pie with Half-ears of Corn.

Cost $4.30

FRUGAL FACT: *A delicious gluten-free alternative to the traditional Chicken Potpie.*

Chicken Succotash

1 cup brown rice ($.40)
2 tablespoons butter ($.20)
½ onion, chopped ($.15)
2 cups shredded, leftover, cooked
   chicken ($1.50)
1 cup frozen corn kernels ($.50)

1 cup frozen lima beans ($.50)
1 cup 2-percent or whole milk ($.10)
1 tomato, diced ($.54)
salt and pepper
2 Red Delicious apples ($.50)

In a medium saucepan, bring 2½ cups of water to a boil, add the brown rice, and bring back to a boil. Reduce the heat, cover, and simmer for 40 to 50 minutes. Fluff the rice with a fork before serving.

In a large skillet, melt the butter, add the chopped onions, and sauté for 4 to 5 minutes, or until translucent. Add the shredded cooked chicken, corn kernels, lima beans, and milk and cook for another 5 minutes, or until the vegetables have thawed and the sauce has thickened. Just before serving, add the diced fresh tomato. Season with salt and pepper to taste.

Slice the apples.

Serve Chicken Succotash over Brown Rice and Sliced Apples.

Cost $4.45

FRUGAL FACT: *Plan this meal two or three days after roasting a whole chicken to use up the leftover chicken meat.*

Chicken and Fried Plantains

1 whole chicken ($4.40/3 = $1.47)
2 teaspoons garlic powder ($.05)
salt and pepper
2 plantains ($.66)

2 to 3 cups canola or vegetable oil ($1)
1 cup white rice ($.20)
ketchup ($.10)

Place the whole chicken in a slow cooker with 1 to 2 cups of water. (Adding extra water will help dilute the stock that will be made while the chicken cooks. Instructions on homemade chicken stock can be found below and on page 273). Season the chicken with the garlic powder, salt, and pepper. Set the slow cooker to low, and cook the chicken for 8 hours.

Cut the top off the plantain and make a lengthwise slice down the skin of the plantain. Peel the skin from the plantains, and cut the plantain flesh into 1½-inch-long chunks. In a medium saucepan, add oil to the depth of 1 inch and heat over medium-heat. When the oil is hot, add the plantain chunks and fry for 5 minutes. Remove carefully from the oil using slotted spoon and drain on paper towels placed on a cutting board. Stand the plantains upright and smash down with a potato masher or large rolling pin. Once all plantains have been flattened, return them to the oil and fry again for 4 to 5 minutes, until the plantains turn yellowish in color. Remove them from the oil with a slotted spoon and set on paper towels to absorb excess oil. Serve the fried plantains with ketchup.

In a medium saucepan, bring 2½ cups of water to a boil, add the rice, and bring back to a boil. Reduce the heat, cover, and simmer for 20 minutes. Fluff the rice with a fork before serving. Season with salt and pepper.

Once the chicken is cooked, remove it from the slow cooker and place it on a cutting board or a serving platter. Let it cool for about 10 minutes before carving.

Carve off as much chicken meat as you wish. Plan to use about one-third of the chicken for this meal, and shred and save the other chicken for future meals. Strain the stock that is leftover in the slow cooker and freeze. Save the bones and or carcass to make homemade Chicken Stock (page 273).

Serve Chicken with Rice and Fried Plantains.

Cost $3.48

FRUGAL FACT: *Look for sale prices for whole chickens that are less than $1/pound. Meat from a whole chicken that costs $4 to $5 can be stretched into three meals, making the cost for chicken for each meal well under $2.*

Cinnamon Chicken

1½-pound package bone-in chicken thighs, or drumsticks ($2.34)
1 teaspoon ground cinnamon ($.05)
salt and pepper
2 whole garlic cloves ($.10)
2 tablespoons extra-virgin olive oil ($.20)
½ onion, quartered ($.15)
1 can (15 ounces) stewed tomatoes, drained ($.59)

1 tablespoon dried Italian seasoning ($.05)
½ package (8 ounces) vermicelli pasta, broken ($.48)
½ cup Parmesan cheese ($.50)
4 carrot sticks ($.40)
salt and pepper

Place the chicken pieces in the insert of a slow cooker and add 1 cup of water. Sprinkle the cinnamon, salt, and pepper over the chicken pieces. Place the whole garlic cloves, olive oil, quartered onion pieces, drained stewed tomatoes, and Italian seasoning around the chicken in the slow cooker. Set the slow cooker on low, and cook the chicken for 8 hours.

When the chicken is just about done, bring 3 cups of water to a boil in a medium saucepan. Add the broken vermicelli pasta and cook according to the package directions. Drain the pasta and return it to the pot. Sprinkle with the Parmesan cheese.

Peel and cut the carrots into rounds or sticks. In a small saucepan, boil the carrots in ½ cup of water for 5 to 6 minutes, or until tender. Drain. Season with salt and pepper to taste.

Serve Cinnamon Chicken with Parmesan Vermicelli and Boiled Carrots.

Cost $4.86

FRUGAL FACT: *Chicken thighs and drumsticks generally cost $.50/pound less than boneless, skinless chicken breasts. Add one of these other chicken cuts to your meal plans to save a little extra money each month.*

Ginger Chicken Stir-fry

2 boneless, skinless chicken breasts ($1.66)

2 teaspoons olive oil ($.05)

1 teaspoon vinegar ($.02)

juice of 1 orange (about ¼ cup) ($.20)

½ teaspoon ground ginger ($.03)

1 red bell pepper ($1)

1 green bell pepper ($.68)

salt and pepper

1 cup brown rice ($.40)

1 pound fresh green beans ($.89)

Dice the chicken breast into cubes. In a large bowl, marinate the diced chicken in the olive oil, vinegar, orange juice, and ground ginger for at least 30 minutes in the refrigerator.

Remove the stems and seeds from the bell peppers, and cut the peppers into ½-inch squares.

Once the chicken has marinated, place the chicken and marinade in skillet on the stovetop over high heat. Add the green and red bell peppers and stir-fry until the chicken is cooked through and the peppers are tender. Season with salt and pepper to taste.

In a medium saucepan, bring 2½ cups of water to a boil, add brown rice, and bring back to a boil. Reduce the heat, cover, and simmer for 40 to 50 minutes. Fluff the rice with a fork before serving.

Snap off the stems of the green beens. Steam the green beans in a stovetop steamer for 4 to 5 minutes, or microwave for 4 to 5 minutes in a microwave-safe bowl, covered with plastic wrap.

Serve Ginger Chicken Stir-fry over Brown Rice with Steamed Green Beans.

Cost $4.93

FRUGAL FACT: *Marinate meats in the baking dish or pan that you plan to cook them in. When grilling, marinate meats in a shallow dish or serving platter.*

Ginger–Sweet Potato Chicken Bake

2 boneless, skinless chicken breasts
  ($1.66)
2 sweet potatoes ($.99)
1 can (8 ounces) pineapple tidbits, in
  100 percent pineapple juice ($.59)
2 teaspoons extra-virgin olive oil
  ($.10)

1 teaspoon ground ginger ($.10)
1 teaspoon garlic powder ($.05)
1 teaspoon ground cinnamon ($.05)
salt and pepper
1 cup brown rice ($.40)
2 cups frozen green beans ($1)

Dice the chicken breasts into ½- to 1-inch cubes.

Peel the sweet potatoes and cut into 1-inch cubes.

Drain the pineapple, reserving about ½ cup of the juice to use when cooking the rice.

Preheat the oven to 350 degrees. In a 9×13-inch baking dish, combine the diced chicken breast, sweet potato pieces, and pineapple tidbits. Add the extra-virgin olive oil, ground ginger, garlic powder, ground cinnamon, and salt and pepper. Gently toss the ingredients in the baking dish.

Bake the chicken and sweet potatoes in the preheated oven for 20 minutes, uncovered. Remove the dish from the oven, cover with aluminum foil, and bake another 30 to 40 minutes, or until the chicken has cooked through. (Covering the dish will prevent the sweet potatoes from drying out.)

In a medium saucepan, bring 2½ cups of water to a boil, add the brown rice, and bring back to a boil. Reduce the heat, cover, and simmer for 40 to 50 minutes. Fluff the rice with a fork before serving.

Cook the frozen green beans according to the package directions. Season with salt and pepper to taste.

Serve Ginger–Sweet Potato Chicken Bake with Brown Rice.

Cost $4.97

FRUGAL FACT: *If you have to thaw chicken and cut it as well, cut it before it is completely thawed. It is easier to cut or dice chicken when it is partially frozen.*

Chicken Verde and Spanish Rice

3 boneless, skinless chicken breasts ($2.52)

1 tablespoon fajita seasoning ($.05)

¾ to 1 cup homemade Salsa Verde (page 278), or 1 can (5 ounces) green chilies ($.75)

1 cup white rice ($.20)

1 can (12 ounces) diced tomatoes with chilies ($.37)

1 teaspoon garlic powder ($.05)

1 teaspoon ground cumin ($.05)

2 cups frozen corn kernels ($1)

salt and pepper

Preheat the oven to 350 degrees. Place the chicken breasts in an 8×8-inch baking dish. Sprinkle with the fajita seasoning. Pour the homemade Salsa verde or can of green chilies over the chicken and cover with aluminum foil. Bake in the preheated oven for 30 to 40 minutes, or until the chicken breasts have cooked through. The cooking times may vary depending on the thickness of each chicken breast.

In a medium saucepan, bring 2½ cups of water to boil, add the rice, the diced tomatoes and green chilies with their juices, and the garlic powder, and cumin. Bring back to a boil. Reduce the heat, cover, and simmer for 20 minutes. Fluff the rice with a fork before serving.

Cook the frozen corn according to the package directions. Season with salt and pepper to taste.

Serve Chicken Verde with Spanish Rice and Corn.

Cost $4.99

FRUGAL FACT: *Stock up on cans of diced tomatoes with green chilies by matching coupons with sale prices.*

Grilled Chicken with Summer Salad

3 to 4 boneless, skinless chicken
   breasts ($2.52)
marinade for chicken (page 283)
   (page 284) ($.50)
½ head romaine lettuce ($.75)

1 plum tomato, seeded and diced
   ($.49)
homemade Balsamic Vinaigrette
   Dressing (page 280) ($.75)

Marinate the chicken breasts with your favorite marinade for at least 30 minutes in the refrigerator. Grill the chicken for 6 to 8 minutes on each side, or until chicken is no longer pink in the middle. The grilling time may vary depending on the thickness of each chicken breast.

Using a plastic lettuce knife to prevent browning, chop ½ head of romaine lettuce. Toss with the diced plum tomato.

Prepare the vinaigrette dressing. Toss the dressing with the salad just before serving.

Serve Grilled Chicken with Balsamic Summer Salad.

Cost $5.01

FRUGAL FACT: *Plan to eat leftover lettuce for lunch the following day.*

Honey-Lime Chicken

3 boneless, skinless chicken breasts
($2.52)
1 tablespoon lime juice ($.10)
3 tablespoons honey ($.20)
2 large tomatoes ($.99)

salt and pepper
2 tablespoons balsamic vinegar ($.10)
6 red potatoes ($.80)
2 teaspoons extra-virgin olive oil
($.20)

Whisk the lime juice and honey together. Place the chicken breasts in a skillet and pour the honey-lime mixture over chicken breasts and let marinate at least 30 minutes in the refrigerator.

Once the chicken has marinated, place the skillet over medium-high heat. Sauté the chicken breasts for 6 to 8 minutes on each side, or until the chicken is cooked through. The cooking time will vary depending on the thickness of the chicken breasts.

Thinly slice the tomatoes and lay flat in baking dish. Sprinkle with salt and pepper. Drizzle balsamic vinegar over the tomato slices. Place in the refrigerator and let the tomatoes marinate for at least 30 minutes. Serve chilled.

Scrub the red potatoes and dice them into 1-inch cubes. Sauté the diced potatoes in a skillet in the extra-virgin olive oil. Cover and cook for about 10 minutes, until the potatoes are cooked through. Stir two or three times while sautéing. Season with salt and pepper.

Serve Honey-Lime Chicken with Sautéed Red Potatoes and Balsamic Tomatoes.

Cost $4.90

FRUGAL FACT: *Add fresh basil from your garden to the tomatoes while they are marinating.*

Italian Turkey Burgers

1 pound ground turkey ($1.49)
1 box (10 ounces) frozen spinach, thawed and squeezed of excess water ($.50)
1 can (14.5 ounces) diced tomatoes with garlic and onion, drained ($.59)
1 teaspoon dried Italian seasoning ($.05)
1 teaspoon garlic powder ($.05)
1 teaspoon onion powder ($.05)
salt and pepper
1 tablespoon olive oil ($.10)
4 slices provolone cheese ($.75)
4 store-bought or homemade Hamburger Buns (page 266) ($.48)
4 large white potatoes ($.60)
1 teaspoon canola oil ($.02)
3 carrot sticks ($.30)

Preheat the oven to 350 degrees. Make the potatoes first. Scrub the potatoes and then slice lengthwise into wedges, about ⅛-inch thick. Place the potato wedges in bowl and toss with 1 teaspoon canola oil and salt and pepper. Lay the wedges out in a single layer on a greased baking sheet. Bake for 20 minutes, flip the wedges, and then bake another 15 minutes until golden brown.

Meanwhile peel the carrots and cut into sticks.

In a mixing bowl, combine the ground turkey, well-squeezed thawed spinach, drained, diced tomatoes, Italian seasoning, garlic powder, onion powder, and a few shakes of salt and pepper. Form into 4 burger-size patties.

In a large skillet over medium-high heat, heat the olive oil. Place the patties in the skillet and cook for 4 to 5 minutes on each side, or until cooked through. (The patties will be soft when you add them to the skillet. They will firm up as they cook and a slight crust will form on the outside.)

When the patties have finished cooking, top with the provolone slices and let cheese melt. Serve the burgers on store-bought or homemade hamburger buns.

Serve Italian Turkey Burgers with Oven Fries and Carrot Sticks.

Cost $4.98

FRUGAL FACT: *Watch for sale prices on 1-pound packages of ground turkey. The sales for ground turkey are often unadvertised, so check each time you browse the meat department at the store.*

Curried Pumpkin Soup, *page 212*

North Carolina Pulled Pork Sandwiches, *page 179*

Shrimp Scampi, *page 205*

Kusherie (Egyptian Lentils), *page 244*

Orange Beef and Broccoli Stir-Fry, *page 157*

Grammy's Pasta Salad, *page 54*

Potato Pizza, this time topped with pepperoni, *page 248*

Apple-Dijon Pork Roast, *page 166*

Jerk Turk–Island Turkey

2 tablespoons oil ($.10)

2 tablespoon Caribbean jerk
   seasonings ($.15)

1½ pounds turkey breast or legs
   ($2.49)

6 medium white potatoes ($.80)

2 tablespoons butter or olive oil ($.20)

½ to 1 cup milk ($.10)

salt and pepper

2 cups frozen corn kernels ($1)

In a small bowl, whisk together the oil and jerk seasonings. Pour the marinade over the turkey breast or legs, and let marinate for at least 30 minutes in the refrigerator.

Preheat the oven to 350 degrees. Bake the turkey breast or legs for 50 to 60 minutes, or until the turkey is cooked through. Internal temperature should reach 165°.

Meanwhile, peel and quarter the potatoes. Boil in a large pot for about 10 minutes, or until tender. Drain and return to the pot. Add the milk a little at a time, the butter, salt, and pepper, and mash with a potato masher. (Add the milk 2 tablespoons at a time, until the potatoes reach the desired consistency.)

Cook the frozen corn kernels according to package directions. Season with salt and pepper to taste.

Serve Jerk Turk–Island Turkey with Mashed Potatoes and Corn.

Cost $4.84

FRUGAL FACT: *Buy a small turkey or turkey breast when they are on sale around the holidays. Cut into smaller pieces with poultry shears and then freeze in 1- or 1½-pound portions.*

Lemon Chicken on Pasta

3 boneless, skinless chicken breasts ($2.52)

2 tablespoons olive oil ($.20)

¼ cup lemon juice ($.15)

¼ teaspoon garlic powder ($.02)

salt and pepper

1 package (16 ounces) angel hair pasta or spaghetti ($.97)

2 tablespoons olive oil ($.20)

1 pound fresh green beans ($.99)

In a small bowl, whisk 1 tablespoon of olive oil and lemon juice with the garlic powder and a few dashes of salt and pepper.

Place the chicken breasts in 8×8-inch glass baking dish. Pour the marinade over the chicken and let marinate for at least 30 minutes in the refrigerator.

Preheat oven to 350 degrees. Bake the chicken breasts for 55 to 60 minutes, or until the chicken is cooked through. The cooking time may vary depending on the thickness of the chicken breasts.

In a large pot, cook the pasta according to the package directions. Drain and return to the pot. Toss with remaining tablespoons olive oil, salt, and pepper.

Rinse the green beans and snap off the ends. Place in small saucepan with ½ cup of water and 2 teaspoons olive oil. Season with salt and pepper. Cover and cook over medium heat for 5 minutes. Drain and serve warm.

Serve Lemon Chicken on Pasta with Steamed Green Beans.

Cost $4.95

FRUGAL FACT: *Consider buying lemon juice in a large bottle and keeping it in the fridge. It's a more frugal option than buying fresh lemons and squeezing them. Add a splash of lemon juice to rice, seafood dishes, or use in place of vinegar in salad dressings.*

Grilled Margarita Chicken

Juice of 1 lime ($.33)
½ teaspoon lime grated zest
1 teaspoon finely chopped fresh
   cilantro ($.25)
3 boneless, skinless chicken breasts
   ($2.52)

1 tablespoon chicken or poultry
   seasoning ($.10)
1 cup brown rice ($.40)
4 ear corn ($1)
2 tablespoons butter ($.20)

In a small bowl, mix the lime juice, lime zest, and finely chopped cilantro. Place the chicken breasts in a shallow dish and sprinkle with the chicken or poultry seasoning. Pour the lime marinade over the chicken and let marinate in the refrigerator for at least 30 minutes.

Grill the chicken for 8 to 10 minutes on each side, or until chicken breasts are cooked through. The cooking time may vary depending on the thickness of the chicken breasts and the heat of the grill.

In a medium saucepan, bring 2½ cups of water to a boil, add the brown rice, and bring back to a boil. Reduce the heat, cover, and simmer for 40 to 50 minutes. Fluff the rice with a fork before serving.

Remove the husks and silk from the ears of corn and boil them in a large pot of water for 4 to 5 minutes, or place the ears of corn in a microwave-safe baking dish, cover with plastic wrap, and microwave for 7 to 9 minutes. Butter the corn.

Serve Grilled Margarita Chicken with Brown Rice and Buttery Corn on the Cob.

Cost $4.80

FRUGAL FACT: *Grow several pots of your favorite herbs in a kitchen window. Small packages of fresh herbs can cost the same or more than a plastic pot, dirt, and a few seeds. Growing your own will give you an endless supply of fresh herbs.*

Mango Chicken

1 cup brown rice ($.40)
½ cup chopped scallions ($.20)
1 tablespoon olive oil ($.10)
3 boneless, skinless chicken breasts
   ($2.52)

1 large, ripe mango ($.75)
1 pound fresh green beans ($.89)
1 tablespoon olive oil ($.10)
salt and pepper

In a medium saucepan, bring 2½ cups of water to a boil, add the brown rice, and bring back to a boil. Reduce the heat, cover, and simmer for 40 to 50 minutes. Fluff the rice with a fork before serving.

In a medium skillet, sauté the chopped scallions in olive oil. Add the chicken breasts and sauté for 2 to 3 minutes on each side until browned.

Peel the mango and cut on either side of the pit to remove the mango flesh. Slice the mango flesh into thin strips. Add the thinly sliced mango plus ½ cup of water to the chicken in the skillet. Cover and simmer for 20 to 25 minutes, or until the chicken is cooked through and the mangoes have softened.

Snap the ends off of the green beans. Steam the green beans in a stovetop steamer for 4 to 5 minutes, or sauté in 1 tablespoon of olive oil for 4 to 5 minutes. Season with salt and pepper to taste.

Serve Mango Chicken over Brown Rice with Green Beans.

Cost $4.96

FRUGAL FACT: *This is a delicious meal to make when mangoes are on sale for less than $1, or when you can buy frozen mangoes with a coupon. When choosing a fresh mango, gently squeeze the mango. If your thumb can easily leave a dent in the mango, it will be ready to use in this dish. Avoid mangoes with holes and/or brown spots.*

Maple Chicken

4 tablespoons pure maple syrup ($.50)
2 tablespoons butter, melted ($.20)
1 teaspoon paprika ($.05)
1 teaspoon ground cinnamon ($.05)
salt and pepper

2 large bone-in, split chicken breasts ($1.76)
1 cup brown rice ($.40)
1 pound fresh green beans ($.89)
2 tablespoons olive oil ($.20)

In a small bowl, whisk together the maple syrup, melted butter, paprika, cinnamon, and a pinch of salt.

Preheat the oven to 350 degrees. Place the split breasts on a broiler pan or roasting rack in a roasting pan. Brush with the maple sauce. Bake in the preheated oven for 55 to 60 minutes. After about 30 minutes of cooking, brush any remaining maple sauce over the chicken. Continue baking for another 25 minutes, for a total of 55 to 60 minutes.

In a medium saucepan, bring 2½ cups of water to a boil, add the brown rice, and bring back to a boil. Reduce the heat, cover, and simmer for 40 to 50 minutes. Fluff the rice with a fork before serving.

Snap off the ends of the green beans and place in a small sauce pan with 1 cup of water and the olive oil. Season with and pepper. Bring to boil, and then remove from the heat. Cover and let, green beans finish cooking about 5 minutes.

Serve Maple Chicken with Brown Rice and Green Beans.

Cost $4.25

FRUGAL FACT: *Best sale prices for bone-in, split chicken breast can be as low as $.99/pound. Be on the lookout for these great prices!*

Mexican Chicken Skillet

1 cup dried black beans ($.40)

1 cup white rice ($.20)

1 can (15 ounces) diced tomatoes with green chilies ($.59)

2 cups frozen corn kernels ($1)

½ onion, chopped ($.15)

2 cups shredded, leftover, cooked chicken ($1.50)

1 teaspoon ground cumin ($.05)

1 teaspoon garlic powder ($.03)

salt and pepper

½ cup shredded Cheddar cheese ($.38)

2 handfuls tortilla chips ($.50)

Soak the black beans overnight, or bring to a boil in a generous amount of water, remove from the heat, and let soak in the hot water for at least 2 hours. Drain and rinse the beans. Add the soaked beans to a saucepan with at least 2 inches of water covering the beans. Bring to a boil. Reduce the heat to medium, cover, and cook for about 1½ hours, or until the beans have softened.

In a medium saucepan, bring 2½ cups of water to a boil, add the rice, and bring back to a boil. Reduce the heat, cover, and simmer for 20 minutes. Fluff the rice with a fork before serving.

To a large skillet, add the diced tomatoes with green chilies, the frozen corn kernels, chopped onion, cooked, shredded chicken, ground cumin, garlic powder, salt, and pepper. Cook over medium heat for about 15 minutes while the rice is cooking.

Once the rice and black beans have finished cooking, add them to the skillet with the chicken mixture. Season with salt and pepper to taste. Simmer for 10 minutes, to give the flavors time to mix and mingle in the skillet!

Sprinkle the cheese over the still warm mixture in the skillet and let it melt.

Serve Mexican Chicken Skillet. Scoop with tortilla chips!

Cost $4.80

FRUGAL FACT: *Although canned beans are not as healthy as cooking dried beans, it may save a little extra time in the kitchen. Substitute 1 can (15 ounces) of no salt added black beans in place of the 1 cup of cooked dried black beans.*

Mini Meatloaves

1 acorn squash ($1.29)
1 tablespoon honey ($.05)
1 pound ground chicken ($1.49)
½ onion, finely chopped ($.15)
1 cup bread crumbs ($.25)
1 egg ($.10)
2 tablespoons ketchup ($.05)

1 teaspoon garlic powder ($.03)
salt and pepper
½ cup BBQ sauce ($.25)
6 large white potatoes ($.80)
½ to 1 cup milk ($.12)
2 tablespoons butter ($.20)

Preheat the oven to 350 degrees. Cut the acorn squash in half. Place cut side down in a baking dish with about ¼ inch of water. Cover with aluminum foil and bake in the preheated oven for 50 to 60 minutes. Remove and let cool 10 minutes before handling. Scoop out and discard the seeds, and then scoop out the flesh and mash. Drizzle the squash with honey or maple syrup.

In a large bowl, combine the ground chicken, chopped onion, bread crumbs, egg, ketchup, garlic powder, and a few dashes of salt and pepper. Scoop the meat mixture into muffin tins or mini loaf pan tins. Bake at 350 degrees for 30 minutes, or until the meatloaves are cooked through. Serve with BBQ sauce.

While the meatloaves are baking, peel and quarter the potatoes. In a large pot, boil the potatoes for about 10 minutes, or until tender. Drain and return to the pot. Add the milk a little at a time, the butter, salt, and pepper and mash with a potato masher. (Add the milk 2 tablespoons at a time, until the potatoes reach the desired consistency.)

Serve Mini Meatloaves with BBQ Sauce, Mashed Potatoes, and BBQ Acorn Squash.

Cost $4.99

FRUGAL FACT: *Ground chicken goes on sale every 8 to 12 weeks for $1.49/pound. Like the ground turkey, it is often an unadvertised special, so be on the lookout for this sale price.*

Oven-Fried Chicken Drumsticks

6 chicken drumsticks ($2.12)
4 tablespoons butter ($.25)
1 tablespoon paprika ($.05)
1 tablespoon garlic powder ($.05)
1 tablespoon onion powder ($.05)

½ teaspoon salt
6 to 8 slices of homemade French
    Bread (page 264) ($.48)
2 cups frozen lima beans ($1)

Prepare the dough for the bread in a bread machine or in a mixing bowl.

Preheat the oven to 350 degrees. Melt the butter in small mixing bowl. Combine the paprika, garlic powder, onion powder, and salt in another small shallow bowl. Dip each drumstick in the melted butter, and then roll through the seasonings bowl. Place the seasoned drumsticks into an 8×8-inch glass baking dish. Bake in the preheated oven for 35 to 45 minutes, or until the juices run clear. The cooking time may vary depending on the size and width of the drumsticks.

Cook the frozen lima beans according to the package directions.

Finish preparing the bread as directed in the recipe.

Serve Oven-Fried Chicken Drumsticks with French Bread and Lima Beans.

Cost $4.00

FRUGAL FACT: *Slice and freeze the remaining French bread. Pull from freezer and toast for a future meal, when you need a quick bread.*

Provolone-Wrapped Chicken

8 to 10 chicken tenderloins ($2.52)
2 tablespoons extra-virgin olive oil
  ($.10)
salt and pepper
4 to 5 slices provolone cheese, cut in
  half ($.75)

2 cup frozen peas ($1)
homemade Cloverleaf Dinner Rolls
  (page 258) ($.48)
1 to 2 tablespoons butter ($.10)

Prepare the dough for cloverleaf rolls in a bread machine or in a mixing bowl.

Preheat the oven to 350 degrees. Place the chicken tenderloins in a 8×8-inch glass baking dish and drizzle the olive oil over the top. Sprinkle with salt and pepper. Bake in the preheated oven for 25 to 35 minutes, or until the chicken is cooked through. Remove the chicken from the oven. Carefully wrap half a piece of provolone cheese around each chicken tenderloin. The cheese will melt over the warm chicken strips.

Cook the frozen peas according to the package directions.

Finish preparing the bread as directed in the recipe.

Serve Provolone-Wrapped Chicken with homemade Cloverleaf Dinner Rolls and Peas.

Cost $4.95

FRUGAL FACT: *Pairing inexpensive and homemade bread with other expensive ingredients will help keep overall meal costs at a minimum.*

Chicken Quesadillas with Corn and Black Bean Salsa

....

½ cup dried black beans ($.20)
2 chicken breasts ($1.66)
1 teaspoon canola oil ($.04)
1 cup frozen corn kernels ($.50)
1 teaspoon vinegar ($.05)
salt and pepper
6 whole wheat tortillas ($.97)
2 cup shredded cheddar cheese ($1.50)
sour cream, homemade Salsa Fresca (page 277), homemade Guacamole
     (page 279) (optional)

Soak the dried black beans overnight or bring to a boil in a generous amount of water, remove from the heat, and let soak for at least 2 hours in the hot water. Drain and rinse the beans. Add the soaked beans to a saucepan with at least 2 inches of water covering them. Bring to a boil. Cover, reduce the heat to medium, and cook for 1½ hours, or until the beans are soft. Drain.

Sauté the chicken in a skillet with oil for 6 to 8 minutes on each side, or until the chicken is no longer pink in the middle. Remove the chicken from the skillet and let cool. Shred or cut the chicken into ½-inch pieces to be used in the quesadillas.

Cook the frozen corn according to the package directions. Drain.

Preheat the oven to 350 degrees. In a small bowl, combine the cooked black beans, cooked corn, vinegar, and the remaining oil. Season the corn and black bean salsa with salt and pepper to taste.

Place a tortilla flat on a baking sheet. Sprinkle with the shredded cheese and shredded chicken. Place another tortilla on top. Repeat to make 3 quesadillas. Bake in the preheated oven for 10 to 15 minutes, or until the cheese has melted.

Serve Chicken Quesadillas with Corn and Black Bean Salsa.

Cost $4.98

FRUGAL FACT: *Thaw 1 to 1½ cups of bulk cooked black beans to use in this recipe. If you have leftover chicken on hand, use 2 cups of leftover shredded, cooked chicken instead of the chicken breasts. Purchase and freeze tortillas when they are on sale, and thaw, wrapped in foil, in a warm 200-degree oven.*

Rosemary-Orange Chicken

2 bone-in, split chicken breasts ($1.79)

3 oranges ($1)

2 tablespoons rosemary, dried or fresh ($.20)

salt and pepper

2 large sweet potatoes ($.99)

2 cup frozen peas ($1)

Place ½ cup water and split chicken breasts in the insert of a slow cooker. Squeeze the juice of 2 oranges over the chicken. Sprinkle the rosemary, salt, and pepper over the chicken. Slice the third orange into ⅛- to ¼-inch slices and arrange over the top of the chicken. Set the slow cooker on low, and cook the chicken for 8 hours.

Preheat the oven to 350 degrees. Make a few slits in the sweet potatoes using a small sharp knife. Bake the sweet potatoes for 1 hour in a baking dish with ¼-inch water, covered with aluminum foil. Remove from the oven and let cool about 10 minutes. Peel off the skins and mash the pulp.

Cook the frozen peas according to the package directions.

When the cooking is finished, remove the chicken from the slow cooker and allow to cool slightly. Pull the chicken meat off the bone. Save and freeze the chicken bones to make homemade chicken stock (page 273).

Serve Rosemary-Orange Chicken with Sweet Potatoes and Peas.

Variation: Slit one of the oranges and stuff it inside the chest cavity of a whole roasting chicken.

Cost $4.98

FRUGAL FACT: *The breast meat portion on a bone-in, split chicken breast is often larger than the boneless, skinless chicken breasts. Buy bone-in split breasts for more meat, for less money.*

Sour Cream Chicken Enchiladas

1 container (16 ounces) fat-free sour
   cream ($.50)
1 can (6 ounces) green chilies ($.59)
1 cup homemade Chicken Stock
   (page 273) ($.10)
1½ cups shredded, leftover, cooked
   chicken ($1.12)

salt and pepper
10 taco-size corn tortillas ($.69)
1 cup shredded Cheddar cheese
   ($.75)
2 cups frozen corn kernels ($1)

In a large skillet, whisk together the sour cream, green chilies, and 1 cup of chicken stock. Add more chicken stock, 1 tablespoon at a time, until the enchilada sauce reaches the desired consistency. Season the sauce with salt and pepper to taste. Scoop out 1 cup of the sauce and set it aside.

Stir the shredded chicken into the enchilada sauce and simmer about 10 minutes, to allow the flavors to mingle and infuse.

Preheat the oven to 350 degrees. Spoon the sauce onto the tortillas. Roll and place seam side down in a glass baking dish. Ten enchiladas will fit comfortably in a 9×13-inch baking dish.

Spread the reserved sauce over the tortillas.

Sprinkle the cheese over the top and bake the enchiladas in the preheated oven for 15 to 20 minutes, or until the sauce is bubbly and the cheese has melted.

Cook the frozen corn kernels according to the package directions. Season with salt and pepper to taste.

Serve Sour Cream Chicken Enchiladas with Corn.

Cost $4.75

Spaghetti Squash and Chicken Bake

....

2 boneless, skinless chicken breasts
    ($1.66)
1 teaspoon extra-virgin olive oil ($.05)
salt and pepper

1 spaghetti squash ($1.99)
1 cup Homemade Spaghetti Sauce
    (page 275) ($.32)
2 large sweet potatoes ($.99)

Dice the chicken breasts into ½-inch pieces and marinate in the olive oil, salt, and pepper for at least 30 minutes in the refrigerator.

While the chicken is marinating, preheat the oven to 350 degrees. Cut the spaghetti squash in half lengthwise. Place seed side down in glass baking dish with about ¼ inch of water. Bake in the preheated oven for 60 minutes. Remove and let cool before handling. Leave the oven on. Scoop out and discard the seeds, then scrape out flesh into 8×8-inch glass baking dish.

Add the diced chicken and 2 cups of spaghetti sauce to the squash in the baking dish. Bake in the preheated oven for 45 to 55 minutes, or until the chicken pieces are cooked through.

Make a few slits in the sweet potatoes using a small sharp knife. Bake the sweet potatoes at 350 degrees for 1 hour in baking dish with ¼-inch water, covered with aluminum foil. Remove from the oven and let cool about 10 minutes. Peel off the skins and mash the pulp. Serve with cinnamon and butter.

Serve Spaghetti Squash and Chicken Bake with Sweet Potatoes.

Cost $5.01

FRUGAL FACT: *In a pinch for time, substitute 1 cup of store-bought spaghetti sauce. If you don't plan to use remaining spaghetti sauce, freeze it in 1- or 2-cup portions for future meals. If your family likes it, you can go over the budget with a few pennies of garlic powder added to the marinade.*

Sweet Potato–Crusted Chicken

2 cups leftover crumbs from sweet
    potato chips ($.20)
½ teaspoon salt
½ teaspoon black pepper
¼ teaspoon ground cinnamon ($.01)
3 boneless, skinless chicken breasts
    ($2.52)

1 egg ($.10)
1 tablespoon canola oil ($.15)
1 butternut squash ($.69)
6 red potatoes ($1)
2 tablespoons extra-virgin olive oil ($.20)
1 teaspoon garlic powder ($.05)

Preheat the oven to 350 degrees. In a food processor or blender, grind the potato chips or leftover crumbs to make about 2 cups of sweet potato "crumbs". Place the ground potato chips in a bowl and mix in the cinnamon, salt, and pepper. In another small bowl, whisk the egg with the oil.

Dip the chicken breast in egg-oil mixture, and then dip into the sweet potato "crumbs" pressing to cover both sides of the chicken. Place the chicken in a 8×8 glass baking dish. Repeat for each chicken breast. Bake the chicken in the preheated oven for 45 to 55 minutes, or until the chicken is no longer pink in the middle. The cooking time may vary depending on thickness of the chicken breasts. Leave the oven on.

Cut the butternut squash in half lengthwise and place cut side down in glass baking dish. Add ¼ inch of water to the baking dish and cover with aluminum foil. Bake at 350 degrees for 50 to 60 minutes. Remove from the oven and let cool for 5 to 10 minutes before handling. Scrape out and discard the seeds, then scrape out squash flesh. Mash the squash and season with salt and pepper to taste.

Scrub the red potatoes and then dice into 1-inch cubes. Sauté the diced potatoes in a skillet in extra-virgin olive oil. Cover and cook for about 10 minutes, until the potatoes are cooked through. Stir two or three times while sautéing. Season with salt and pepper.

Serve Sweet Potato–Crusted Chicken with Butternut Squash and Sautéed Red Potatoes.

Cost $4.92

FRUGAL FACT: *Save and freeze the last bits of potato chips in a freezer-safe plastic container to use for potato chip–crusted chicken.*

Tex-Mex Chicken

....

1 cup dried pinto beans ($.40)
2 boneless, skinless chicken breasts,
    diced ($1.66)
1 cup homemade Salsa Fresca
    (page 277) or store-bought salsa
    ($1.01)

1 can (6 ounces) green chilies ($.59)
2 tablespoons flour ($.05)
salt and pepper
1 cup rice ($.20)
4 ears of corn ($1)
sour cream (optional)

Soak the dried pinto beans overnight or bring to a boil in a generous amount of water, remove from the heat and let soak for at least 2 hours in the hot water. Drain and rinse the beans. Add the soaked beans to a medium saucepan with at least 2 inches of water covering them. Bring to a boil. Cover, reduce the heat to medium, and cook for 1½ hours, or until the beans are soft. Drain and return to the saucepan.

Add the diced chicken breasts, salsa, green chilies, flour, and 2 cups of water to the saucepan with the cooked beans. Season with salt and pepper. Cover and simmer for 30 minutes, stirring occasionally, until the chicken pieces have cooked through.

In a medium saucepan, bring 2½ cups of water to a boil, add the brown rice, and bring back to a boil. Reduce the heat, cover, and simmer for 40 to 50 minutes. Fluff the rice with a fork before serving.

Remove the husks and silk from the ears of corn and boil in a large pot of water for 4 to 5 minutes, or place the ears of corn in a microwave-safe baking dish, cover with plastic wrap, and microwave for 7 to 9 minutes.

Serve Tex-Mex Chicken over Rice with Corn on the Cob.

Cost $4.89

FRUGAL FACT: *Substitute 2 cups of precooked pinto beans, or 1 can (15 ounces) pinto beans.*

Turkey and Cornbread

2 carrots ($.20)
1 cup chopped celery ($.15)
1 turkey breast (about 5 pounds)
($5.66/3 = $1.88)
½ cup flour ($.10)
½ cup yellow cornmeal ($.10)
2 tablespoons sugar ($.05)

2 teaspoons baking powder ($.05)
½ teaspoon salt
½ cup milk ($.04)
1 egg ($.11)
2 tablespoons honey ($.15)
2 cups frozen peas ($1)

Peel and chop the carrots and celery.

Place the turkey breast in a slow cooker with the chopped carrots and celery and 1 to 2 cups water. Season with salt and pepper. Set the slow cooker on low, and cook the turkey for 8 hours. When the cooking is finished, set the turkey aside, strain turkey stock, and freeze the stock as directed on page 273.

Preheat the oven to 350 degrees. In a mixing bowl, combine the flour, yellow cornmeal, sugar, baking powder, and ½ teaspoon salt. Whisk in the milk and egg to form a batter. Pour the batter into a 8×8-inch glass baking dish and bake the cornbread at 350 degrees for 15 to 20 minutes, or until a toothpick, inserted in the center, comes out clean. Serve the cornbread warm with honey.

Cook the frozen peas according to the package directions.

Serve Turkey with Warm Cornbread and Honey and Peas.

Cost $3.83

FRUGAL FACT: *A 5-pound turkey prepared in the slow cooker will yield enough turkey meat for at least three meals. Use ⅓ for this meal, and then pull off extra turkey meat from the bones, shred, and freeze in 2- to 3-cup portions to use for two or more future meals. By dividing out the cost of the larger turkey breast over 2 to 3 meals, the cost for each meal is less than $2 for the turkey meat.*

White Chicken Chili

....

2 boneless, skinless chicken breasts
   ($1.66)
½ onion, chopped ($.15)
2 cups Homemade Basic White Sauce
   (page 53) ($.40)
1 can (6 ounces) green chilies ($.59)
2 garlic cloves, crushed ($.10)

1 cup dried Great Northern beans
   ($.25)
1 pound asparagus ($.99)
1 tablespoon extra-virgin olive oil
   ($.10)
salt and pepper

Prepare 2 cups of the basic white sauce.

Dice chicken breast into ½-inch pieces. Place the diced chicken, chopped onion, crushed garlic, canned green chilies, dried beans, and 4 cups of water in a slow cooker. Pour the white sauce over the chicken and other ingredients in the slow cooker. Set the slow cooker to low, and cook the chili for 8 hours.

In a skillet sauté the asparagus in 1 tablespoon olive oil for approximately 5 to 6 minutes, stirring every other minute. When the asparagus is tender-crisp and turns bright green, it is ready to serve. Remove the asparagus from the skillet to prevent overcooking.

Serve White Chicken Chili with Sautéed Asparagus.

Cost $4.24

FRUGAL FACT: *Pair colorful vegetables with "white" meals, such as this chili, to ensure proper balance of nutrients in each meal.*

SIX

Beef Meals

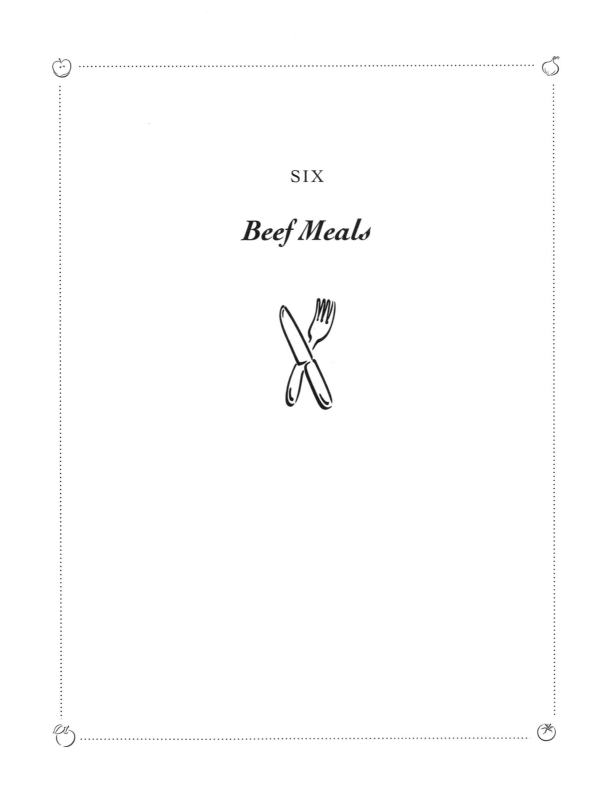

Beef and Lentil Bake

1 cup green lentils ($.40)
2 cups shredded, leftover, cooked beef roast ($1.50)
1 cup white rice ($.20)
1 can (8 ounces) tomato sauce ($.33)
2 tablespoons brown sugar ($.05)
2 teaspoons vinegar ($.05)
1 teaspoon Worcestershire sauce ($.05)
1 cup shredded Cheddar cheese ($.75)
4 carrot sticks ($.40)
1 to 2 teaspoons extra-virgin olive oil ($.05)
2 tablespoons honey ($.15)

To a medium saucepan, add the green lentils and 3 cups water. Bring to a boil, reduce the heat to medium, and simmer, tightly covered, for 30 minutes, or until the lentils are tender. Once the cooking is complete, drain off any excess liquid.

Preheat the oven to 350 degrees. In a medium saucepan, bring 2½ cups of water to a boil, add the rice, and bring back to a boil. Reduce the heat, cover, and simmer for 20 minutes. Fluff the rice with a fork before serving.

In a small bowl whisk the tomato sauce with the brown sugar, Worcestershire sauce, and vinegar.

In an 8×8-inch glass baking dish, combine the drained, cooked lentils, rice, shredded, cooked beef, and the sauce. Top with the cheese. Bake in the preheated oven for 20 minutes, or until the cheese has melted.

Peel and thinly slice the carrots into ⅛-inch rounds. Heat 1 to 2 teaspoons olive oil in skillet. Add the carrots and ¼ cup of water and cook for 2 to 3 minutes. Add the honey and stir well. Cook another 3 to 4 minutes, stirring often.

Serve Beef and Lentil Bake on Rice with Honey-Glazed Carrots.

Cost $3.93

FRUGAL FACT: *Purchasing frequently used ingredients with a longer shelf life, such as rice or pasta, in bulk sizes will reduce the "per meal" cost for the ingredients. For example, 1 cup of rice from a 10-pound bag comes out to be $.20, whereas 1 cup of rice from a 1-pound bag could be more than $.50.*

Beef Burrito Skillet

½ cup dried kidney beans ($.25)
¾ pound ground beef ($1.12)
1 cup homemade Salsa Fresca
    (page 277), or store-bought
    salsa ($.40)
2 teaspoons ground cumin ($.10)
salt and pepper

4 corn tortillas, cut in 1½-inch
    squares ($.25)
1 cup shredded Cheddar cheese ($.75)
2 cups frozen corn kernels ($1)
sour cream, homemade Guacamole
    (page 279), lettuce, tomato ($1) for
    garnish

Soak the dried kidney beans overnight, or bring to a boil in a generous amount of water, remove from the heat, and let soak for at least 2 hours in the hot water. Drain and rinse the beans. Add the soaked beans to a medium saucepan with at least 2 inches of water covering them. Bring to a boil. Cover, reduce the heat to medium, and cook 1½ hours, or until the beans are soft.

While the beans finish cooking, brown the ground meat in a skillet and drain the excess fat. Return the meat to the skillet and add the cooked beans, salsa, cumin, salt and pepper, and ½ cup of water. Bring the sauce to a boil, reduce the heat, and simmer for 5 to 10 minutes.

Stir in the corn tortilla strips, and top with the cheese. Remove the skillet from the heat. Cover and let sit for 5 minutes, to allow the cheese to melt.

Garnish with sour cream, guacamole, lettuce and/or tomato.

Cook the frozen corn kernels according to the package directions. Season with salt and pepper to taste.

Serve Beef Burrito Skillet with Corn.

Cost $4.87

FRUGAL FACT: *When 16-ounce bags of shredded cheese go on sale for less than $1.50 or $2, be sure to grab a few extra bags and stash them in the freezer.*

Beef Curry with Raisins

1 pound beef sirloin or beef roast, diced ($2.25)

2 cups homemade Beef broth (page 274) (free)

1 tablespoon curry powder plus ½ teaspoon curry powder ($.30)

1 Granny Smith apple, peeled and diced ($.25)

1 cup raisins ($.69)

½ teaspoon ground allspice ($.05)

2 tablespoons butter ($.20)

2 cups water

1 cup quick-cooking couscous ($.40)

1½ cups frozen broccoli ($.75)

Add the diced beef sirloin or roast with 2 cups of homemade beef broth to a slow cooker. Mix in 1 tablespoon curry powder and the peeled and diced apple. Set the slow cooker on low, and cook the curry for 8 hours. When there are approximately 30 minutes left on the slow cooker timer, add the raisins and the allspice.

To small saucepan, add the butter and the water. Stir in the couscous and the ½ teaspoon curry powder. Bring to a boil, remove from heat, cover tightly, and let stand for 5 minutes.

Cook the frozen broccoli according to the package directions. Drain and chop coarsely.

Just before serving, fluff the couscous with a fork, add the chopped broccoli, and toss until well combined.

Serve Beef Curry with Raisins over Broccoli Couscous.

Cost $4.79

FRUGAL FACT: *Raisins are often on sale at the national drugstore chains.*

Beef Enchiladas

1 cup dried pinto beans ($.40)
1 onion, finely chopped ($.30)
2 garlic cloves, crushed ($.10)
4 teaspoons ground cumin ($.20)
1 can (8 ounces) tomato sauce ($.33)
2 cups homemade Chicken Stock
  (page 273) ($.20)
2 tablespoons vegetable oil ($.05)

2 tablespoons cornstarch ($.05)
2 to 3 tablespoons chili powder ($.10)
1 teaspoon sugar ($.02)
10 corn tortillas ($.69)
¾ pound ground chuck ($.90)
2 cups shredded Cheddar cheese
  ($1.50)
1 cup white rice ($.20)

Soak the pinto beans overnight, or bring to a boil with a generous amount of water, remove from heat, and let soak at least 2 hours in the hot water. Drain and rinse the beans. Add the soaked pinto beans with half of the finely chopped onion, crushed garlic cloves, 2 teaspoons ground cumin, and a dash of salt and pepper to a slow cooker. Add enough water to cover the beans by 1 inch. Cook the beans on Low for 8 hours. Once cooked, mash with a potato masher.

Prepare the enchilada sauce. In a skillet, whisk together the tomato sauce, homemade chicken broth, and vegetable oil. When combined, vigorously whisk the cornstarch into the sauce so it doesn't get clumpy. Add the chili powder, remaining ground cumin, sugar, and salt and pepper to taste. Simmer for 8 to 10 minutes.

Preheat the oven to 350 degrees. Brown the ground chuck with the remaining chopped onion and drain the excess fat. Return the beef to the skillet and add 1 cup of the enchilada sauce.

Spread ¼ to ½ cup of the enchilada sauce in the bottom of a 9×13-inch baking dish. Place an open tortilla down into the sauce in the baking dish. Add some ground beef and sauce along the midline of the tortilla. Sprinkle with a bit of cheese. Roll up the tortilla. Repeat using all the tortillas and the beef sauce. Spread any remaining sauce over the top of the enchiladas. Sprinkle the remaining cheese over the top of the enchiladas.

Bake in the preheated oven for 15 to 20 minutes, or until the cheese has melted and sauce is bubbly.

In a medium saucepan, bring 2½ cups of water to a boil, add the rice, and bring back to a boil. Reduce the heat, cover, and simmer for 20 minutes. Fluff the rice with a fork before serving.

Serve Beef Enchiladas with Rice and Refried Beans.

Cost $5.04

FRUGAL FACT: *Double or triple the enchilada sauce portion of this recipe and freeze unused portions for another enchilada meal.*

Beef Fajitas

1 pound beef steak, cut into strips ($1.99)
2 tablespoons canola oil ($.10)
1 teaspoon ground cumin ($.05)
1 teaspoon garlic powder ($.02)
salt
1 green bell pepper ($.68)

½ onion ($.15)
8 burrito-size flour or wheat tortillas ($.99)
4 ears of corn ($1)
sour cream, homemade Salsa Fresca (page 277), homemade Guacamole (page 279) (optional)

In a medium bowl, toss the beef steak strips with the oil, ground cumin, garlic powder, and salt. Let marinate for at least 30 minutes in the refrigerator.

Remove the stem and seeds from the bell pepper, and thinly slice the pepper lengthwise. Peel the half onion and thinly slice in half-moons.

In a large skillet over high heat, sauté the marinated beef steak strips, with thinly sliced bell pepper and onion, for 6 to 8 minutes, or until the beef strips have cooked through and the pepper and onions have softened.

Wrap the tortillas in aluminum foil, or place them in a tortilla warmer. Warm in a 300-degree oven for 10 to 15 minutes, or until the tortillas in the middle of the stack have warmed through.

Wrap the sautéed beef and vegetables in the warm tortillas. Garnish with sour cream, homemade salsa, or homemade guacamole, if desired.

Remove the husks and silk from the corn and boil in large pot of water for 4 to 5 minutes.

Serve Beef Fajitas with Corn on the Cob.

Cost $4.98

FRUGAL FACT: *Substitute leftover beef roast for the beef steak strips. Shred the leftover beef roast and marinate as indicated above.*

Beef and Rice Casserole

¾ pound ground beef ($1.12)
½ onion, chopped ($.15)
1 cup white rice ($.20)
1 teaspoon olive oil ($.03)
1 can (15 ounces) diced tomatoes
 with their juices ($.59)
1 teaspoon dried Italian seasoning
 ($.05)

1 teaspoon garlic powder ($.05)
salt and pepper
1 cup shredded Cheddar cheese
 ($.75)
2 boxes (10 ounces each) frozen leaf
 spinach ($1)

In a skillet, brown the ground beef with the chopped onion. Drain the excess fat. Set aside.

Preheat the oven to 350 degrees. Add the rice plus 3 cups of water, olive oil, diced tomatoes, Italian seasoning, garlic powder, and salt and pepper to an 8×8-inch glass baking dish. Add the drained, cooked ground beef and onions. Stir to combine, and cover with aluminum foil.

Bake the casserole in the preheated oven for 1 hour. Remove from the oven, uncover, and fluff with a fork. Top with the shredded cheese, and return the casserole to the oven. Bake for another 10 minutes, or until the cheese has melted.

Cook the frozen spinach according to the package directions. Season with salt and pepper to taste.

Serve Beef and Rice Casserole with Spinach.

Cost $3.94

FRUGAL FACT: *It is generally cheaper to purchase a block of cheese and shred it yourself. Shred a 32-ounce block of cheese and freeze it in 1- or 2-cup portions.*

Beef Roast with Potatoes and Squash

....

1½ pounds beef roast ($2.73)
1 cup water
salt and pepper
2 white potatoes, cut in large dice
   ($.50)

3 carrot sticks ($.30)
½ onion, chopped ($.15)
1 large butternut squash ($1.25)

Place the beef roast in the insert of a slow cooker with the water. Sprinkle with salt and pepper.

Peel and dice the carrots, potatoes, and onion. Spread the vegetables around the beef roast. Set the slow cooker on low, and cook the beef and veggies for 8 hours.

Preheat the oven to 350 degrees. Cut the butternut squash in half lengthwise and place cut side down in a glass baking dish. Add ¼ inch of water to the baking dish and cover it with aluminum foil. Bake in the preheated oven for 50 to 60 minutes. Remove from the oven and let cool for 5 to 10 minutes before handling. Scrape out and discard the seeds, then scrape out the squash flesh. Mash the squash and season with salt and pepper to taste.

When the roast has finished cooking, remove it from the slow cooker along with all the cooked vegetables. Save the broth for use in a future meal (page 274).

Serve sliced Beef Roast with Roasted Potatoes, Squash, Carrots, and Onions.

Cost $4.93

FRUGAL FACT: *10-pound bags of potatoes are regularly on sale for less than $3 through the winter months.*

Beef Tacos

1 cup white rice ($.20)
¾ pound ground beef ($1.12)
½ onion, chopped ($.15)
2 teaspoons ground cumin ($.10)
salt and pepper
8 taco shells ($.75)

1 cup shredded iceberg lettuce
  ($.25)
1 plum tomato, chopped ($.54)
1 cup Cheddar cheese ($.75)
½ cup sour cream ($.15)
4 ears corn ($1)

In a medium saucepan, bring 2½ cups of water to a boil, add the rice, and bring back to a boil. Reduce the heat, cover, and simmer for 20 minutes. Fluff the rice with a fork before serving.

In a large skillet, brown the ground beef with chopped onion. Drain excess fat. Return the beef to the skillet and add the ground cumin, salt, and pepper, and ¼ cup of water. Simmer for 4 to 5 minutes.

Add the cooked beef to the taco shells and top with the shredded lettuce, diced tomato, shredded Cheddar cheese and sour cream.

Remove the husks and silk from the ears of corn and boil the corn in a large pot of water for 4 to 5 minutes, or place the ears of corn in microwave-safe baking dish, cover with plastic wrap, and microwave for 7 to 9 minutes.

Serve Beef Tacos with Rice and Corn on the Cob.

Cost $4.91

FRUGAL FACT: *Coupons for name-brand taco shells and sour cream are released several times throughout the year. Match the coupon with a sale or store promotion for the lowest price on taco shells and sour cream.*

Cheeseburger Pie

3 large sweet potatoes ($1.49)
¾ pound ground beef ($1.12)
½ onion, finely chopped ($.15)
1 can (15 ounces) diced tomatoes,
   drained ($.59)
½ cup milk ($.25)
3 eggs ($.30)

¾ cup flour ($.15)
1 teaspoon baking powder ($.05)
½ teaspoon baking soda ($.02)
½ teaspoon pepper
½ teaspoon salt
1 cup shredded Cheddar cheese ($.75)

Preheat the oven to 350 degrees. Make a few slits on the sweet potatoes with a small sharp knife. Bake the sweet potatoes for 1 hour in a baking dish with ¼ inch water, covered with aluminum foil. Remove from the oven and let cool about 10 minutes. Peel off skins and mash the pulp. Increase the oven temperature to 400 degrees.

In a skillet, brown the ground beef with the chopped onions and drain the excess fat.

Place the meat in bottom of a greased 10-inch pie dish. Add the well-drained canned tomatoes to the meat and mix to combine.

In a medium bowl, whisk the milk, eggs, flour, salt, and pepper. Pour over the meat mixture.

Bake the cheeseburger pie at 400 degrees for 25 minutes. Remove from the oven, top with the shredded cheese, and bake another 5 minutes, or until the cheese has melted and a knife inserted in the middle comes out clean. Let cool a few minutes before cutting and serving.

Serve Cheeseburger Pie with Mashed Sweet Potatoes.

Cost $4.87

FRUGAL FACT: *This is a great meal in which to use previously cooked/frozen ground beef. Simply thaw the cooked ground beef in the refrigerator, or microwave and skip step #2.*

Simple Cheeseburgers

1¼ pound ground beef ($1.86)
1 tablespoon steak seasoning ($.10)
4 slices mild cheddar cheese ($.75)
4 homemade Hamburger Buns
   (page 266) ($.50)

ketchup, mustard, and relish for
   serving ($.25)
4 ears of corn ($.80)
¼ watermelon ($.75)

Prepare the dough for the hamburger buns in a bread machine or in a mixing bowl.

Finish preparing the buns as directed in the recipe.

Form the ground beef into burger-size patties. Sprinkle with the steak seasoning.

Grill the burgers for 5 to 8 minutes on each side, or until cooked through. The cooking time will vary based on the thickness of the patties and the heat of the grill. Place the cheese slices on the cooked burgers and place the burgers on the top rack of the grill until the cheese melts.

Serve the burgers on homemade buns with your favorite condiments.

Remove the husks and silk from the corn and boil the corn in large pot of water for 4 to 5 minutes, or place the ears of corn in a microwave-safe dish, cover with plastic wrap, and microwave for 7 to 9 minutes.

Slice the watermelon into wedges.

Serve Cheeseburgers with Corn on the Cob and Watermelon.

Cost $5.01

FRUGAL FACTS: *First, compare prices of store-brand cheese slices versus name-brand cheese slices. Because there are few coupons released for sliced cheese, consider buying the store brand as a more frugal option. Second, grab hamburger buns when they are on sale for $1 or less and stash them in the freezer. They'll help when you're in a time crunch. Finally, if you want to include the corn, remember to keep this recipe for the summer months when corn is really inexpensive. During those months, I've seen corn priced as low as $.10 an ear.*

Chili-Topped Potatoes

....

1 cup dried red kidney beans ($.40)
1 cup dried black beans ($.40)
6 large baking white potatoes ($.80)
½ pound ground beef ($.75)
1 can (15 ounces) diced tomatoes with their juices ($.59)
2 garlic cloves ($.10)
1 tablespoon chili powder ($.10)
salt and pepper
1 cup shredded Cheddar cheese ($.75)
½ cantaloupe ($.75)

Soak the red and black beans together overnight, or bring to a boil in a generous amount of water, remove from the heat and let soak for at least 2 hours in the hot water. Drain and rinse the beans. In a medium saucepan, add the soaked beans plus enough water to cover them with at least 2 inches. Cover and cook over medium-low heat for 1½ to 2 hours, or until soft. Drain and return to the saucepan.

Preheat the oven to 400 degrees. Wrap the potatoes in aluminum foil and cut 2 slits in the top of each wrapped potato. Bake the potatoes in the preheated oven for 45 minutes to 1 hour, or until the potatoes are soft. The cooking time will vary depending on the size of the potatoes. If you prefer crispier potatoes, do not wrap them in foil before cutting the slits.

In a medium skillet, brown the ground beef and drain the excess fat.

Add the cooked beef, diced tomatoes, crushed garlic, chili powder, and salt and pepper to the cooked beans in the saucepan. Simmer for 20 minutes.

Once the potatoes are cooked, open them up and mash a well into the middle to hold the chili. Top with chili and shredded cheese. If necessary, place the potatoes with the chili and cheese under the broiler for 4 to 5 minutes to melt the cheese.

Slice the cantaloupe into wedges or dice the cantaloupe into bite-size pieces.

Serve Chili-Topped Potatoes with Sweet Cantaloupe.

Cost $4.79

FRUGAL FACT: *Cantaloupe prices fluctuate throughout the seasons. Best sale price is around $1.50 to $2. Diced cantaloupe can be frozen and tossed into a smoothie for breakfast or a snack.*

Chili-Cornbread Cups

¾ pound ground beef ($1.12)
1 cup dried red kidney beans ($.50)
1 can (15 ounces) crushed tomatoes ($.37)
½ onion, chopped ($.15)
1 to 2 tablespoons chili powder ($.25)
½ teaspoon salt plus salt and pepper to season
½ cup flour ($.10)
½ cup yellow cornmeal ($.10)
2 tablespoons sugar ($.05)
2 teaspoons baking powder ($.05)
½ cup milk ($.04)
1 egg ($.11)
2 cups frozen green beans ($1)

Soak the beans overnight, or bring to a boil in a generous amount of water, remove from the heat and let soak at least 2 hours in the hot water. Drain and rinse the beans. To a medium saucepan, add the soaked beans plus enough water to cover them with at least 2 inches. Cover and cook over medium-low heat for 1½ to 2 hours, or until soft.

In a saucepan, combine the ground beef, cooked beans, crushed tomatoes, chopped onion, ½ cup of water, chili powder, and salt and pepper. Cook over medium-high heat for 10 to 15 minutes, or until the beef has cooked through. The consistency of the chili will need to be thick, so simmer to reduce any excess liquid.

While the chili is simmering, prepare the cornbread. Preheat the oven to 350 degrees. In a mixing bowl, combine the flour, yellow cornmeal, sugar, baking powder, and ½ teaspoon salt. Whisk in the milk and egg to form a batter.

Spoon the chili in the bottom of regular-size or jumbo-size muffin tins, until about halfway full. Pour the corn muffin batter over the chili in each well, leaving about ¼ inch of space at the top.

Bake in the preheated oven for 25 minutes, or until the cornbread has cooked through. Let cool a few minutes before scooping out the chili-cornbread cups.

Cook frozen green beans according to the package directions.

Serve Chili-Cornbread Cups with Green Beans.

Cost $3.84

FRUGAL FACT: *If you have a smaller family, consider cooking an entire 1½-pound package of ground beef and then use the cooked meat for two different meals to save both time and money.*

Cowboy's Pie

4 large long white potatoes ($.60)
1 to 1½ cups milk ($.10)
3 tablespoons butter ($.30)
salt and pepper
2 cups of shredded leftover, cooked,
   beef roast ($1.75)

3 tablespoons BBQ Sauce ($.10)
1 cup shredded Cheddar cheese
   ($.75)
2 large heads broccoli ($.79)

Peel and quarter the potatoes. Boil them in water to cover for about 10 minutes, or until tender. Drain and return them to the saucepan. Add the milk little by little, the butter, salt and pepper, and mash with a potato masher. (Add the milk 2 tablespoons at a time, until the mashed potatoes reach the desired consistency.)

Preheat the oven to 350 degrees. Shred the leftover, cooked beef roast and mix with BBQ sauce.

Spread the mashed potatoes in the bottom of 8×8-inch baking dish. Top with BBQ shredded beef roast. Sprinkle the cheese over the beef roast.

Bake in the preheated oven for 15 minutes, or until the cheese begins to turn golden.

Cut the broccoli into spears and trim the stems. Steam the broccoli in a stovetop steamer for 4 to 5 minutes, or microwave for 4 to 5 minutes in a microwave-safe bowl, covered with plastic wrap.

Serve Cowboy's Pie with Steamed Broccoli.

Cost $4.59

FRUGAL FACT: *Consider doubling or tripling the amount when making the mashed potatoes and freeze the extra in freezer ziplock bags or a freezer-safe plastic container.*

Slow Cooker Steak and Potatoes

1 pound cube steak ($3.03)
2 tablespoons Worcestershire sauce ($.20)
4 large baking potatoes ($.60)

salt and pepper
ketchup or sour cream ($.20)
1 pound fresh green beans ($.89)
2 teaspoons olive oil ($.05)

Place the cube steak into the insert of a slow cooker with 1 cup of water. Sprinkle the Worcestershire sauce over the meat.

Cut the potatoes into quarters and place on top of the cube steak in the slow cooker. Sprinkle with salt and pepper. Set the slow cooker on low, and cook the steak and potatoes for 8 hours. Remove the meat and potatoes from the slow cooker. Serve the potatoes with ketchup, or mash them with sour cream.

Snap off the ends of the green beans and place in a small saucepan with ½ cup of water and the olive oil. Season with salt and pepper. Cover and cook over medium heat for 5 minutes. Drain and serve warm.

Serve Slow Cooker Steak and Potatoes with Green Beans.

Cost $4.97

FRUGAL FACT: *Coupons for name-brand meats can be found periodically both online and in newspapers.*

Garden Fresh Chili

¾ pound ground beef ($1.12)
1 cup dried red kidney beans ($.40)
1 onion, chopped ($.30)
1 green bell pepper, chopped ($.68)
1 tomato, diced ($.59)
1 can (8 ounces) tomato sauce ($.33)

1 tablespoon chili powder ($.05)
salt and pepper
6 red potatoes ($.80)
2 tablespoons olive oil ($.20)
1 cup frozen peas ($.50)

In a skillet, brown the ground beef. Drain the excess fat.

Add the cooked ground beef, dried beans, 2 cups of water, chopped onion, chopped bell pepper, diced tomato, tomato sauce, chili powder, salt, and pepper into the insert of a slow cooker and stir to combine. Set the slow cooker on low and cook the chili for 8 hours.

Scrub the red potatoes and then dice into 1-inch cubes. Sauté the diced potatoes in a skillet with the extra-virgin olive oil. Cover and cook for about 10 minutes, until the potatoes are cooked through. Stir two or three times while sautéing. Season with salt and pepper.

Cook the frozen peas according to the package directions.

Serve Garden Fresh Chili with Sautéed Red Potatoes and Peas.

Cost $4.97

FRUGAL FACT: *Consider the lower cost of this meal if you harvested the tomato, green pepper, onion, and peas from your own garden.*

Italian Meatball Hoagies

1 cup homemade Spaghetti Sauce
  (page 275) ($.32)
1 pound ground beef ($1.49)
½ cup bread crumbs ($.15)
1 egg ($.10)
2 tablespoons extra-virgin olive
  oil ($.10)

4 hoagie rolls ($1)
4 slices provolone cheese ($.75)
2 apples ($.50)
1 package sweet potato chips
  ($.50)

Preheat the oven to 400 degrees. In a medium bowl, combine ½ cup of the spaghetti sauce, the ground beef, bread crumbs, and egg. Mix well with your hands or a spoon. Form into 1- to 1½-inch meatballs.

In a large skillet, warm the extra-virgin olive oil. Add the meatballs and brown the edges, about 2 minutes on each side. Transfer the meatballs to 9×13-inch baking dish. Bake the browned meatballs in the oven for about 15 minutes.

Meanwhile, in a small saucepan, heat up the remaining sauce.

Slice the hoagie rolls lengthwise and lay out open-faced. Spread a spoonful of the homemade spaghetti sauce along the bottom bun. Place 4 cooked meatballs over the sauce, and add a few more spoonfuls of sauce over the meatballs. Cut the cheese slice in half and place the 2 halves next to each other immediately adding the meatballs and sauce to allow cheese to melt.

Slice the apples and set out the store-bought sweet potato chips in a bowl.

Serve Italian Meatball Hoagies with Sliced Apples and Sweet Potato Chips.

Cost $4.91

FRUGAL FACT: *Grab hoagie rolls or sub sandwich rolls from the bakery when they're marked down for quick sale. Freeze the rolls if they will not be used right away.*

Lentil Meatloaf

....

1½ pounds ground beef ($2.24)
1 cup leftover BBQ lentils (page 232)
  ($.25)
½ cup sour cream ($.25)
1 egg ($.10)
1 teaspoon paprika ($.05)
1 teaspoon garlic powder ($.05)

salt and pepper
ketchup ($.20)
1 medium acorn squash ($.69)
2 tablespoons butter ($.20)
2 tablespoons brown sugar ($.05)
homemade Italian Breadsticks
  (page 262) ($.50)

Prepare the dough for Italian Breadsticks in a bread machine or in a mixing bowl.

Preheat the oven to 350 degrees. Mix the ground beef, egg, sour cream, leftover BBQ lentils, salt, pepper, and spices in a mixing bowl. Combine well, but lightly, with your hands until all the ingredients are incorporated.

Place the meat mixture into 9×5-inch loaf pan. Sprinkle ketchup in a zigzag design along the top! Bake the meatloaf for 1 hour, or until cooked through. Slice and serve with additional ketchup.

Cut the acorn squash in half lengthwise and place face down in a glass baking dish. Add ¼ inch of water to the baking dish and cover with foil. Bake at 350 degrees for 50 to 60 minutes. If you have only one oven, you can bake it along with the meatloaf. Remove from the oven and let cool for 5 to 10 minutes before handling. Scrape out and discard the seeds, then scrape out the squash flesh. Mix the squash with the butter and brown sugar before serving.

Finish preparing the bread as directed in the recipe.

Serve Lentil Meatloaf with Candied Acorn Squash and Homemade Italian Breadsticks.

Cost $4.58

FRUGAL FACT: *Creative uses for leftovers keep both your family and your pocketbook happy.*

Meat and Potato Lasagna

6 large potatoes ($.80)
¾ pound ground beef ($.76)
½ onion ($.15)
1 zucchini ($.79)
1 teaspoon garlic powder ($.03)
salt and pepper

1 can (15 ounces) crushed tomatoes ($.59)
1 tablespoon brown sugar ($.03)
½ teaspoon salt
1 cup shredded Cheddar cheese ($.75)
2 cups frozen corn kernels ($1)

Preheat the oven to 350 degrees. Peel the potatoes and slice crosswise about ⅛-inch thick. Boil the potatoes about 6 to 8 minutes until soft. Drain carefully and pat dry.

In a skillet, brown the ground beef with the chopped onion and diced zucchini. Add the garlic powder, salt, and pepper while browning. Drain the excess fat.

In a medium bowl, mix the crushed tomatoes with the brown sugar, salt, and shredded cheese.

In 9×13-inch baking dish, layer the sliced potatoes and meat mixture until all are used up. Pour the tomato-cheese sauce over the top.

Bake the lasagna in the preheated oven for 20 to 25 minutes, or until all the cheese has melted and the sauce is bubbly.

Cook the frozen corn kernels according to the package directions.

Serve Meat and Potato Lasagna with Corn.

Cost $4.90

FRUGAL FACT: *March is "frozen food" month. Frozen vegetables can be purchased for their lowest prices during the month of March, so stock up.*

Meatloaf

2 slices bread or 1 leftover homemade roll ($.10)

1½ pounds ground beef ($2.23)

2 eggs ($.20)

½ cup milk ($.05)

½ cup finely chopped onion ($.05)

1 teaspoon Worcestershire sauce ($.05)

2 teaspoons garlic powder ($.05)

1 teaspoon chopped fresh parsley ($.05)

3 tablespoons ketchup ($.10)

2 tablespoons prepared mustard ($.05)

1 tablespoon brown sugar ($.02)

2 large heads broccoli ($.79)

homemade Italian Breadsticks (page 262) ($.50)

Prepare the dough for the breadsticks in a mixing bowl or in a bread machine.

Preheat the oven to 350 degrees. To make homemade bread crumbs, place 2 slices of bread or leftover sliced homemade roll from the freezer on a baking sheet and place in the oven for about 30 minutes, until the bread is crispy and lightly browned. Cool the bread, place in a mini grinder or food processor, and pulverize into bread crumbs. Substitute 1 cup of store-bought bread crumbs, if necessary. Leave the oven on.

In a large mixing bowl, combine the ground beef with the eggs, milk, finely chopped onion, Worcestershire sauce, garlic powder, homemade bread crumbs, and chopped parsley. Mix until incorporated and a loaf can be formed with the meat mixture. Place the meat mixture into a 9×5-inch loaf pan and press into the pan. Bake the meatloaf in the preheated oven for 1 hour, or until it is no longer pink in the middle.

In a small bowl, whisk together the ketchup, mustard, and brown sugar. Set aside.

After the meatloaf has been cooking for an hour, remove it from the oven and drain the excess fat from the pan. Brush the top of the loaf with the ketchup mixture, return the meatloaf to the oven, and bake for 10 more minutes.

Finish preparing the bread as directed in the recipe.

Remove the stems from the broccoli and separate the broccoli into florets. Steam the broccoli florets in a stovetop steamer for 4 to 5 minutes, or microwave for 4 to 5 minutes in a microwave-safe bowl, covered with plastic wrap.

Serve Meatloaf with Steamed Broccoli and Homemade Italian Breadsticks.

Cost $4.24

FRUGAL FACT: *Thinly slice leftover meatloaf and serve in a sandwich, or use leftover meatloaf in spaghetti sauce.*

Mexican Rice Casserole

1 can (8 ounces) tomato sauce ($.33)
¾ pound ground beef ($1.12)
1 tablespoon chili powder ($.10)
1 tablespoon ground cumin ($.10)
1 teaspoon garlic powder ($.05)
1 teaspoon onion powder ($.05)
½ teaspoon salt

½ teaspoon pepper
1 cup white rice ($.20)
1 cup shredded Monterey Jack cheese ($.75)
¼ watermelon ($.75)
4 ears corn ($1)

In a medium saucepan, bring 2½ cups of water to a boil, add the rice, and bring back to a boil. Reduce the heat, cover, and simmer for 20 minutes. Fluff the rice with a fork before serving.

Preheat the oven to 350 degrees. Brown ground beef and drain the excess fat. Return the beef to the skillet, stir in ½ cup water, the tomato sauce, chili powder, ground cumin, garlic powder, onion powder, salt, and pepper. Simmer for 5 minutes.

Combine the ground beef and sauce with the rice in an 8×8-inch baking dish. Top with the shredded cheese. Bake the casserole for 10 to 15 minutes, or until the cheese melts.

Slice the watermelon.

Remove the husks and silk from the ears of corn and boil the corn in a large pot for 4 to 5 minutes.

Serve Mexican Rice Casserole with Corn on the Cob and Watermelon.

Cost $4.45

FRUGAL FACT: *Double this recipe and make an extra casserole in a disposable foil pan. Freeze the casserole to have on hand for when a friend or neighbor needs a meal. Instructions for thawing/cooking are as follows: If frozen, bake, covered with foil, at 350 degrees for 1½ hours. If thawed, bake, covered with foil, at 350 degrees for 30 minutes.*

Orange Beef and Broccoli Stir-Fry

1 pound beef strips for stir-fry ($1.68)
1 tablespoon canola oil ($.05)
2 tablespoons soy sauce ($.10)
juice of 1 orange ($.33)
1 orange, peeled and sliced ($.33)

2 cups frozen broccoli ($1)
salt and pepper
1 cup brown rice ($.40)
2 cups frozen corn kernels ($1)

In a small bowl, toss the stir-fry beef with the canola oil, the soy sauce, and the orange juice. Let marinate in the refrigerator for at least 30 minutes.

In a medium saucepan, bring 2½ cups of water to a boil, add the brown rice, and bring back to a boil. Reduce the heat, cover, and simmer for 40 to 50 minutes. Fluff the rice with a fork before serving.

In a large skillet or wok, combine the marinated stir-fry beef with the sliced fresh orange, frozen broccoli, and season with salt and pepper. Stir-fry for 8 to 10 minutes over high heat, until the beef is cooked through and the broccoli is hot. The cooking time may vary depending on the thickness of the stir-fry beef pieces.

Cook the frozen corn according to the package directions.

Serve Orange Beef and Broccoli Stir-fry over Brown Rice with Corn.

Cost $4.89

FRUGAL FACT: *Keep an eye out for unadvertised meat sales or* REDUCED FOR QUICK SALE *stickers for the less common cuts of meat like stir-fry beef.*

Pronto Beef and Rice

1 butternut squash ($.69)
¾ pound ground beef ($1.12)
2 cups homemade Beef Broth
  (page 274)
1 can (8 ounces) tomato sauce ($.33)

1 can (12 ounces) diced tomatoes with
  green chilies ($.38)
1 cup brown rice ($.40)
2 cups frozen green beans ($1)

Preheat the oven to 350 degrees. Cut the butternut squash in half lengthwise and place cut side down in a glass baking dish. Add ¼ inch of water to the baking dish and cover with aluminum foil. Bake in the preheated oven for 50 to 60 minutes. Remove from the oven and let cool for 5 to 10 minutes before handling. Scrape out the seeds and discard, then scrape out the squash flesh. Mash the squash and season with salt and pepper to taste.

In a large skillet, brown the ground beef and drain the excess fat. Return it to the skillet. Add the beef broth, diced tomatoes with green chilies, and brown rice. Bring to a boil. Reduce the heat, cover, and simmer for 20 to 25 minutes, or until the rice is cooked.

Cook the frozen green beans according to the package directions.

Serve Pronto Beef and Rice with Butternut Squash and Green Beans.

Cost $3.92

FRUGAL FACT: *Stockpile diced tomatoes with green chilies when they are on sale and you have coupons. Coupons can be bought "in bulk" on e-bay to build your stockpile.*

Shepherd's Pie

6 large white potatoes ($.80)
2 tablespoons butter ($.20)
½ to 1 cup milk ($.10)
salt and pepper
¾ pound ground beef ($1.12)
1 can (15 ounces) diced tomatoes, drained ($.59)

1 cup frozen mixed vegetables, thawed ($.50)
1 cup shredded Cheddar cheese ($.75)
1 acorn squash ($.69)
2 tablespoons butter ($.20)
2 tablespoons brown sugar ($.05)

Preheat the oven to 350 degrees. Peel, quarter, and boil the potatoes for 10 minutes in a medium saucepan. Drain and transfer them to a mixing bowl. Mash the potatoes with the butter, milk, and salt and pepper.

Brown the ground beef and drain the excess fat. Return it to the skillet. Add the diced tomatoes and simmer for 5 minutes. Place the ground beef and tomatoes in the bottom of a 8×8-inch baking dish. Sprinkle the thawed mixed vegetables on top.

Spread the mashed potatoes over the beef and veggies. Sprinkle with the cheese. Bake in the preheater oven for 10 to 15 minutes, or until the cheese has melted.

Cut the acorn squash in half lengthwise and place cut side down in a glass baking dish. Add ¼ inch of water to the baking dish and cover with aluminum foil. Bake at 350 degrees for 50 to 60 minutes. Remove and let cool for 5 to 10 minutes before handling. Scrape out and discard the seeds, then scrape out the squash flesh and mash. Serve with butter and brown sugar.

Serve Shepherd's Pie with Candied Acorn Squash.

Cost $5.00

FRUGAL FACT: *Double or triple the mashed potatoes and freeze the unused potatoes in meal-size portions for a quick side dish in a future meal.*

Skirt Steak and Pepper Kabobs

1 pound skirt steak ($1.99)
2 tablespoons olive oil ($.10)
1 teaspoon ground cumin ($.05)
2 teaspoon lime juice ($.05)
1 garlic clove, crushed ($.05)

1 cup rice ($.20)
1 green bell pepper ($.68)
1 red bell pepper ($.99)
¼ watermelon, sliced ($.75)

Cut the skirt steak into 1-inch strips.

In small bowl, whisk together the olive oil, cumin, lime juice, and crushed garlic. Toss the marinade with the skirt steak strips in a shallow dish. Marinate in the refrigerator for at least 30 minutes.

In a medium saucepan, bring 2½ cups of water to a boil, add the rice, and bring back to a boil. Reduce the heat, cover, and simmer for 20 minutes. Fluff the rice with a fork before serving.

Remove the stems and seed the bell peppers. Cut into 1-inch squares, in preparation for the skewers.

Once the skirt steak has finished marinating, roll up the strips and put them on skewers, alternating bell with the peppers squares.

Grill the skewers for 5 to 6 minutes on each side, or until the steak is cooked through. Rotate often to avoid charring the peppers.

Cut the watermelon into slices.

Serve Skirt Steak and Pepper Kabobs over Rice with Watermelon.

Cost $4.86

FRUGAL FACT: *Substitute the skirt steak for stew meat or stir-fry beef.*

Stuffed Green Peppers

4 large green bell peppers ($2)
½ cup white rice ($.10)
½ pound ground beef, cooked ($.75)
1 can (12 ounces) diced tomatoes with green chilies ($.50)
½ cup frozen organic corn kernels ($.25)
½ cup shredded Cheddar cheese ($.37)
2 medium sweet potatoes ($.99)

In a medium saucepan, bring 1¼ cups of water to a boil, add the rice, and bring back to a boil. Reduce the heat, cover, and simmer for 20 minutes. Fluff the rice with a fork before serving.

Add the diced tomatoes with green chilies, frozen corn, and cooked ground beef to the saucepan with the cooked rice. Mix well.

Cut off the tops of each bell pepper and remove the stem and seeds.

Scoop the rice and meat mixture into each bell pepper. Place the bell peppers into the slow cooker. Set the slow cooker on low, and cook the stuffed peppers for 8 hours. About 15 minutes before serving, add the shredded cheese to the top of each pepper. Let the cheese melt.

Preheat the oven to 350 degrees. Make a few slits in the sweet potatoes with a small sharp knife. Place the potatoes in a baking dish with ¼ inch of water and cover with aluminum foil. Bake the potatoes for 1 hour. Remove from the oven and let cool about 10 minutes. Peel off the skins and mash the pulp.

Serve Stuffed Bell Pepper with Mashed Sweet Potatoes.

Cost $4.96

FRUGAL FACT: *This meal will only come in under $5 if the peppers are bought on sale for $.50 or less! Watch for those prices in the mid to late summer.*

Sweet Potato Beef Roast

1¾ pound beef roast ($4.03/2 = $2.02)
1 teaspoon garlic powder ($.05)
salt and pepper
3 sweet potatoes, peeled and quartered
   ($1.49)

½ teaspoon ground ginger ($.05)
1 teaspoon ground cinnamon ($.05)
2 boxes (10 ounces each) frozen
   chopped spinach ($1)

Place the beef roast and 1 cup of water in the insert of a slow cooker. Sprinkle with the garlic powder, salt, and pepper.

Peel and quarter the sweet potatoes. Place the potatoes in the slow cooker around and on top of the beef roast. Sprinkle the ground ginger and cinnamon over the sweet potatoes. Set the slow cooker on low, and cook the beef and potatoes for 8 hours.

When the cooking is finished remove the roast and sweet potatoes. Slice the roast, and strain juices from cooker, and save for beef broth (page 274). Save the other half of the cooked beef roast and use in Cowboy's Pie (page 148) or Hearty Beef Stew (page 208).

Cook the frozen spinach according to package directions.

Serve Sliced Beef Roast with Sweet Potatoes and Spinach.

Cost $4.66

FRUGAL FACT: *Match coupons for brand-name, boxed, frozen vegetables with a sale price and the brand-name boxed vegetables will be cheaper than the store-brand boxed vegetables.*

Tex-Mex Chili

1 pound ground beef ($1.49)
1 onion, finely chopped ($.30)
2 garlic cloves, crushed ($.10)
1 can (15 ounces) stewed or diced
    tomatoes with their juices ($.59)
1 can (8 ounces) sliced black olives
    ($.69)

½ cup dried red kidney beans ($.15)
2 teaspoons ground cumin ($.10)
1 teaspoon chili powder ($.05)
salt and pepper
4 ears corn ($1)
2 tablespoons butter ($.20)
sour cream for serving ($.25)

In large saucepan, brown the ground beef with the finely chopped onion and crushed garlic. Drain the excess fat and return the ground beef to the saucepan. Add the diced tomatoes with their juices, the black olives, red kidney beans, and 3 cups of water. Season with the cumin, chili powder, salt, and pepper and stir to combine. Cover and simmer for at least 1½ hours, or until the beans are soft.

Remove the husks and silk from the ears of corn and boil the corn in large pot of water for 4 to 5 minutes, or place the ears of corn in microwave-safe baking dish, covered with plastic wrap and microwave for 7 to 9 minutes. Serve with butter.

Serve Tex-Mex Chili with Sour Cream and Buttery Corn on the Cob.

Cost $4.92

FRUGAL FACT: *Since there are rarely coupons released for olives, be sure to buy a few extra cans of store-brand olives when they are on sale.*

Round Steak and Mashed Potatoes

¾ pound eye of round, cut in thin
   steaks ($2.88)
1 tablespoon steak seasoning (free)
5 medium white potatoes ($.66)
½ cup sour cream ($.20)

2 tablespoon butter ($.20)
1 garlic clove, crushed ($.05)
salt and pepper
4 ears corn ($1)

Set the steaks on a plate and sprinkle with the seasonings. Cover the steaks with aluminum foil and refrigerate for at least 30 minutes to allow the seasoning and salt to tenderize the meat.

Grill the steaks for 3 to 4 minutes on each side, until cooked through. The cooking time may vary depending on the thickness of the steaks.

Peel and quarter the potatoes. Boil in water to cover for about 10 minutes, or until tender. Drain and return to the saucepan. Add the sour cream, butter, garlic, salt, and pepper and mash with a potato masher. Add milk, 2 tablespoons at a time, until you reach the desired consistency.

Remove the husks and silk from the ears of corn and boil the corn in large pot of water for 4 to 5 minutes, or place corn the ears of in microwave-safe baking dish, cover with plastic wrap, and microwave for 7 to 9 minutes.

Serve Round Steak with Mashed Potatoes and Corn on the Cob.

Cost $4.99

FRUGAL FACT: *How can you say that the steak seasoning is "free"? I watch for name-brand spices that are on sale for $1. Match with a $.50 coupon that doubles to $1, and the spices are free! This doesn't always happen, but it always pays to be on the lookout for bargains like this.*

SEVEN

Pork Meals

Apple-Dijon Pork Roast

1 pork shoulder roast (about
   2½ pounds) ($4.01/2 = $2.01)
½ cup applesauce ($.15)
¼ cup apple juice ($.05)
¼ cup Dijon mustard ($.25)
6 red potatoes ($.80)

2 tablespoons extra-virgin olive oil
   ($.20)
1 teaspoon dried Italian seasoning
   ($.05)
salt and pepper
2 heads broccoli ($.79)

Place the roast in the insert of a slow cooker with ½ cup of water.

In a small bowl, whisk together the applesauce, apple juice, and Dijon mustard. Pour over the roast. Set the slow cooker on low, and cook the roast for 8 hours.

Scrub the red potatoes and then dice into 1-inch cubes. Sauté the diced potatoes in a skillet in the extra-virgin olive oil. Stir in Italian seasoning. Cover and cook for about 10 minutes, or until the potatoes are cooked through. Stir two or three times while sautéing. Season with salt and pepper.

Remove the stems from the broccoli and separate the broccoli into florets. Steam the florets in a stovetop steamer for 4 to 5 minutes, or microwave for 4 to 5 minutes in a microwave-safe bowl, covered with plastic wrap.

When the pork has finished cooking, slice the roast, and spoon some sauce over each serving.

Serve Apple-Dijon Pork with Sautéed Red Potatoes and Steamed Broccoli.

Cost $4.30

FRUGAL FACT: *This 2½-pound roast costs only $4 and can be used for two meals, as a small family will not eat 2½ pounds of meat in one meal.*

Apple-Walnut Pork

1 cup brown rice ($.40)

1 pound leftover, cooked pork roast, shredded ($1.69)

1 Granny Smith apple, peeled and diced ($.25)

½ cup apple juice ($.25)

¼ cup honey ($.30)

½ cup chopped walnuts ($.75)

2 cups frozen green beans ($1)

salt and pepper

In a medium saucepan, bring 2½ cups of water to a boil, add the brown rice, and bring back to a boil. Reduce the heat, cover, and simmer for 40 to 50 minutes. Fluff the rice with a fork before serving.

To a skillet, add the peeled and diced apple, apple juice, honey, and walnuts. Sauté for 4 to 6 minutes until the juices reduce. Add the shredded leftover pork roast and stir into the sauce. Simmer for 3 to 4 minutes.

Cook the frozen green beans according to the package directions.

Serve Apple-Walnut Pork with Brown Rice and Green Beans.

Cost $4.64

FRUGAL FACT: *Many people are not fans of leftovers, but this meal is perfect for disguising leftover pork roast meat. Sautéing with apple juice and adding new textures with the apples and walnuts give the pork an entire new look and taste.*

Bacon-Wrapped Pork Roast

1 pork shoulder roast (1 to 1½ pounds) ($2.24)
1 heaping tablespoon raspberry or apricot jelly ($.10)
2 strips bacon, cut in half crosswise ($.25)
2 tablespoons extra-virgin olive oil ($.20)
1 pound asparagus ($.99)
salt and pepper
2 garlic cloves, crushed ($.10)
2 tablespoons butter or margarine, melted ($.10)
½ teaspoon salt
½ French bread, store-bought or homemade (page 264) ($.50)

Spray the insert of a slow cooker with nonstick cooking spray. Place the pork roast in bottom of the slow cooker. Spread the jelly over the top of the roast. Lay the bacon strips over the pork and jelly. Set the slow cooker on low, and cook the pork for 8 hours. When the roast has finished cooking, remove it from the slow cooker and let cool about 10 minutes.

In a skillet, heat the olive oil over medium-high heat. Add the asparagus spears and sauté for 3 to 4 minutes, until tender-crisp and bright green. Season the asparagus with salt and pepper.

In a small bowl, combine the crushed garlic, melted butter, and salt. Whisk briefly. Slice the French bread and butter it with the garlic butter.

Slice the roast and serve each piece with a slice of bacon.

Serve Bacon-Wrapped Pork Roast with Sautéed Asparagus and warm French Garlic Bread.

Cost $4.48

FRUGAL FACT: *Ask the meat manager at your grocery store when they mark down the meat products. Ask if there is a section with* REDUCED FOR QUICK SALE *cuts that you can take home and use right away or freeze. You can also ask the bakery manager if they* have an "Oops, we baked too much" section for bread products that need to be sold quickly. Bread can be eaten right away or frozen for a busy day, when a quick meal is in order.

Cowboy Beans and Rice

1 cup dried pinto beans ($.40)
2 cups shredded, cooked pork meat ($1.60)
½ onion, chopped ($.20)
1 can (6 ounces) tomato paste ($.19)
1 cup white rice ($.20)

chili powder, to taste ($.10)
½ to 1 cup homemade Salsa Verde (page 278) ($.99)
2 cups frozen corn ($1)
salt and pepper

Soak the dried pinto beans overnight, or bring to a boil in a generous amount of water, remove from the heat, and let soak for at least 2 hours in the hot water. Drain and rinse the beans. Add the soaked beans to a medium saucepan with at least 2 inches of water covering them. Bring to a boil. Cover, reduce the heat to medium, and cook for 1½ hours, or until the beans are soft. Drain the beans.

Return the drained beans to the saucepan, add the shredded pork meat, chopped onion, tomato paste, rice, and 2 cups of water, the chili powder, and salt and pepper to taste. Bring to a boil, reduce the heat, and simmer for at least 20 minutes until the rice is cooked. The consistency should be thick like a chili.

Cook the frozen corn according to the package directions. Combine the corn with homemade Salsa Verde, or your favorite salsa.

Serve Cowboy Beans and Rice with Corn Salsa.

Cost $4.18

FRUGAL FACT: *This is another great meal for using up leftover pork roast meat. Be sure to use coupons when buying canned tomato paste.*

Cranberry Pork Chops

4 pork chops (about 1½ pounds total) ($2.52)

½ bag fresh cranberries ($.50) or 1 can whole cranberries ($.79)

½ cup apple juice ($.10)

¼ cup granulated sugar ($.02)

3 tablespoons brown sugar ($.01)

1 teaspoon ground cloves ($.05)

2 large sweet potatoes ($.99)

½ cup frozen peas ($.75)

Place the pork chops in the insert of a slow cooker with ½ cup of water.

In a bowl, toss the fresh or canned cranberries, apple juice, white and brown sugars, and the ground cloves. Pour over the pork chops in the slow cooker. Set the slow cooker on low, and cook the pork chops for 8 hours.

Preheat the oven to 350 degrees. Make a few slits in the sweet potatoes using a small sharp knife. Put the sweet potatoes in a baking dish with ¼ inch of water and cover with aluminium foil. Bake the sweet potatoes in the preheated oven for 1 hour. Remove from the oven and let cool about 10 minutes. Peel off the skins and mash the pulp.

Cook the peas according to the package directions.

Serve Cranberry Pork Chops with Mashed Sweet Potatoes and Peas.

Cost $4.94

FRUGAL FACT: *Fresh cranberries can be frozen whole and used for future meals. Look for them for just $1/pound. around the Thanksgiving holiday. Grab an extra bag and toss it in the freezer to use in future meals.*

Country Ribs with Oven Fries

....

1 to 2 cups store-bought BBQ sauce ($.50)

1½ pounds country-style pork ribs ($1.98)

1 onion, chopped ($.40)

2 garlic cloves, crushed ($.10)

10 small white potatoes ($.80)

2 tablespoons olive oil ($.20)

chili powder or Cajun seasoning (optional)

salt and pepper

2 heads broccoli ($.79)

Place ¼ cup of BBQ sauce in the insert of the slow cooker with ½ cup of water. Place the ribs on top of the BBQ sauce. Sprinkle the chopped onion and crushed garlic around and on top of ribs. Pour 1 cup, or so, of BBQ sauce over the ribs. Set the slow cooker on low, and cook the ribs for 8 hours.

Preheat the oven to 400 degrees. Peel the potatoes and cut lengthwise into wedges. Toss the wedges in large bowl with olive oil, salt, and pepper. Place the wedges on a baking sheet in a single layer. (Overlapping pieces will create a longer cooking time.) Sprinkle with chili powder or Cajun seasonings if you wish to add some kick to the oven fries. Bake the wedges for 20 minutes, then turn the wedges and bake another 10 to 15 minutes, or until the wedges are golden and sizzle.

Remove stems from the broccoli and separate the broccoli into florets. Steam the florets in a stovetop steamer for 4 to 5 minutes, or microwave for 4 to 5 minutes in a microwave-safe bowl, covered with plastic wrap.

Serve BBQ Country Ribs with Oven Fries and Steamed Broccoli.

Cost $4.77

FRUGAL FACT: *A fantastic meal for all those "Meat and Potato" guys out there!*

Garlic Pork Chops

4 pork chops (about 1¼ pounds) ($2.52)

1 tablespoon extra-virgin olive oil ($.20)

4 garlic cloves, crushed ($.10)

6 large white potatoes ($.80)

1 to 1½ cups milk ($.15)

2 tablespoons butter ($.20)

salt and pepper

2 cups frozen green beans ($1)

In a large skillet, marinate the pork chops in the olive oil and the equivalent of 2 crushed garlic cloves for at least 30 minutes in the refrigerator. Place the skillet over medium-high heat and sauté the chops for 5 to 6 minutes on each side, or until no longer pink in the middle. The cooking time may vary depending on thickness of the chops.

Scrub, peel, and quarter the potatoes. Boil for 10 minutes in large saucepan with water to cover. When the potato pieces have softened, drain off the liquid and return the cooked potatoes to the saucepan. Add 1 cup of the milk, butter, the remaining crushed garlic cloves, and salt and pepper. Mash together with a potato masher. Add more milk if you prefer creamier potatoes.

Cook the frozen green beans according to the package directions. Season with salt and pepper to taste.

Serve Garlic Pork Chops with Garlic Mashed Potatoes and Green Beans.

Cost $4.97

FRUGAL FACT: *Marinate your meat in the dish you plan to cook it in to save time and energy when it comes time for the dishes.*

Grilled BLT Sandwiches

8 slices bacon ($1)
1 plum tomato, thinly sliced ($.49)
8 slices whole wheat bread ($.60)
2 tablespoons butter ($.20)
3 to 4 tablespoons mayonnaise ($.10)

4 slices provolone cheese ($.75)
4 iceberg lettuce leaves ($.10)
2 carrot sticks ($.20)
2 apples ($.50)

Cook the bacon in skillet or microwave. To prepare the bacon in the microwave, place 2 pieces of paper towel on a large plate. Place the bacon strips on top of the paper towels, then cover with 1 piece of paper towel. Cook on high timing for 1 minute for each slice, so cook 4 slices for 4 minutes. Once cooked and cooled, tear the bacon strips so they will fit on the sandwich bread.

Slice the tomato and wash the lettuce leaves.

Butter the outside side of the bread slices. Spread the mayonnaise on the inside side of the bread. Place the cheese, bacon strips, tomato slices, and lettuce in the sandwich. Place the sandwich butter side down on a greased electric griddle or in a skillet. Cook each side for 2 to 3 minutes, or until the bread is golden brown and cheese has melted.

Peel and cut the carrots into sticks. Slice the apples.

Serve Grilled BLT Sandwiches with Sliced Apples and Carrot Sticks.

Cost $3.94

FRUGAL FACT: *Coupons for bread and buns can be found regularly in newspaper inserts. Stockpile and freeze them when they are on sale, and a coupon can be used with the sale price.*

Grilled Pork Chops

4 pork chops (about 1¼ pounds)
($2.52)
½ cup pork rub or brine
(pages 285 and 286) ($.25)

2 fresh peaches, sliced ($.79)
4 ears corn ($1)
2 tablespoons butter ($.20)
chili powder ($.05)

At least 30 minutes before grilling, marinate the pork chops in 1 cup of the rub or brine in the refrigerator. Grill the marinated chops for 4 to 5 minutes on each side, or until no longer pink in the middle. The cooking time may vary depending on thickness of the chops.

Slice the peaches.

Remove the husks and silk from the ears of corn and boil the corn in a large pot of water for 4 to 5 minutes, or place the ears of corn in a microwave-safe baking dish, cover with plastic wrap, and microwave for 7 to 9 minutes. Serve the corn with butter and a few sprinkles of chili powder.

Serve Grilled Pork Chops, Sliced Peaches, and Chili Corn Cob.

Cost $4.81

FRUGAL FACT: *Do you always eat at the dinner table or patio table? Consider having a picnic in your own backyard, or living room. Add a little spice to your family's mealtime!*

Ham and Swiss Roll Ups

8 burrito-size flour tortillas ($.99)
4 tablespoons Dijon mustard ($.25)
8 slices leftover ham ($1)
4 slices Swiss cheese ($.85)
2 mangoes ($1.36)
leftover side dish or salad ($.50)

Lay the tortillas out flat on a clean work surface. Spread Dijon mustard along the midline. Add a slice of ham and half a slice of Swiss cheese to each tortilla. Roll up tightly.

Peel the mangoes. Cut flesh away from the large pit in the center and dice the flesh.

Serve the Ham and Swiss Roll Ups with Diced Mangoes and a leftover side dish or salad.

Cost $4.95

FRUGAL FACT: *A great way to use up leftover ham after a holiday meal!*

Honey-Baked Lentils

1 cup green lentils ($.40)
4 slices bacon ($.50)
2 tablespoons mustard ($.05)
¼ teaspoon ground ginger ($.05)
½ onion, finely chopped ($.15)

1 teaspoon salt
⅓ cup honey ($.50)
1 cup brown rice ($.40)
2 cups frozen fried okra ($1)
½ cup canola oil ($.50)

To a medium saucepan, add the green lentils and 3 cups water. Bring to a boil, and then reduce the heat to medium. Cover tightly and simmer for 30 minutes, or until the lentils are tender. Drain off any excess liquid.

Cook the bacon in the microwave or a skillet. To prepare the bacon in the microwave, place 2 pieces of paper towel on a large plate. Place the bacon strips on top of the paper towel, then cover with 1 piece of paper towel. Cook on high for 1 minute for each slice, so cook 4 slices for 4 minutes.

Preheat the oven to 350 degrees. In a small a bowl, mix the mustard, ginger, and finely chopped onion with 1 cup water.

Add the cooked lentils to an 8×8-inch baking dish. Pour the spice mixture over the cooked lentils. Crumble 2 pieces of bacon and mix in with the lentils. Crumble the remaining 2 pieces of bacon and sprinkle over the top. Drizzle with the honey.

Bake in the preheated oven for 15 to 20 minutes, or until bubbling.

In a medium saucepan, bring 2½ cups of water to a boil, add the brown rice, and bring back to a boil. Reduce the heat, cover, and simmer for 40 to 50 minutes. Fluff the rice with a fork before serving.

Cook the frozen fried okra in a saucepan with the oil according to the package directions. Drain the fried okra on a plate lined with paper towels.

Serve Honey-Baked Lentils over Brown Rice with Fried Okra.

Cost $3.65

FRUGAL FACT: *Purchase local, unprocessed honey from the farmers' market.*

Honey-Glazed Pork Chops

2 tablespoons brown sugar ($.05)
3 tablespoons honey ($.20)
salt and pepper
4 pork chops (about 1¼ pounds)
   ($2.52)

1 cup brown rice ($.40)
1 pound asparagus ($.99)
2 tablespoons olive oil ($.20)

In a small bowl, whisk together the brown sugar, honey, and salt and pepper.

Place the pork chops in a large skillet, and paint the honey glaze on each side of each chop. Cook over medium-high heat for 5 to 6 minutes on each side, or until the chops are no longer pink in the middle. The cooking time may vary depending on the thickness of the pork chops.

In a medium saucepan, bring 2½ cups of water to a boil, add the brown rice, and bring back to a boil. Reduce the heat, cover, and simmer for 40 to 50 minutes. Fluff the rice with a fork before serving.

In a skillet, heat the olive oil over medium-high heat. Add the asparagus spears and sauté for 3 to 4 minutes, until they are tender-crisp and turn bright green. Season the asparagus with salt and pepper.

Serve Honey-Glazed Pork Chops with Brown Rice and Sautéed Asparagus.

Cost $4.36

FRUGAL FACT: *Pork chops are often on sale in smaller packages of 3 to 4 pork chops for $1.99/pound. If you eat pork chops regularly, consider buying a larger "family pack" with 12 to 16 pork chops for prices as low as 1.49/pound. Divide the pork chops into portions that will feed your family and freeze them in freezer ziplock bags or in vacuum-sealed bags.*

North Carolina Pulled Pork Sandwiches

4 to 6 homemade Hamburger Buns
  (page 266) ($.50)
1 pound, leftover, cooked, pork roast
  ($1.69)
1 cup store-bought BBQ sauce ($.20)
1 cup mayonnaise or Miracle Whip
  ($.25)
1 teaspoon lemon juice ($.05)

1 teaspoon vinegar ($.02)
½ teaspoon salt
½ to 1 teaspoon garlic pepper ($.02)
2 tablespoons sugar ($.02)
1 bag (12 ounces) coleslaw mix
  ($2.18/2=$1.09)
¼ watermelon ($.75)

Prepare the dough for homemade hamburger buns in a bread machine or in a mixing bowl.

In a microwave-safe bowl, combine the leftover shredded pork roast with BBQ sauce. Microwave the pork until hot. The time will depend on how much meat you are reheating.

In a small bowl, whisk together the mayonnaise or Miracle Whip with the lemon juice, vinegar, salt, garlic pepper, and sugar. Pour over the coleslaw mix, and stir to combine.

Finish preparing the buns as directed in the recipe.

Pile the BBQ pulled pork on the homemade hamburger buns, and top with the coleslaw.

Cut the watermelon into slices or diced pieces.

Serve North Carolina Pulled Pork Sandwiches with Watermelon.

Cost $4.90

FRUGAL FACT: *Since this meal only uses a small portion of the coleslaw for the sandwiches, plan to eat the leftovers the following night with grilled chicken or steak.*

Peachy Pork Chops

homemade French Bread ($.25)
1 large or 2 small peaches ($.79)
4 pork chops (about 1¼ pounds) ($2.52)

salt and pepper
1 pound green beans ($.89)
2 tablespoons olive oil ($.20)

Prepare the dough for homemade French Bread in a bread machine or in a mixing bowl.

Cut the peaches into thin slices. Put the pork chops in a skillet and spread the peaches over the top. Add ½ cup of water, and sprinkle with salt and pepper. Cover and cook the pork chops (with the peaches) over medium heat for 5 to 6 minutes on each side, or until no longer pink in the middle. The cooking time may vary depending on thickness of the pork chops.

Snap off the ends of the green beans. Heat the olive oil in a skillet until hot. Toss the beans in, season with salt and pepper, and sauté until cooked, but still crisp and flavorful.

Finish preparing the bread as directed in the recipe.

Serve Peachy Pork Chops with Sautéed Green Beans and warm French Bread.

Cost $4.65

FRUGAL FACT: *Use fresh peaches that were purchased on sale, then sliced up and frozen. When thawed, peaches become slightly "mushy." Since peaches are being cooked down in this recipe, frozen ones are perfect to use.*

Pork and Beans

....

2 cups dried pinto beans ($.80)
1 pound leftover, cooked, pork roast meat ($1.69)
½ onion, minced ($.15)
1 cup ketchup ($.25)
3 to 4 tablespoons mustard ($.05)
¼ cup brown sugar ($.10)
1 tablespoon cider vinegar ($.05)
1 teaspoon garlic powder ($.02)
salt and pepper
4 ears corn ($1)
1 teaspoon lime juice ($.10)
2 to 3 teaspoons chili powder ($.10)

Soak the pinto beans overnight, or bring to a boil in a generous amount of water, remove from the heat, and let soak for at least 2 hours in the hot water. Drain and rinse the beans. Add the soaked beans to a medium saucepan with at least 2 inches of water covering them. Bring to a boil. Cover, reduce the heat to medium, and cook for 1½ hours, or until the beans are soft. Drain the beans and return to the saucepan.

Add the shredded leftover pork, minced onion, ketchup, mustard, brown sugar, vinegar, garlic powder, and salt and pepper and stir through. Set the saucepan over medium-low heat and simmer the pork and beans 15 to 20 minutes.

Remove the husks and silk from the ears of corn and boil in large pot of water for 4 to 5 minutes, or place the ears of corn in microwave-safe baking dish, cover with plastic wrap, and microwave for 7 to 9 minutes. Sprinkle with lime juice and chili powder.

Serve Pork and Beans with Chili-Lime Corn.

Cost $4.31

FRUGAL FACT: *Cook the pork and beans in the slow cooker, by placing all the ingredients (except the corn, lime juice, and chili powder) plus 4 to 5 cups of water into the slow cooker. Mix well, set the slow cooker on low, and cook for 8 hours—come home after a long day at work to a simple and delicious meal.*

Cajun-Seasoned Pork Chops

3 large sweet potatoes ($1.49)
2 tablespoons oil ($.10)
4 pork chops (about 1¼ pounds)
  ($2.52)

1 to 2 teaspoons Cajun seasoning
  ($.10)
2 cups frozen green beans ($1)
salt and pepper

Preheat the oven to 350 degrees. Make a few slits in the sweet potatoes using a small sharp knife. Place the sweet potatoes in a baking dish with ¼ inch of water and cover with foil. Bake the sweet potatoes in the preheated oven for 1 hour. Remove from the oven and let cool about 10 minutes. Peel off the skins and mash the pulp.

Heat the oil in large skillet, and add the pork chops. Sprinkle the pork chops with the Cajun seasoning. Sauté the pork chops for 4 to 5 minutes on each side, or until no longer pink in the middle. The cooking time may vary depending on the thickness of the pork chops.

Cook the frozen green beans according to the package directions. Season with salt and pepper to taste.

Serve Cajun-Seasoned Pork Chops with Mashed Sweet Potatoes and Green Beans.

Cost $4.87

FRUGAL FACT: *Baking and steaming the sweet potatoes as directed above gives them a sweeter flavor than cooking them in the microwave or roasting them in the oven. There is no need for extra sugar or butter when the sweet potatoes are baked and steamed!*

Pork Roast with Mashed Red Potatoes

....

1 pork roast (about 2½ pounds)
($4.05/2 = $2.03)
1 teaspoon garlic powder ($.05)
salt and pepper
6 red potatoes ($.80)

¼ cup low-fat sour cream ($.10)
¼ to ½ cup fat-free milk ($.10)
2 tablespoons butter ($.20)
2 garlic cloves, crushed ($.10)
2 cups organic frozen peas ($1)

Place the pork roast in the slow cooker with ½ cup of water. Season it with the garlic powder, salt, and pepper. Set slow cooker on low, and cook the roast for 8 hours.

Scrub and cut the red potatoes into quarters. Boil for about 10 minutes, until softened. Drain and return to the saucepan. Mash with a potato masher. Add the sour cream, milk, butter, and crushed garlic. Add more milk for creamier potatoes or less milk for chunkier potatoes. Season with salt and pepper to taste.

Cook the frozen peas according to the package directions.

When the cooking is finished, remove the pork from the slow cooker. Slice the roast into ⅓- to ½-inch slices. Save the leftover pork meat to use in a future meal, like North Carolina Pulled Pork Sandwiches (page 179) or Pork and Beans (page 181).

Serve Sliced Pork Roast with Mashed Red Potatoes with Garlic and Peas.

Cost $4.54

FRUGAL FACT: *Searing (browning each side) of the roast in a large skillet or saucepan before putting it into a slow cooker or roasting pan will seal in juices and the roasted meat will be more moist and tender. If you are short on time, and can't sear the roast before cooking it, add 1/2 to 1 cup of water to the roasting pan or slow cooker to add more moisture into the cooking environment.*

Pork Roast with Apples and Asparagus

....

1 pork roast (about 1 pound) ($1.99)
salt and pepper
½ onion, chopped ($.15)
3 Macintosh apples, peeled and
   sliced ($1)
1 teaspoon ground cinnamon ($.05)

2 tablespoons brown sugar ($.05)
2 tablespoons lemon juice ($.10)
1 cup brown rice ($.40)
1 pound asparagus ($.99)
2 tablespoons olive oil ($.20)

Place ½ cup of water in the insert of a slow cooker. Place the roast into the slow cooker and sprinkle with salt and pepper. Distribute the chopped onions around the roast.

In a bowl, combine the apples, lemon juice, cinnamon, and brown sugar. Toss well. Pour over the roast in the slow cooker. Set the slow cooker on low, and cook the pork roast for 8 hours.

In a medium saucepan, bring 2½ cups of water to a boil, add the brown rice, and bring back to a boil. Reduce the heat, cover, and simmer for 40 minutes. Fluff the rice with a fork before serving.

In a skillet, sauté the asparagus in the olive oil for 5 to 6 minutes, stirring every other minute. The asparagus will be tender-crisp and turn bright green when it is ready to serve. Remove from the skillet to prevent overcooking.

Serve Pork Roast with Brown Rice and Sautéed Asparagus.

Cost $4.93

FRUGAL FACT: *A delicious meal for a busy fall day. Apple prices are lowest during the fall and the slow cooker will do all the hard work while you are out running errands all afternoon.*

Pork Roast with Apples and Pears

homemade French Bread (page 264) ($.25)

1 pork shoulder roast (1 to 1¼ pounds) ($1.84)

1 cup apple cider or juice ($.30)

salt and pepper

½ onion, diced ($.15)

1 Golden Delicious apple ($.40)

1 Anjou pear ($.59)

1 pound asparagus ($.99)

3 tablespoons extra-virgin olive oil ($.25)

Prepare the dough for the homemade French bread in a mixing bowl or in a bread machine.

Place the pork roast into the insert of a slow cooker. Pour the apple cider or juice over the top. Sprinkle with salt and pepper.

Slice, and peel if you like, the apple and the pear. Toss the sliced apples, sliced pears, and diced onions around the pork roast. Set the slow cooker on low and cook the pork and fruit for 8 hours.

Finish preparing the bread as directed in the recipe.

In a skillet, sauté the asparagus in the olive oil for 5 to 6 minutes, stirring every other minute. The asparagus will be tender-crisp and turn bright green. Remove the asparagus from the skillet to prevent overcooking.

Serve Pork Roast with Apples and Pears, Sautéed Asparagus, and warm French Bread.

Cost $4.72

FRUGAL FACT: *Every time you stop in the grocery store, "drive through" the meat department on the lookout for unadvertised specials and reduced-price meats. Incorporate meat with the reduce price sticker into your meal plan, or freeze for a future meal.*

BBQ Pulled Pork Sandwiches

....

1 pound leftover, cooked, pork roast
   meat ($1.69)
1 cup store-bought BBQ Sauce ($.50)
6 carrot sticks ($.60)
1 cup raisins ($.70)
3 to 4 tablespoons mayonnaise or
   Miracle Whip ($.10)

1 small can crushed pineapple,
   drained, reserve 1 tablespoon of the
   juice ($.50)
homemade Hamburger Buns
   (page 266) ($.48)

Prepare the dough for the homemade hamburger buns in a bread machine or in a mixing bowl.

Shred the leftover pork roast meat and toss in a bowl with the BBQ sauce. Warm the meat and BBQ sauce in a microwave-safe bowl or over medium heat in a skillet.

Prepare the carrot and raisin salad. In large bowl, mix the peeled and grated carrots, raisins, mayonnaise, crushed pineapple, and reserved pineapple juice.

Finish preparing the bread as directed on page 266.

Once the hamburger buns are ready and sliced, fill with the BBQ pulled pork.

Serve BBQ Pulled Pork Sandwiches with Carrot-Raisin Salad.

Cost $4.57

FRUGAL FACT: *When adding a large pork roast to your meal plan for the week or month, get in the habit of adding pulled pork sandwiches a few days after serving the pork roast.*

Sweet and Sour Pork

1 cup rice ($.20)
2 tablespoons olive oil ($.10)
3 tablespoons honey ($.20)
1 tablespoon cornstarch ($.01)
Juice of 1 orange ($.33)
⅓ cup white vinegar ($.15)

1 tablespoon soy sauce ($.05)
1 pound pork, cubed for stew ($1.99)
¼ fresh pineapple, diced ($.75)
½ green bell pepper, seeded and chopped ($.34)
2 large heads broccoli ($.79)

In a medium saucepan, bring 2½ cups of water to a boil, add the rice, and bring back to a boil. Reduce the heat, cover, and simmer for 20 minutes. Fluff the rice with a fork before serving.

In a large skillet or wok, prepare the sweet and sour sauce. Whisk together the oil, honey, and cornstarch. Add the orange juice and about ¼ cup water, the vinegar, and soy sauce. Stir in the cubed pork pieces, diced pineapple chunks, and chopped bell peppers. Cook over medium heat until the pork pieces have cooked through, 10 to 12 minutes, stirring often. The cooking time will vary depending on the thickness of the pork pieces.

Remove stems from broccoli and separate broccoli into florets. Steam the florets in a stovetop steamer for 4 to 5 minutes, or microwave for 4 to 5 minutes in a microwave-safe bowl, covered with plastic wrap.

Serve Sweet and Sour Pork over Rice with Steamed Broccoli.

Cost $4.91

FRUGAL FACT: *Eat the leftover pineapple for lunch and serve the remaining green pepper in a salad.*

Asian Pork Chops

1 tablespoon lemon juice ($.05)
½ cup soy sauce ($.25)
3 garlic cloves, crushed ($.15)
1 teaspoon ground ginger ($.10)
salt and pepper

4 pork chops (about 1¼ pounds) ($2.52)
1 cup brown rice ($.40)
4 carrot sticks ($.40)
3 tablespoons honey ($.25)
1 teaspoon olive oil ($.03)

In a small bowl, whisk together the lemon juice, soy sauce, crushed garlic cloves, ground ginger, and salt and pepper. Pour the marinade over the pork chops in a baking dish or in plastic ziplock bag. Let marinate for at least 30 minutes in the refrigerator.

In a medium saucepan, bring 2½ cups of water to a boil, add the brown rice, and bring back to a boil. Reduce the heat, cover, and simmer for 40 minutes. Fluff the rice with a fork before serving.

Once the pork chops have marinated, add the chops with the marinade to a large skillet and place over medium-high heat. Cook the pork chops, covered, for 6 to 8 minutes on each side, or until no longer pink in the middle. The cooking time may vary depending on the thickness of the pork chops.

Peel and cut carrots crosswise into ¼- to ⅛-inch rounds. Add the rounds to a small saucepan with the honey, olive oil, and ¼ cup of water. Cook for 5 to 6 minutes over medium heat, until the carrots are slightly tender, but still crunchy and nicely glazed.

Serve Thai Garlic Pork Chops with Brown Rice and Honey-Glazed Carrots.

Cost $4.34

FRUGAL FACT: *If you purchase a larger family pack and divide the pork chops into freezer ziplock bags, you can add the prepared marinade with the pork in the freezer bag and freeze it all together. The pork will marinate as it thaws in the refrigerator and before you cook.*

EIGHT

Fish and Seafood

Baked Lime Tilapia

1 tablespoon lime juice ($.05)
2 teaspoons olive oil ($.05)
1 teaspoon dill ($.05)
salt and pepper

4 frozen tilapia fillets ($2.99)
1 cup brown rice ($.40)
splash of lemon juice ($.01)
2 large heads broccoli ($.79)

In a small bowl, whisk together the lime juice, olive oil, dill, and a few dashes of salt and pepper.

Place the thawed tilapia fillets in a glass baking dish. Pour the lime-dill sauce over the fish and marinate at least 30 minutes in the refrigerator. Preheat the oven to 350 degrees.

Bake fish in the preheated oven for 15 to 20 minutes, until the fillets are opaque and flake easily. The cooking time may vary depending on the thickness of the fillets.

In a medium saucepan, bring 2½ cups of water to a boil, add the brown rice, and bring back to a boil. Add a splash of lemon juice. Reduce the heat, cover, and simmer for 40 to 50 minutes. Fluff the rice with a fork before serving.

Remove the stems from broccoli and separate the broccoli into florets. Steam the broccoli florets in a stovetop steamer for 4 to 5 minutes, or microwave for 4 to 5 minutes in a microwave-safe bowl, covered with plastic wrap.

Serve Baked Lime Tilapia with Brown Rice and Steamed Broccoli.

Cost $4.34

FRUGAL FACT: *Fresh herbs can be grown through the winter months on a kitchen windowsill and outside during warmer months.*

Breaded Cod

1 cup brown rice ($.40)
4 frozen breaded cod fillets ($2.99)
juice of 1 lemon ($.33)

2 heads broccoli ($.79)
store-bought tartar sauce ($.20)

In medium saucepan, bring 2½ cups of water to a boil, add the brown rice, and bring back to a boil. Reduce the heat, cover, and simmer for 40 to 50 minutes. Add the final squeeze of lemon juice to the rice as it cooks. Fluff the rice with a fork before serving.

Cook the breaded cod according to the package directions. Squeeze the juice of 1 lemon over the fillets when you remove them from the oven.

Cut the broccoli into spears and trim the stems. Steam the broccoli in a stovetop steamer for 4 to 5 minutes, or microwave for 4 to 5 minutes in a microwave-safe bowl, covered with plastic wrap.

Serve Breaded Cod and Tartar Sauce with Brown Rice and Steamed Broccoli.

Cost $4.71

FRUGAL FACT: *Lemons are often on sale for 3/$1 or 4/$1 during the winter months. Be sure to compare the prices of each individual fruit versus the price per fruit found in the bags.*

Cod with Sautéed Red Potatoes

....

4 frozen cod fillets ($2.99)
4 red potatoes ($.60)
2 tablespoons extra-virgin olive oil ($.20)
salt and pepper

1 acorn squash ($.69)
2 tablespoons butter ($.20)
1 tablespoon brown sugar ($.05)
store-bought tartar sauce ($.20)

Bake the cod fillets in the oven according to the package directions.

Scrub the red potatoes and dice them into 1-inch cubes. Sauté the red potatoes in a skillet with the extra-virgin olive oil. Cover and cook for about 10 minutes, until potatoes are cooked through. Stir two or three times while sautéing. Season with salt and pepper.

Preheat the oven to 350 degrees. Cut the acorn squash in half lengthwise and place cut side down in a glass baking dish. Add ¼ inch of water to the baking dish and cover with aluminum foil. Bake the squash for 50 to 60 minutes. Remove from the oven and let cool for 5 to 10 minutes before handling. Scrape out and discard the seeds, then scrape out the squash flesh. Add butter and brown sugar to the flesh for a sweeter side dish.

Serve Cod Fillets with Tartar Sauce, Sautéed Red Potatoes, and Acorn Squash.

Cost $4.93

FRUGAL FACT: *Look for winter squash sales around the Thanksgiving and Christmas holiday seasons.*

Fish Tacos 'n Chips

....

2 frozen whiting fillets ($1.50)
1 teaspoon seafood seasoning ($.05)
salt and pepper
4 large potatoes ($.60)
3 tablespoons canola oil ($.10)
ketchup ($.10)
2 heads broccoli ($.79)
4 burrito-size tortillas ($.50)
store-bought tartar sauce ($.20)
handful shredded lettuce ($.15)
handful shredded cheese ($.42)

Preheat the oven to 400 degrees. Place each frozen fillet onto a sheet of aluminum foil. Sprinkle with the seafood seasoning, salt, and pepper. Fold the foil around the fish. Place the foil fish packets directly onto the oven rack. Bake in the preheated oven for 15 to 20 minutes, or until the fish is flaky in the middle. The cooking time may vary depending on the thickness of the fish fillets. Remove the packets from the oven and let cool 5 minutes before handling. Slice each fillet into ½-inch-wide strips to fit into the tortillas.

Slice the potatoes lengthwise into wedges or "fries," about ⅛-inch thick. Place the wedges in a bowl and toss with the oil and salt and pepper. Lay them out in a single layer on a baking sheet. Bake the potato wedges at 350 degrees for 20 minutes. Flip them and bake another 15 minutes until golden brown. Serve the "chips" with ketchup.

Cut the broccoli into spears and trim the stems. Steam the broccoli in a stovetop steamer for 4 to 5 minutes, or microwave for 4 to 5 minutes in a microwave-safe bowl, covered with plastic wrap.

Assemble the fish tacos. Lay the tortillas out flat on a clean work surface and spread tartar sauce down the middle of the tortilla. Add the fillet slices, shredded lettuce, and shredded cheese.

Serve Fish Tacos 'n Chips with Broccoli.

Cost $4.46

FRUGAL FACT: *When there is just a handful or two of shredded cheese left in the bag, stash the bag in the freezer for use in meals that only call for a small amount of cheese. Shredded cheese thaws in 10 to 15 minutes on the counter.*

Honey-Dijon Tilapia

4 frozen tilapia fillets ($2.99)
2 tablespoons honey ($.13)
1 tablespoon rice vinegar ($.03)
1 tablespoon Dijon mustard ($.05)

salt and pepper
1 pound sweet potatoes ($.79)
2 cups frozen peas ($1)

Preheat the oven to 400 degrees. In a bowl, whisk together the honey, vinegar, Dijon mustard, and salt and pepper.

Place the thawed tilapia fillets on aluminum foil. Pour the Honey-Dijon sauce over the fish. Wrap the foil around the fish fillets.

Place the foil packet straight onto the oven rack. Bake in the preheated oven for 10 to 15 minutes, until the fish flakes easily. The cooking time may vary depending on the thickness of the fillets.

Make a few slits in the sweet potatoes using a small, sharp knife. Put the sweet potatoes in a baking dish with ¼ inch of water and cover with aluminum foil. Bake the sweet potatoes at 350 degrees for 1 hour. Remove and let cool about 10 minutes. Peel off the skins and mash the pulp.

Cook the frozen peas according to the package directions. Season with salt and pepper to taste.

Serve Honey-Dijon Tilapia with Mashed Sweet Potatoes and Peas.

Cost $4.99

FRUGAL FACT: *Individually wrapped, vacuum-sealed fish fillets are the most frugal way to incorporate fish into your meals.*

Creamy Lemon-Dill Catfish

Juice of 1 lemon ($.33)
½ teaspoon lemon rind
½ cup mayonnaise ($.10)
½ teaspoon dill ($.05)
salt and pepper

4 frozen catfish fillets ($2.99)
4 red potatoes ($.60)
4 tablespoons extra-virgin olive oil
   ($.40)
1 pound asparagus ($.99)

To make the creamy lemon-dill sauce, whisk together the lemon juice, lemon rind, mayonnaise, dill, and a few dashes of salt and pepper in a small bowl. Set the sauce aside.

Bake the frozen catfish fillets as directed on the package. When they have finished baking, let them cool for 5 to 10 minutes. Pour the lemon-dill sauce over the catfish just before serving.

Scrub the red potatoes and dice into 1-inch cubes. Sauté the potatoes in a skillet in 2 tablespoons of the extra-virgin olive oil. Cover and cook for about 10 minutes, until the potatoes are cooked through. Stir two or three times while sautéing. Season with salt and pepper.

In a skillet, sauté the asparagus in the remaining 2 tablespoons olive oil for 5 to 6 minutes, stirring every other minute. The asparagus will be tender-crisp and turn bright green when it is ready to serve. Remove the asparagus from skillet to prevent overcooking.

Serve Creamy Lemon-Dill Catfish with Sautéed Red Potatoes and Asparagus.

Cost $4.95

FRUGAL FACT: *Purchase mayonnaise with a coupon when it goes on sale to keep the costs low on meals that call for mayonnaise.*

Broiled Lemon-Pepper Fish

½ cup mayonnaise ($.10)
2 teaspoons lemon-pepper seasoning
   (free)

1 pound frozen tilapia fillets ($2.99)
1 cup white rice ($.20)
1 medium zucchini ($.75)

Preheat the broiler to 450 degrees. In a small bowl, whisk the mayonnaise with the lemon-pepper seasoning.

Lay the tilapia fillets in one layer on a broiling pan. Spread lemon-pepper mayo over the top of the tilapia. Broil the tilapia at 450 degrees for 10 minutes, or until the fillets flake easily. The cooking time may vary depending on the thickness of the fillets.

In a medium saucepan, bring 2 ½ cups of water to a boil, add the rice, and bring back to a boil. Reduce the heat, cover and simmer for 20 minutes. Fluff the rice with a fork before serving.

Wash and slice the zucchini crosswise into ¼-inch rounds. Place the zucchini in a microwave-safe bowl with ½ cup of water and cover with plastic wrap. Steam in the microwave for 5 to 6 minutes, or until the zucchini flesh is translucent.

Serve Broiled Lemon-Pepper Tilapia with Rice and Steamed Zucchini.

Cost $4.04

FRUGAL FACT: *Look for $.50 or $.75 coupons for name-brand spices and use them when the spices go on sale for $1 or less. If your grocery store doubles coupons, you can get FREE spices by combining the coupon with the sale price!*

Honey-Mustard Salmon

3 tablespoon honey ($.20)
3 tablespoon yellow prepared mustard ($.05)
4 frozen salmon fillets (4 to 6 ounces each) ($3)

1 cup brown rice ($.40)
1 pound asparagus ($.99)
2 tablespoons extra-virgin olive oil ($.20)

In a small bowl, whisk together the honey and mustard until well blended.

Place the thawed salmon fillets in a 9×13-inch baking dish. Pour the honey-mustard sauce over the salmon. Let marinate for at least 30 minutes in the refrigerator.

In medium saucepan, bring 2½ cups of water to a boil, add the brown rice, and bring back to a boil. Reduce the heat, cover, and simmer for 40 to 50 minutes. Fluff the rice with a fork before serving.

Preheat the oven to 350 degrees. Bake the salmon for 10 to 15 minutes, or until the fillets flake easily. The cooking time may vary depending on the thickness of the fillets.

In a skillet, sauté the asparagus in the olive oil for 5 to 6 minutes, stirring every other minute. The asparagus will be tender-crisp and turn bright green when it is ready to serve. Remove the asparagus from heat immediately to prevent overcooking.

Serve Honey-Mustard Salmon with Brown Rice and Sautéed Asparagus.

Cost $4.84

FRUGAL FACT: *Coupons are released for name-brand mustards throughout the year. Use your coupons when condiments are on sale, especially around the time of the "grilling holidays," like Memorial Day and Fourth of July, to get the best bang for your buck!*

Scallops with Roasted Red Pepper Pasta

1 large red bell pepper ($1)
1 package (16 ounces) angel hair
   pasta ($.97)
1 cup homemade Vegetable or Chicken
   Stock (pages 272 and 273) ($.10)
¾ pound frozen bay scallops, thawed
   ($2.00)

2 teaspoons Dijon mustard ($.03)
4 tablespoons butter ($.40)
salt and pepper
1 cup frozen broccoli pieces ($.50)

Preheat the oven to 450 degrees. Remove the stem and seeds from the bell pepper. Roast the pepper on a baking sheet at 450 degrees for 8 to 10 minutes. Remove from the oven, let cool for 5 to 10 minutes, then cut into ½-inch dice.

Cook the angel hair pasta according to the package directions.

To a large skillet, add 1 cup vegetable or chicken stock. Add the thawed bay scallops and simmer for 3 to 4 minutes. Remove the scallops with a slotted spoon and place on a plate near the stovetop. Whisk the Dijon mustard and butter into the cooking stock, reduce the heat, and simmer the sauce for 4 to 5 minutes. Return the scallops to the pan with the sauce and simmer for 4 to 5 minutes more. Season with salt and pepper.

Cook 1 cup frozen broccoli as directed on the package. Drain and squeeze dry.

Drain the angel hair pasta, and toss with the roasted red pepper pieces, broccoli, scallops, and sauce.

Serve Scallops with Roasted Red Pepper and Pasta.

Cost $5.00

FRUGAL FACT: *Look for sale prices of $3 or less for 16-ounce bags of frozen fish fillets, scallops, shrimp, and other seafood. Also, a great sale price for red, orange, and yellow peppers is $1 each. Be sure to snag this great price on an otherwise more expensive vegetable.*

Poached Salmon over Dill Rice

1 pound frozen salmon fillets ($2.99)
3 tablespoons lemon juice ($.15)
1 teaspoon fresh dill plus some for
    sprinkling ($.05)

2 heads broccoli ($.79)
1 cup brown rice ($.40)

Slice the salmon fillet into 4 smaller fillets. Select a microwave-safe glass baking dish that will hold the fillets in one layer. Add ½ to 1 cup of water and lemon juice to the dish, making sure that the entire bottom surface of the dish is covered. Place the baking dish with the liquid in the microwave and cook on high for 3 to 4 minutes, or until the liquid is hot. Add the fillets to the dish, and cover with plastic wrap. Cook on high for 5 minutes, or until the salmon becomes opaque. Remove the fillets from the microwave and let cool 5 minutes. Sprinkle the fillets with some finely chopped fresh dill.

In a medium saucepan, bring 2¼ cups of water to a boil. Add the rice and 1 teaspoon of the fresh dill, and return to a boil. Reduce the heat, cover, and simmer 20 minutes. Fluff the rice with a fork before serving.

Remove stems from the broccoli and separate broccoli into florets. Steam the florets in stovetop steamer for 4 to 5 minutes, or microwave for 4 to 5 minutes in a microwave-safe bowl, covered with plastic wrap.

Serve Poached Salmon over Dill Rice with Steamed Broccoli.

Cost $4.38

FRUGAL FACTS: *First, you can really only make this for $5.00 or less when salmon is on sale. Recently, I have seen salmon priced at $2.99 per pound. When it goes that low, this dish can certainly be included on a weekly menu plan. If you buy salmon at the $4.00 per pound average that I usually see it at, it puts you a few cents over your limit. So, it's worth saving this recipe for times when salmon is on sale. Second, several times throughout the winter months, broccoli goes on sale for less than $1/bunch. Keep an eye out for it.*

Tilapia with Wild Rice Blend

4 fresh tilapia fillets ($3.29)
2 teaspoons lemon juice ($.04)
2 teaspoons seafood seasoning ($.10)

1 cup wild rice blend ($.60)
1 large summer squash ($.79)
1 tablespoon butter ($.10)

Preheat the oven to 350 degrees. Place the tilapia fillets in a glass baking dish. Squeeze the lemon juice over the fish. Sprinkle the fish with the seafood seasonings. Bake in the preheated oven for 10 to 15 minutes, or until the fish flakes easily. The cooking time may vary depending on thickness of the fillets.

In a medium saucepan, bring 3 cups of water to a boil. Add the wild rice blend (mix of wild rice and white rice), and return to a boil. Reduce the heat, cover, and simmer 20 minutes. Fluff the rice with a fork before serving.

Slice the summer squash crosswise into ⅛-inch rounds. Place the rounds in a microwave-safe bowl with ½ cup of water and the butter. Cover with plastic wrap and microwave for 5 to 6 minutes, or until the squash is translucent. Remove the plastic wrap carefully to avoid steam burns, and drain off the water. Serve warm, seasoned with salt and pepper to taste.

Serve Tilapia Fillets with Wild Rice and Steamed Summer Squash.

Cost $4.92

FRUGAL FACT: *The best prices on fresh fish can be found during the Lenten season (late February through March or early April).*

Tuna Melts

2 cans (6 ounces each) tuna, drained ($1.36)

3 tablespoons sandwich spread ($.15)

8 slices bread ($.50)

2 tablespoons butter ($.20)

4 slices provolone cheese ($.75)

2 pears ($.89)

2 cups frozen peas ($1)

In a small bowl, mix the drained tuna with the sandwich spread.

Butter the "toasting sides" of each piece of bread. Place the tuna on the bread and top with the cheese slice. Toast the tuna melt on an electric griddle or in a hot skillet for 2 to 3 minutes each side, until the cheese has melted and the bread has toasted.

Slice and dice the pears; you can peel the pears first if you wish.

Cook the frozen peas according to the package directions.

Serve Tuna Melts with Sliced Pears and Steamed Peas.

Cost $4.85

FRUGAL FACT: *Incorporate a "lunch-type" meal into your dinner plans once a month. Match coupons with sale price to stockpile canned tuna.*

Shrimp Scampi

2 garlic cloves, crushed ($.10)
2 tablespoons extra-virgin olive oil ($.20)
about 25 small cooked frozen shrimp ($2.50)
2 tablespoons butter ($.20)

salt and pepper
1 package (16 ounces) thin spaghetti (spaghettini) ($.97)
¼ cup grated Parmesan cheese ($.25)
1 pound fresh green beans ($.79)

Cook the thin spaghetti according to the package directions, meanwhile preparing the shrimp and sauce. Drain the pasta.

In a large skillet, sauté the crushed garlic in the olive oil for 2 to 3 minutes. Add the shrimp and butter, sprinkle with salt and pepper, and sauté for 3 to 4 minutes more.

Add the cooked thin spaghetti to the skillet with the shrimp and sauce. Toss to combine and simmer for 3 to 4 minutes. Sprinkle the grated Parmesan over the shrimp and pasta.

Snap off the ends of the green beans, and steam in a stovetop steamer for 4 to 5 minutes, or boil the green beans in small saucepan with 1 to 2 cups of water for 6 to 8 minutes. Drain and serve warm.

Serve Shrimp Scampi with Spaghetti and Green Beans.

Cost $5.01

FRUGAL FACT: *Purchase a 41 to 60 ct. bag of frozen cooked shrimp when it is on sale for $5, and split the shrimp for use in two different meals.*

NINE

Soups and Stews

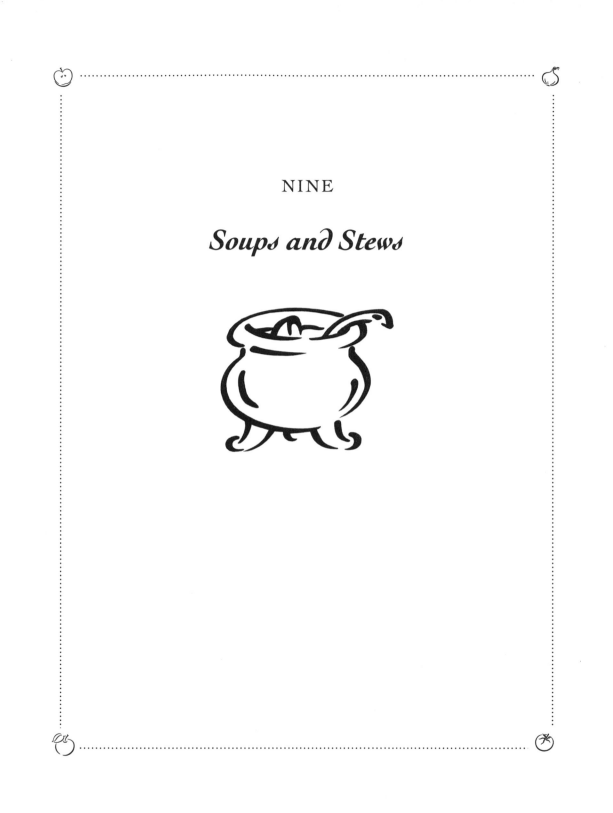

Hearty Beef Stew

2 tablespoons canola oil ($.10)
1½ pounds stewing beef ($2.12)
3 cups water or homemade Beef Broth
   (page 274) (free)
1 can (15 ounces) petite diced
   tomatoes with their juices ($.59)
3 carrots ($.30)

4 small white potatoes ($.50)
1 cup frozen green beans ($.50)
2 garlic cloves, crushed ($.10)
salt and pepper
6 homemade Cloverleaf Dinner Rolls
   (page 258) ($.48)

Prepare the dough for the homemade cloverleaf dinner rolls in a bread machine according to the recipe.

In a large saucepan, heat the oil and add the beef. Sear and brown each side of each piece of stewing beef. Then add water or homemade beef broth. Bring to a boil. Lower the heat.

Peel and dice carrots and potatoes. Add the diced carrots, diced potatoes, diced tomatoes, green beans, crushed garlic, and salt and pepper to the beef stew. Cook for 20 to 30 minutes, then reduce the heat and simmer until the beef and vegetable are tender and the stew is ready to serve. If you prefer a thicker stew, whisk in 1 tablespoon of cornstarch.

Form the dough into rolls and bake the rolls according to the recipe.

Serve Hearty Beef Stew with Homemade Cloverleaf Dinner Rolls.

Cost $4.69

FRUGAL FACT: *Making your own beef broth will save between $2 and $3 per meal. Details for making homemade beef broth from a beef roast and other stocks can be found on page 274.*

Chicken and Sweet Potato Stew

4 tablespoons extra-virgin olive oil ($.40)

1 onion, chopped ($.30)

2 celery stalks, chopped ($.10)

2 garlic cloves, crushed ($.10)

salt and pepper

2 cups homemade Chicken Stock (page 273) ($.20)

2 cups shredded chicken ($1.50)

1 large sweet potato, peeled and diced ($.69)

1 can (15 ounces) diced tomatoes with their juices ($.59)

1 cup white rice ($.20)

1 pound fresh green beans ($.99)

To a large saucepan, add 2 tablespoons of the olive oil, the chopped onion, chopped celery, crushed garlic, and salt and pepper. Sauté the vegetables for 4 to 5 minutes, or until onions become opaque.

Add the homemade Chicken Stock, shredded chicken, peeled and diced sweet potato, diced tomatoes, and 1 cup of water. Cook for 40 minutes over medium heat.

In a medium saucepan, bring 2½ cups of water to a boil, add the rice, and bring back to a boil. Reduce the heat, cover, and simmer for 20 minutes. Fluff the rice with a fork before serving.

Snap off the stems of the green beans. Cut the beans into 2-inch pieces, if you wish. In a small skillet, sauté the green beans in the remaining 2 tablespoons olive oil with a few dashes of salt and pepper for 3 to 4 minutes, stirring often, until the green beans are tender-crisp and turn bright green.

Serve Chicken and Sweet Potato Stew over Rice with a side of Sautéed Green Beans.

Cost $4.87

FRUGAL FACT: *When celery goes on sale during the holiday season for less than $.50 a bunch, buy one or two bunches. Wash the stalks and dice into "soup-size" pieces. Place 1- or 2-cup portions in freezer ziplock bags or freezer-safe plastic containers. Freeze for up to 6 months. Chopping soup ingredients in bulk saves time and energy when throwing together a quick soup on a cold winter evening. Simply grab a bag of chopped celery from the freezer, drop it into the soup frozen, and carry on with the rest of your dinner preparation!*

Chicken Tortilla Soup

2 boneless, skinless chicken breasts ($1.66)

3 tablespoons canola oil ($.10)

3 cups homemade Chicken Stock (page 273) (.30)

1 can (12 ounces) diced tomatoes with green chilies ($.37)

½ onion, chopped ($.15)

1 cup milk ($.10)

6 corn tortillas ($.50)

1 cup shredded Cheddar cheese ($.75)

4 ears corn ($1)

Cut the chicken breasts into 1-inch cubes. In a medium saucepan, heat the oil and add the cubed chicken. Sauté the chicken pieces over medium-high heat for 3 to 4 minutes, then add 2 to 3 cups of water or homemade chicken broth. Add the tomatoes with green chilies, the chopped onion, and the milk. Season the soup with salt and pepper. Reduce the heat, and simmer for 20 minutes, or until the chicken pieces have cooked through.

About 10 minutes before serving, cut the tortillas into strips, add the tortillas strips and shredded cheese to the soup.

Remove the husks and silk from the ears of corn and boil the corn in a large pot of water for 4 to 5 minutes, or place the ears of corn in a microwave-safe baking dish, cover with plastic wrap, and microwave for 7 to 9 minutes.

Serve Chicken Tortilla Soup with Corn on the Cob.

Cost $4.93

FRUGAL FACT: *If you have chicken leftover from making a whole chicken, you can freeze the shredded chicken in 2-cup portions to use for recipes that call for diced or shredded chicken.*

Chickpea Stew

1 can (15 ounces) chickpeas, drained and rinsed ($.79)
1 can (15 ounces) diced tomatoes with their juices ($.59)
1 box (10 ounces) frozen chopped spinach ($.50)
1 zucchini, diced ($.79)
½ onion, diced ($.15)

2 garlic cloves, crushed ($.10)
2 tablespoons extra-virgin olive oil ($.20)
salt and pepper
1 cup brown rice ($.40)
4 slices bread ($.50)
2 tablespoons butter ($.20)
garlic salt ($.05)

To the insert of a 4-quart or larger slow cooker, add the chickpeas, diced tomatoes, thawed, undrained spinach, diced zucchini, diced onion, crushed garlic, olive oil, and salt and pepper. Set the slow cooker on low, and cook the stew for 8 hours.

In a medium saucepan, bring 2½ cups of water to a boil, add the brown rice, and bring back to a boil. Reduce the heat, cover, and simmer for 40 to 50 minutes. Fluff the rice with a fork before serving. Place the rice in the bottom of individual serving bowls. Ladle the chickpea stew over the rice.

Toast 4 slices of bread, butter the bread, and sprinkle with garlic salt.

Serve Chickpea Stew over Brown Rice with Toasted Garlic Bread.

Cost $4.27

FRUGAL FACT: *Save and freeze the heels from each loaf of bread you purchase. When you need garlic toast, put the frozen slices into the toaster, then butter and sprinkle with garlic salt. This makes for frugal and easy garlic bread for this stew and many other soups and stews!*

Curried Pumpkin Soup

2 teaspoons extra-virgin olive oil ($.05)
½ onion, finely chopped ($.20)
3 garlic cloves, crushed ($.15)
1 can (28 ounces) pure pumpkin ($1.68)
2 cups homemade Chicken Stock ($.20) (page 273)
1 cup water

3 tablespoons green curry paste ($.25)
few dashes of ground cinnamon ($.03)
1 tablespoon brown sugar ($.05)
salt and pepper
sour cream for serving ($.20)
2 cups frozen green beans ($1)
½ loaf French Bread, homemade or store-bought ($.60)

In a large saucepan, heat the olive oil, and add the finely chopped onion and crushed garlic and sauté 2 to 3 minutes. Add the chicken broth and canned pumpkin, and whisk to combine. Add about 1 cup of water if you prefer a thinner soup. Simmer the soup over medium-low heat.

Whisk in the curry paste, cinnamon, brown sugar, salt, and pepper and simmer until ready to serve. Serve the soup in individual bowls, garnished with a dollop of sour cream.

Slice and warm the French bread.

Cook the frozen green beans according to the package directions.

Serve Curried Pumpkin Soup with French Bread and Green Beans.

Cost $4.41

FRUGAL FACT: *Ask your grocery store's bakery if and when they mark down specialty bread loaves. If you don't have time to make your own bread, then buy the bread at a reduced price and use or freeze it right away.*

Corn and Salsa Soup

6 corn tortillas ($.50)
3 tablespoons vegetable oil ($.0.12)
1 tablespoon ground cumin ($.10)
2 cups frozen corn kernels ($1)
2 garlic cloves, crushed ($.10)
½ onion, chopped ($.15)
salt and pepper
3 cups homemade Chicken or
    Vegetable Stock (pages 273 and
    272) ($.30)

1 can (15 ounces) fire-roasted diced
    tomatoes with their juices ($.59)
1 tablespoon lime juice ($.10)
sour cream for serving ($.20)
½ cup salsa ($.50)
tortilla chips for serving ($1)

Preheat the oven to 400 degrees. Cut the corn tortillas into strips. Toss the strips with 2 tablespoons of the vegetable oil and the ground cumin. Spread out on a baking sheet and bake in the preheated oven for 8 to 10 minutes until crispy and golden brown.

To a saucepan, add the remaining 1 tablespoon of oil and the corn kernels. Cook a few minutes until the kernel edges start to brown. Add the garlic, onion, salt, and pepper. Then add chicken or vegetable stock and then diced tomatoes. Simmer for 10 to 15 minutes, to give the flavors time to mingle.

Ladle the soup into individual serving bowls. Add the tortilla strips, a dash of lime juice, salsa, and a dollop of sour cream to each bowl.

Serve Corn and Salsa, Soup with Tortilla Chips.

Cost $4.65

FRUGAL FACT: *You can make your own tortilla chips by cutting corn tortillas into triangles and following the steps listed in #1. A tasty, homemade tortilla chip!*

Corn Chowder

2 slices bacon ($.40)
2 small white potatoes, peeled and
   diced ($.25)
1 onion, chopped ($.30)
2 cups frozen corn kernels ($1)

1 can (15 ounces) creamed corn ($.69)
3 cups milk ($.30)
1 cup Monterey Jack cheese ($.75)
freshly ground black pepper
2 heads broccoli ($.79)

In a large skillet over medium-high heat, fry the bacon slices for 4 to 5 minutes on each side, until brown and crispy. Remove the bacon from the skillet and tranfer to paper towels to drain the fat. Crumble the bacon pieces and set aside. Drain the excess bacon grease from the skillet, reserving 2 tablespoons.

Add the bacon grease, diced potatoes, chopped onion, and frozen corn kernels to a saucepan and sauté for 3 to 4 minutes in the bacon grease.

Add the creamed corn and milk to the potato mixture. Stir well to combine, whisking if necessary. Bring the soup to a slow bubble. Add the Monterey Jack cheese and stir through. Season with black pepper, to taste. Add the crumbled bacon to each individual serving bowl just before serving.

Remove the stems from the broccoli and separate the broccoli into florets. Steam the broccoli florets in a stovetop steamer for 4 to 5 minutes, or microwave for 4 to 5 minutes in a microwave-safe bowl, covered with plastic wrap.

Serve Corn Chowder with Steamed Broccoli.

Cost $4.68

FRUGAL FACT: *Want to save a little extra time in the kitchen? Double a soup recipe, then freeze the second portion for a future meal. Place the soup in the refrigerator the day before you wish to serve it. Then add the thawed or partially thawed soup to a saucepan and simmer for an hour. Serve with freezer garlic toast. Your home will smell like you worked hard on this soup, when all you really did was pull it out of the freezer!*

Beef and Cranberry Stew

1½ pounds stewing beef ($2.12)
1 cup fresh cranberries ($.50)
½ onion, chopped ($.15)
2 celery stalks, chopped ($.10)
½ cup (8 ounces) white rice ($.10)
1 can (8 ounces) crushed pineapple
   with its juice ($.59)

1 Golden Delicious apple, chopped
   ($.25)
1 cup orange juice ($.15)
2 cups frozen green beans ($1)

Add the stewing beef, fresh cranberries, chopped onion, chopped celery, crushed pineapple, chopped apple, and orange juice to the insert of a slow cooker. Set the slow cooker on low, and cook the stew for 8 hours. After the stew has been cooking for about 7 hours, add the ½ cup of rice plus 1 cup of water and continue to cook the stew for 1 more hour.

Cook the frozen green beans according to the package directions.

Serve Cranberry Stew with a side of Green Beans.

Cost $4.96

FRUGAL FACT: *At the start of the winter months, purchase a larger "family pack" of stewing beef for a lower price than individual meal-size packages. Divide the stewing beef from the larger package into 1- or 1½-pound portions and freeze in freezer ziplock bags.*

Cream of Broccoli Soup

2 bone-in, split chicken breasts ($1.79)
2 tablespoons extra-virgin olive oil ($.20)
1 tablespoon vinegar ($.05)
salt and pepper
2 heads broccoli, trimmed, chopped ($.79)
3 small white potatoes, peeled and diced ($.40)
2 celery stalks, chopped ($.10)
1 cup shredded sharp Cheddar cheese ($.75)
1 can (12 ounces) evaporated milk ($.37)
½ cup milk, 2 percent or whole ($.05)
1 large sweet potato ($.49)

Prepare the sweet potato first. Make a few slits in the sweet potato using a small sharp knife. Put the potato in a baking dish with ¼ inch of water and cover with aluminum foil. Bake the sweet potatoes at 350 degrees for 1 hour. Remove from the oven and let cool about 10 minutes. Peel off the skin and mash the pulp.

Marinate the chicken breasts with the olive oil, vinegar, salt, and pepper in a baking dish in the refrigerator for at least 30 minutes. Preheat the oven to 350 degrees.

Bake the chicken breasts in the preheated oven for 35 to 45 minutes, or until the juices run clear. The cooking time may vary depending on the thickness of the chicken breasts.

To a large saucepan, add the evaporated milk, regular milk, peeled and diced white potatoes, celery, and chopped broccoli. Bring to boil, reduce the heat, and simmer for 30 minutes.

Pour the soup into a blender or food processor in batches if necessary. Blend until smooth and creamy. Return the processed soup to the pot and bring to a low simmer. Slowly add handfuls of the cheese, stirring constantly until the cheese is completely incorporated.

Serve Cream of Broccoli Soup with Baked Chicken and Mashed Sweet Potatoes.

Cost $4.99

FRUGAL FACT: *Broccoli can be blanched and frozen. When it goes on sale for less than $1/pound, purchase more than you need for that week and blanch it in boiling water, cool quickly in a large bowl of ice water, drain, and then freeze in freezer ziplock bags or freezer-safe plastic containers for future meals.*

Creamy Butternut Squash Soup

homemade Honey Wheat Rolls
   (page 260) ($.50)
1 large butternut squash ($.69)
2 tablespoons butter ($.10)
1 small onion, chopped ($.20)
1 celery stalk, chopped ($.05)
2 small white potatoes, diced ($.20)
3 garlic cloves, crushed ($.15)

dashes of ground cinnamon, cloves,
   and ginger ($.10)
2 cups homemade Chicken or Vegetable
   Stock (pages 273 and 272) ($.20)
¼ cup apple juice ($.10)
1½ cups whole milk ($.20)
salt and pepper
2 cups frozen peas ($1)

Prepare the dough for homemade Honey Wheat Rolls in a bread machine or in a mixing bowl.

Microwave the whole squash for 5 to 6 minutes. Using hot pads, remove from the microwave and let cool for 10 minutes. Slice off the skin, scoop out and discard the seeds, and cut the squash flesh into 1-inch cubes.

In a large saucepan, melt the butter and add the squash cubes, chopped onion, chopped celery, diced potatoes, and crushed garlic. Sauté the vegetables for 7 to 8 minutes. Add the spices, chicken or vegetable stock, apple juice, and milk. Simmer 30 to 40 minutes, until all vegetables are soft and tender.

Pour the soup into a blender or food processor, in batches if necessary. Blend until smooth and creamy.

Cook the frozen peas according to the package directions.

Finish preparing the bread as directed in the recipe.

Serve Creamy Butternut Squash Soup with Peas and homemade Honey Wheat Rolls.

Cost $3.49

FRUGAL FACT: *During the late fall season, stores will sometimes sell squash for one price per individual squash, not a price pre pound. If your store offers this deal, be sure to grab the largest squash to get the most for your money.*

Winter Vegetable Stew

1 small butternut squash ($.69)
1 small acorn squash ($.69)
1 box frozen chopped (10 ounces) spinach ($.50)
2 carrots, peeled and diced ($.20)
2 teaspoons extra-virgin olive oil ($.05)
1 can (15 ounces) chickpeas, rinsed and drained ($.79)

4 cups homemade Vegetable or Chicken Stock (pages 272 and 273) ($.40)
1 teaspoon garlic powder ($.02)
salt and pepper
2 teaspoon honey ($.05)
3 tablespoons green curry paste ($.25)
1 cup white rice ($.20)

Microwave the butternut squash for 3 minutes. Remove from the microwave using hot pads, and let cool. Microwave the acorn squash for 3 minutes. Remove and let cool. (Peeling and cutting winter squashes is much easier after their skins have been softened in the microwave.) Once the squashes have cooled, peel off the skins with a vegetable peeler or knife. Cut the squashes in half lengthwise and scoop out and discard the seeds. Cut the flesh of both squashes into ½-inch-square cubes.

Microwave the spinach according to the package directions, until thawed. Do not drain.

Peel and cut the carrots into rounds.

To a large saucepan, add the olive oil and chickpeas and sauté 2 to 3 minutes. Add the homemade vegetable or chicken stock and bring to a boil. Add the squash cubes, diced carrots, and thawed frozen spinach.

Add the garlic powder, salt, and pepper, curry paste, and honey to the stew. Stir to combine. Cover and cook for at least 30 minutes over medium-low heat.

In a medium saucepan, bring 2½ cups of water to a boil, add the rice, and bring back to a boil. Reduce the heat, cover, and simmer for 20 minutes. Fluff the rice with a fork before serving.

Serve Winter Vegetable Stew over Steamed Rice.

Cost $3.84

FRUGAL FACT: *One-dish stews are not only delicious and filling, but keep the kitchen cleanup and dirty dishes to a minimum as well.*

Green Pepper Soup

3 large sweet potatoes ($1.49)
2 tablespoons butter ($.20)
¼ to ½ cup walnuts or pecans ($.50)
½ pound ground beef ($.75)
1 green bell pepper, chopped ($.79)
½ onion, chopped ($.15)
½ cup white rice ($.15)

1 can (15 ounces) diced tomatoes with their juices ($.59)
1 can (8 ounces) tomato sauce ($.25)
1 tablespoon brown sugar plus some for the sweet potatoes ($.10)
4 to 5 cups water
salt and pepper

Preheat the oven to 350 degrees. Make a few slits in the sweet potatoes using a small sharp knife. Put the sweet potatoes in a baking dish with ¼ inch of water and cover with aluminum foil. Bake the sweet potatoes for 1 hour. Remove from the oven and let cool about 10 minutes. Peel off the skins and mash the pulp. Add the butter, crushed walnuts or pecans, and brown sugar to each serving.

In a large saucepan, brown the ground beef and drain the excess fat. Return the meat to the saucepan.

To the cooked ground beef, add the chopped bell pepper, chopped onion, rice, diced tomatoes, tomato sauce, brown sugar, salt and pepper, and 4 cups of water. Simmer over medium-low heat for 20 to 30 minutes, or until the rice is cooked through.

Serve Green Pepper Soup with Candied Sweet Potatoes.

Cost $4.99

FRUGAL FACT: *Green peppers and onions can be sliced and/or diced and frozen in 1- or 2-cup portions in freezer ziplock bags. Toss frozen green peppers and onions right into soups, or use to make fajitas.*

Barley and Lentil Soup

1 cup lentils ($.40)
2 cups homemade Vegetable or Chicken Stock (pages 272 and 273) ($.20)
1 teaspoon salt
1 onion, chopped ($.30)
1 can (15 ounces) diced tomatoes with their juices ($.59)
1 box (10 ounces) frozen spinach ($.50)
1 teaspoon chopped, fresh parsley ($.05)
½ teaspoon cayenne pepper ($.05)
dash of salt
1 cup barley ($.40)
1 head romaine lettuce ($1.49)
1 plum tomato ($.39)
homemade Honey-Mustard Salad Dressing (page 281) ($.50)

To a large saucepan, add the lentils and the homemade stock, 1 cup of water, and salt. Bring to a boil. Reduce heat and continue cooking at a rolling boil for ten minutes. Add the chopped onion, diced tomatoes, and frozen spinach. Stir to combine. Mix in the parsley, cayenne, and salt to taste. Cook over medium-low heat for 10 to 15 minutes.

Add the barley plus 2 cups of water. Continue cooking for 15 minutes. Serve immediately, so that the barley does not overcook.

Rinse and cut the lettuce with a plastic lettuce knife to prevent browning. Toss the lettuce and the diced tomato with the dressing.

Serve Barley and Lentil Soup with Romaine Salad.

Cost $4.87

FRUGAL FACT: *Using a plastic lettuce knife to cut lettuce will prevent the edges of the portion of lettuce you don't use right away from browning. Purchasing a large head of lettuce is more frugal that buying a bag of precut and washed lettuce.*

Mexican Bean Soup

½ cup dried small red beans ($.20)
½ cup dried black beans ($.20)
1 can (6 ounces) tomato sauce ($.33)
1 can (12 ounces) diced tomatoes with
    green chilies ($.37)
½ onion, chopped ($.20)
1 cup frozen corn kernels ($.50)
2 teaspoons ground cumin ($.10)

1 teaspoon chili powder ($.05)
1 teaspoon garlic powder ($.05)
1 teaspoon onion powder ($.05)
1 teaspoon cornstarch ($.05)
salt and pepper
1 cup white rice ($.20)
4 ears corn ($1)

Soak the dried red beans overnight, or bring to a boil with water, remove from the heat, and let soak for at least 2 hours in the hot water. Drain and rinse the beans. Add the soaked beans to a medium saucepan with at least 2 inches of water covering them. Bring to a boil. Cover, reduce the heat to medium, and cook 1½ hours, or until the beans are soft.

As beans are cooking, add ½ can of tomato sauce; reserve the other half for the rice. Add the can of diced tomatoes with green chilies, the chopped onion, corn kernels, 1 teaspoon of ground cumin, chili powder, garlic powder, and onion powder. Whisk in the cornstarch to thicken soup. Season the soup with salt and pepper to taste.

In a medium saucepan, bring 2½ cups of water to a boil, add the rice, and bring back to a boil. Reduce the heat and cover. While the rice is cooking, add the remaining ½ can of tomato sauce and 1 teaspoon ground cumin. Cover the rice and simmer for 20 minutes. Fluff the rice with a fork before serving.

Remove husks and silk from the ears of corn and boil in the large pot of water for 4 to 5 minutes, or place the ears of corn in a microwave-safe baking dish, cover with plastic wrap, and microwave for 7 to 9 minutes.

Serve Mexican Bean Soup with Spanish Rice and Corn on the Cob.

Cost $3.30

FRUGAL FACT: *Walgreens often has great sale prices ($.25 or $.33 each) on canned tomato sauce.*

Beefy Minestrone Soup

1 pound stewing beef ($1.49)

2 cups homemade Beef Broth (page 274) (free)

1 head broccoli, chopped ($.39)

1 can (15 ounces) diced tomatoes with their juices ($.59)

¼ cup dried red kidney beans ($.10)

½ onion, chopped ($.15)

2 celery stalks, chopped ($.20)

1 teaspoon dried Italian seasoning ($.05)

salt and pepper

½ cup elbow macaroni ($.25)

2 large sweet potatoes ($.98)

2 tablespoons butter ($.20)

1 teaspoon ground cinnamon ($.03)

To the insert of a slow cooker, add the stewing beef, homemade beef broth, chopped broccoli, diced tomatoes, dried red kidney beans, chopped onion, chopped celery, Italian seasoning, and salt and pepper. Set the slow cooker on low, and cook the soup for 8 hours. After 7½ hours, add ½ cup of elbow macaroni and stir into the soup. Cook for 30 more minutes.

Meanwhile, preheat the oven to 350 degrees. Make a few slits in the sweet potatoes using a small sharp knife. Put the sweet potatoes in a baking dish with ¼ inch of water and cover with aluminum foil. Bake the sweet potatoes for 1 hour. Remove from the oven and let cool about 10 minutes. Peel off the skins and mash the pulp. Top with butter and sprinkle with cinnamon.

Serve Beefy Minestrone Soup with Cinnamon Sweet Potatoes.

Cost $4.43

FRUGAL FACT: *Depending on the season and the sale cycle, frozen vegetables are cheaper than fresh vegetables and often on sale. You can substitute 1 cup of frozen chopped broccoli if fresh broccoli is not in season.*

Pasta e Fagioli Soup

¾ pound ground beef ($1.12)
2 carrots, chopped ($.30)
2 celery stalks, chopped ($.20)
½ onion, chopped ($.15)
1 can (15 ounces) diced tomatoes with their juices ($.59)
1 can (6 ounces) tomato sauce ($.33)

1 cup dried red kidney beans ($.40)
2 tablespoons dried Italian seasoning ($.10)
2 teaspoons garlic powder ($.05)
salt and pepper
1 cup elbow macaroni ($.49)
2 heads broccoli ($.79)

In a skillet, brown the ground beef and drain excess fat.

Add the cooked ground beef, chopped carrots, chopped celery, chopped onion, canned tomatoes, tomato sauce, dried beans, and 2 cups of water to a slow cooker. Stir in the Italian seasoning, garlic powder, and salt and pepper. Set the slow cooker on low, and cook the soup for 8 hours.

Add 1 cup of elbow macaroni and stir into the soup when the slow cooker has 30 minutes remaining to cook.

Cut the broccoli into spears and trim the stems. Steam the broccoli in a stovetop steamer for 4 to 5 minutes, or microwave for 4 to 5 minutes in a microwave-safe bowl, covered with plastic wrap.

Serve Pasta e Fagioli Soup with Steamed Broccoli.

Cost $4.52

FRUGAL FACT: *Purchase a large package or roll of ground beef. Divide into 1- to 2-pound portions and make meatballs. Uncooked meatballs can be frozen on baking sheets and then transferred into a freezer ziplock bag. Cook the rest of the ground beef and then freeze in 2- to 3-cup portions for use in future meals.*

Pickapeppa Beef Stew

2 tablespoons canola oil ($.07)
¾ pound stewing beef ($1.11)
5 cups water or homemade Beef Broth
   (page 274) (free)
1 can (15 ounces) diced or stewed
   tomatoes ($.59)
2 carrots, chopped ($.20)
4 large white potatoes, diced ($.60)

2 celery stalks, chopped ($.20)
½ onion, chopped ($.15)
salt and pepper
3 to 4 tablespoons Pickapeppa sauce
   ($.50)
4 ears corn ($1)
homemade Cloverleaf Dinner Rolls
   (page 258) ($.50)

Prepare the dough for homemade cloverleaf dinner rolls in a bread machine or in a mixing bowl.

To a large saucepan, add the oil and stewing beef. Sear and brown the beef cubes on each side to seal in the juices. Once browned, add 5 to 6 cups water or homemade beef broth. Add canned tomatoes, chopped carrots, diced potatoes, chopped celery, chopped onion, and salt and pepper to taste. Add the Pickapeppa sauce to taste. Simmer the stew for 30 to 45 minutes.

Remove husks and silk from the ears of corn and boil the corn in large pot of water for 4 to 5 minutes, or place the ears of corn in microwave-safe baking dish, cover with plastic wrap, and microwave for 7 to 9 minutes.

Form the dough into rolls and bake according to directions in the recipe.

Serve Pickapeppa Beef Stew with Corn on the Cob and warm Cloverleaf Dinner Rolls.

Cost $4.92

FRUGAL FACT: *Look for Pickapeppa sauce among the condiments at your grocery store. This sauce gives the stew a rich and tangy flavor that can only come from Pickapeppa sauce.*

Steak Sauce Stew

1½ pounds leftover, cooked, beef roast or 1½ pounds. stewing beef ($2.24)

3 cups homemade Beef Broth (free)

1 can (15 ounces) diced tomatoes with their juices ($.59)

½ cup brown rice ($.25)

2 carrots, chopped ($.20)

½ green bell pepper, diced ($.39)

1 teaspoon garlic powder ($.05)

1 teaspoon dried Italian seasoning ($.05)

2 tablespoons steak sauce ($.25)

salt and pepper

homemade Honey Wheat Rolls (page 260) ($.50)

Prepare the dough for the homemade rolls in a bread machine or in a mixing bowl.

To a large saucepan, add the leftover beef roast or stewing beef, beef broth, diced tomatoes, 2 cups of water, brown rice, the chopped carrots, diced bell pepper, garlic powder, Italian seasoning, and salt and pepper to taste. Add the steak sauce, bring to boil, and simmer the stew for about 1 hour, or until the veggies are tender and the rice has cooked.

Finish preparing the rolls as directed in the recipe.

Serve Steak Sauce Stew with homemade Honey Wheat Rolls.

Cost $4.52

FRUGAL FACT: *After cooking a large 2- to 3-pound beef roast, save some of the meat for a stew or another meal that calls for diced or shredded beef.*

Creamy Potato Soup

8 small white potatoes peeled and diced ($1)
½ onion, chopped ($.15)
1 celery stalk, chopped ($.10)
2 garlic cloves, crushed ($.10)
½ cup sour cream ($.25)
¼ cup milk ($.02)
1 cup shredded Cheddar or mozzarella cheese ($.75)
4 strips turkey bacon ($.75)
2 heads broccoli ($.79)
2 cups frozen corn kernels ($1)
salt and pepper

Add the potatoes to a large saucepan with 4 to 5 cups of boiling water. Let boil for 8 to 10 minutes, or until soft.

Add the chopped onion, chopped celery, crushed garlic, sour cream, milk, and cheese to the potatoes. Stir to combine. Let simmer for 5 to 10 minutes. Mash with a potato masher. Continue simmering and mashing until the soup reaches the desired consistency.

Place the turkey bacon on plate lined with 2 paper towels. Cover the bacon with another paper towel. Microwave the bacon on high for 3 to 4 minutes. Microwave 30 seconds more, until crispy. Once crispy, let cool and then crumble. Just before serving top the individual soup bowls with the crumbled bacon.

Remove the stems and separate the broccoli into florets. Steam the broccoli florets in a stovetop steamer for 4 to 5 minutes, or microwave for 4 to 5 minutes in a microwave-safe bowl, covered with plastic wrap.

Cook the frozen corn according to the package directions. Season with salt and pepper to taste.

Serve Creamy Potato Soup with Bacon, Steamed Broccoli, and Corn.

Cost $4.91

FRUGAL FACT: *At the start of the fall or winter months, buy an extra bag of onions when they are on sale. Chop all the onions at once and freeze in 1-cup portions in freezer ziplock bags. When it's time to make soup, simply toss the chopped onions into the soup while still frozen.*

TEN

Vegetarian Meals

BBQ Lentils

1 cup green or red lentils ($.40)
1 cup BBQ sauce ($1)
1 tablespoon brown sugar or honey ($.04)
1 garlic clove, crushed ($.10)

1 cup brown rice ($.40)
1 large yellow summer squash or zucchini ($.79)
2 to 3 tablespoons shredded or grated Parmesan cheese ($.15)

In a medium saucepan, bring 1 cup of lentils, 3 cups water, and a dash of salt to a boil. Simmer for 20 minutes, or until the lentils are soft. Once cooked, drain any excess water from the lentils. Mix in the BBQ sauce, brown sugar or honey, and the crushed garlic. Simmer for 4 to 5 minutes.

In another saucepan, bring 2½ cups of water to a boil, add the rice, and bring back to a boil. Reduce the heat, cover, simmer for 40 to 50 minutes. Fluff the rice with a fork before serving.

Slice the squash into ¼-inch rounds and place in the microwave-safe bowl. Cover with plastic wrap and microwave for 4 to 5 minutes, or until the squash is opaque. The cooking time may vary depending on the thickness of the squash rounds. Drain excess water and sprinkle the Parmesan cheese over the hot squash.

Serve BBQ Lentils over Brown Rice with Squash Parmesan.

Cost $2.79

FRUGAL FACT: *Lentils when combined with brown or white rice make a complete protein source.*

Blueberry Wild Rice

1 cup wild rice ($1.50)
3 cups water
2 cups blueberries ($1)
2 tablespoons sugar ($.05)

2 dashes ground cinnamon ($.05)
1 medium butternut squash ($1.09)
2 tablespoons butter ($.10)
1 tablespoon brown sugar ($.05)

In a medium saucepan, cook 1 cup of wild rice with 3 cups of water. Add the blueberries, sugar, and cinnamon. Bring the water and wild rice to a boil. Reduce the heat, cover, and simmer for 30 to 40 minutes, until the wild rice is tender. Fluff the wild rice gently with a fork before serving.

Meanwhile, preheat the oven to 350 degrees. Cut the butternut squash in half lengthwise and place it cut side down in a glass baking dish. Add ¼ inch of water to the baking dish and cover it with aluminum foil. Bake the squash for 50 to 60 minutes. Remove from the oven and let cool for 5 to 10 minutes before handling. Scrape out and discard the seeds, then scrape out the squash flesh. Season warm squash with butter and brown sugar.

Serve Blueberry Wild Rice with Baked Butternut Squash.

Variation: Add 1 cup of dried or fresh cranberries instead of blueberries!

Cost $3.84

FRUGAL FACT: *Stretch this dish a bit further by adding in ¹/₂ cup of white rice plus 1 cup of water to step #1 after the wild rice has been cooking for about 20 minutes. Grab extra blueberries when they're on sale for $1 and freeze them.*

Broccoli-Topped Potatoes

6 large baking potatoes ($1.25)
2 heads broccoli ($.79)
2 tablespoons butter ($.20)
salt and pepper

2 cups shredded Cheddar cheese
 ($1.50)
sour cream for serving ($.25)
½ fresh pineapple ($.99)

Preheat the oven to 400 degrees. Make a few slits in the potatoes using a sharp knife. Wrap the potatoes in aluminum foil and place directly on the oven rack. Bake for 1 hour, or until the potatoes are soft. The cooking time may vary depending on thickness of the potatoes. Remove the potatoes from the oven and let cool.

Cut the broccoli into spears and trim the stems. Steam the broccoli in a stovetop steamer for 4 to 5 minutes, or microwave for 4 to 5 minutes in a microwave-safe bowl, covered with plastic wrap.

Halve and open up the potatoes and fluff the pulp, as if serving a baked potato. Add butter and salt and pepper. Top the potatoes with broccoli pieces and then shredded cheese. If necessary, microwave the potatoes to melt cheese. Serve with sour cream.

Peel and dice the pineapple.

Serve Broccoli-Topped Potatoes with Fresh Pineapple.

Cost $4.96

FRUGAL FACT: *When buying a pineapple, look for a darker yellow-colored pineapple and then smell the bottom of the pineapple. If it has that sweet scent, then it is ready to be eaten! Watch for $1.99 sale price on pineapple during the early spring and throughout the summer.*

Cauliflower Bake

1 large head cauliflower, broken into small pieces ($1.50)

3 tablespoons flour ($.02)

1 container (16 ounces) cottage cheese ($1.79)

salt and pepper

1 cup shredded Cheddar cheese ($.75)

2 peaches ($.79)

In a stovetop steamer, steam the cauliflower pieces for 5 to 6 minutes, or place the cauliflower in a microwave-safe bowl with ½ cup of water. Cover with plastic wrap and microwave for 4 to 5 minutes. Drain excess water.

Preheat the oven to 350 degrees. In a large bowl, mix together the flour, cottage cheese, and salt and pepper. Add the cooked cauliflower and stir to combine.

Place the mixture in 8×8-inch baking dish. Sprinkle the shredded Cheddar cheese over the top. Bake in the preheated oven for 20 minutes, or until the cheese turns golden brown.

Slice the peaches.

Serve Cauliflower Bake with Sliced Peaches.

Cost $4.85

FRUGAL FACT: *Cottage cheese coupons are regularly released in newspaper inserts. Watch for a sale price of $1.50/head for cauliflower.*

Cheese Enchiladas

¼ cup dried black beans, or use frozen previously cooked beans ($.10)
2 tablespoons vegetable oil ($.07)
2 tablespoons cornstarch ($.05)
2 cups homemade Vegetable Stock (page 272) ($.18)
1 can (8 ounces) tomato sauce ($.33)
1 teaspoon salt
2 teaspoons ground cumin ($.07)
1 teaspoon dried oregano ($.05)
1 teaspoon sugar ($.01)
cayenne pepper (optional)
10 taco-size corn tortillas ($.69)
½ onion, chopped ($.15)
3 cups shredded Cheddar cheese ($2.25)
1 cup frozen corn kernels ($.50)
½ homemade Salsa Fresca (page 277) or store-bought salsa ($.25)

Add the beans to a saucepan with 3 cups of water. Boil for 1½ hours, or until tender. Once tender, cool the beans under running cold water in a strainer.

Prepare the enchilada sauce. In a skillet, heat the oil and cornstarch for 1 to 2 minutes, and then whisk in the vegetable broth. Whisk in the tomato sauce, salt, cumin, oregano, and sugar. Let simmer for 5 to 6 minutes before using. If you would like more spice, add cayenne pepper, a half teaspoon at a time, to taste.

Preheat the oven to 350 degrees. Spread about ½ cup of the enchilada sauce in the bottom of an 8×8-inch glass baking dish. Then place a tortilla open in the sauce in the baking dish. Sprinkle with cheese. Roll up the tortilla and lay seam side down in the dish. Repeat using all the tortillas and cheese. Spread the remaining sauce over the top of the enchiladas. Sprinkle with the remaining cheese.

Bake the enchiladas in the preheated oven for 15 to 20 minutes, or until the sauce is bubbling and the cheese has melted.

Cook the frozen corn kernels as directed on the package.

Combine 1 cup of the corn with 1 cup of the cooked beans. Add salsa to the corn and black beans.

Serve Cheese Enchiladas with Corn and Black Bean Salsa.

Cost $4.70

FRUGAL FACT: *Preparing dried beans in a larger batch and then freezing them in smaller 1- or 2-cup portions will save both time and energy in the kitchen.*

Cuban Black Beans and Rice

1 cup dried black beans ($.40)
1 mango ($.79)
2 teaspoons olive oil ($.10)
1 onion ($.30)
2 garlic cloves, crushed ($.10)
1 to 2 teaspoons ground cumin ($.10)
salt and pepper
1 cup white rice ($.20)
4 ears corn ($1)

Soak 1 cup dried black beans overnight, or bring to a boil in a saucepan of water, remove from the heat, and let soak for at least 2 hours in the hot water. Drain and rinse the beans. Add the soaked beans to a medium saucepan with at least 2 inches of water covering them. Bring to a boil. Cover, reduce the heat to medium, and cook for 1½ hours, or until the beans are soft. Reserve 1 cup of the bean cooking liquid, then drain the cooked beans.

Peel the mango and cut away the fresh mango from either side of the pit. Dice the mango into ½-inch pieces.

In a skillet, heat the olive oil, and add onion, garlic, cumin, salt, and pepper and sauté for 3 to 4 minutes. Add the fully cooked beans plus about 1 cup of the reserved liquid. Simmer for 8 to 10 minutes. Remove from the heat and let cool. After about 10 minutes of cooling, add the diced mango pieces to the mixture in the skillet.

In a medium saucepan, bring 2½ cups of water to a boil, add the rice, and bring back to a boil. Reduce the heat, cover, and simmer for 20 minutes. Fluff the rice with a fork before serving.

Remove husks and silk from the ears of corn and boil the corn in large pot for 4 to 5 minutes, or place the ears of corn in microwave-safe baking dish, cover with plastic wrap, and microwave for 7 to 9 minutes.

Serve Cuban Black Beans over Rice and Corn on the Cob.

Cost $2.99

FRUGAL FACT: *Dried beans are not only healthier for you than canned beans; they are more frugal than canned beans!*

Curried Split Peas

1 cup split peas ($.60)
3½ cups water
2 teaspoons salt
2 tablespoons canola oil ($.20)
1 onion, chopped ($.40)
3 garlic cloves, crushed ($.15)
2 tablespoons curry powder or
    3 tablespoons curry paste ($.25)

2 teaspoons ground cumin ($.25)
1 cup white rice ($.20)
3 sweet potatoes ($1.47)
2 tablespoons butter ($.20)
1 teaspoon ground cinnamon ($.02)
sour cream for serving ($.25)

Soak the split peas overnight. If you forget to soak them overnight, add split peas with water to a saucepan and heat to boiling. Remove from the heat and let stand for 1 hour then drain. Bring the split peas and 3 cups of water to boil. Add 1 more cup of water, if necessary. Reduce the heat and simmer 30 to 45 minutes, until soft.

In a skillet, heat the oil. Add the chopped onion and crushed garlic cloves, and sauté about 4 to 5 minutes. Add the curry powder or curry paste, cumin, and salt and sauté another minute. Mix in the cooked split peas and sauté for 1 to 2 more minutes to allow the flavors to infuse. Remove from the heat.

In a medium saucepan, bring 2½ cups of water to a boil, add the rice, and bring back to a boil. Reduce the heat, cover, and simmer for 20 minutes. Fluff the rice with a fork before serving.

Meanwhile, preheat the oven to 350 degrees. Make a few slits in the sweet potatoes using a sharp knife. Put the sweet potatoes in a baking dish with ¼ inch of water and cover with aluminum foil. Bake the sweet potatoes for 1 hour. Remove from the oven and let cool about 10 minutes. Peel off the skins and mash the pulp. Season with cinnamon and butter.

Serve Curried Split Peas over Rice with Mashed Sweet Potatoes.

Cost $3.84

FRUGAL FACT: *Sweet potatoes are at their lowest prices during the major "food holidays," Thanksgiving, Christmas, and Easter. You can buy extra, cook and mash them, and freeze in meal-size portions to use as an an inexpensive vegetable for a future meal.*

Dominican Rice and Beans

1 cup dried red kidney beans ($.40)
1 cup white rice ($.20)
2 tablespoons canola oil ($.15)
2½ cups boiling water
½ teaspoon salt
3 ounces tomato paste (half of small 6 ounce can) (free)
¼ green bell pepper, stemmed, seeded, and diced ($.17)
½ onion, diced ($.15)
1 large sprig fresh cilantro ($.25)
2 teaspoons Adobo Seasoning ($.25)

salt and pepper
2 avocados, peeled and sliced ($1.36)
2 teaspoons lime juice ($.10)

Optional, traditional sides: Avocado slices, fried chicken, tostones (twice-fried plantains), or macaroni salad. Adding these to your meal might push the cost over $5!

Soak the dried kidney beans overnight, or bring to a boil in a saucepan of water, remove from the heat, and let soak for at least 2 hours in the hot water. Drain and rinse the beans. Add the soaked beans to a medium saucepan with at least 2 inches of water covering them. Bring to a boil. Cover, reduce the heat to medium, and cook 1½ hours, or until the beans are soft.

In a saucepan or medium pot, heat the oil. When the oil starts to bubble, add the rice. Stir the rice to coat it with the oil, then stir continuously for approximately 1 minute. Once some rice kernels turn color and start to brown, add 2½ cups of *hot* water, stir well, and season with salt and pepper. Once it returns to a boil, reduce the heat, cover, and cook for 20 minutes.

After the beans have been cooking for about 1 hour, add the tomato paste, diced bell pepper, and diced onion. Add the Adobo seasoning and cilantro sprig (you can remove the cilantro sprig later if you prefer). Let the beans finish cooking for another 30 to 45 minutes.

Cut the avocado in half. Remove the pit. Slice the avocado flesh lengthwise, then scoop out the slices with a spoon. Sprinkle the slices with lime juice.

Serve Dominican Beans over Rice with Avocado Slices and Lime.

Cost $3.02

FRUGAL FACT: *Small cans of tomato paste are often free when on sale and purchased with a coupon! The other half of the can of tomato paste can be added to spaghetti sauce, or another meal with red sauce. It can also be frozen in a plastic container if it won't be used right away.*

Gnocchi and Spinach Bake

2 cups of homemade Basic White
   Sauce (page 276) ($.40)
1 package (16 ounces) vacuum-packed
   potato gnocchi ($1.99)
1 box (10 ounces) frozen chopped
   spinach ($.50)

1 cup shredded Cheddar cheese
   ($.75)
1 pound asparagus ($.99)
1 tablespoon extra-virgin olive oil
   ($.05)

Prepare 2 cups of homemade basic white sauce.

In a medium saucepan, cook the gnocchi in boiling salted water. When all the gnocchi float to the surface, cook for about 2 more minutes. Drain the gnocchi and pour into an 8×8-inch glass baking dish.

Thaw the frozen spinach in the microwave for 4 minutes. Drain excess liquid. Squeeze the spinach and pat dry with paper towels.

Preheat the oven to 350 degrees. Spread the spinach over the gnocchi in the baking dish. Then pour the white sauce over the top and add ½ cup of shredded Cheddar cheese. Stir the ingredients together. Sprinkle the remaining half cup of cheese over the top.

Bake the gnocchi in the preheated oven for 20 minutes, or until the sauce is bubbly and the cheese has melted.

In a skillet, sauté the asparagus in the olive oil for 5 to 6 minutes, stirring every other minute. The asparagus, will be tender-crisp and turn bright green when it is ready to serve. Remove the asparagus from skillet to prevent overcooking.

Serve Gnocchi and Spinach Bake with Sautéed Asparagus.

Cost $4.98

FRUGAL FACT: *The best sale prices for frozen vegetables can be found during the month of March. Don't forget to match with coupons and you can get a box of frozen spinach for just $.50!*

Kusherie *(Egyptian Lentils)*

1 cup elbow macaroni ($.49)
1 cup brown rice ($.40)
1 cup green lentils ($.40)
1 green bell pepper, stemmed, seeded, and diced ($.79)
4 tablespoons canola or vegetable oil ($.14)
1 can (15 ounces) organic tomato sauce ($.24)

1 can (6 ounces) tomato paste ($.33)
1 tablespoon brown sugar ($.05)
2 tablespoons ground cumin ($.20)
salt and pepper
1 teaspoon garlic powder ($.05)
1 white onion ($.30)
4 carrots ($.40)

Clear off stovetop. You will need to use several saucepans and skillets to prepare this meal, but I promise it's all worth it!!!

In a saucepan, cook the elbow macaroni according to the package directions. Drain and set aside.

In another saucepan, cook the brown rice. Bring 2½ cups of water to a boil, add brown rice with a few dashes of salt, and bring the water back to a boil. Reduce the heat to medium-low, cover, and cook for 45 to 50 minutes.

In another saucepan, cook the lentils, with about 4 cups of water, on medium-high heat for 20 minutes. If the water levels get too low, add a cup or so more of water. The lentils are ready when the water has evaporated and the lentils are soft. If the water has not completely evaporated once the lentils have cooked, drain off any excess water. Combine the cooked brown rice and lentils in the pot the lentils cooked in.

In a small skillet, sauté the diced bell peppers in 2 tablespoons of the oil. Add the tomato sauce, and stir in the brown sugar, ground cumin, salt, pepper, and garlic powder. Let simmer about 10 minutes.

When the sauce has finished cooking, pour it into a bowl. Rinse skillet and reuse to brown the onions.

Slice the onions into strips and place in a skillet with the remaining 2 tablespoons of oil. Fry the onions over medium-high heat for about 10 minutes, stirring often, until browned and caramelized.

Add a few spoonfuls of sauce to the cooked elbow macaroni. Place in serving dish. Add the brown rice and lentil mixture next to the macaroni in the serving dish. Top with the remaining tomato sauce, and the caramelized onions.

Peel and cut the carrots into sticks.

Serve *Kusherie*—Egyptian Lentils—with Carrot Sticks!

Cost $3.75

FRUGAL FACT: *Organic canned tomatoes that cost $1.24/can purchased with a $1 coupon are just $.24!*

Lentil Burritos

1 cup brown rice ($.40)
1 cup green lentils ($.40)
1 can (6 ounces) tomato paste ($.19)
½ onion, finely chopped ($.15)
1 packet taco seasoning ($.50), or
    1 teaspoon ground cumin ($.05),
    1 teaspoon chili powder ($.05),
    1 teaspoon garlic powder ($.05),
    1 teaspoon onion powder ($.05)

1 bag taco-size corn or flour tortillas
    ($.69–$1.29)
1 cup shredded Cheddar cheese
    ($.75)
homemade Salsa Fresca (page 277) or
    sour cream for garnish ($.50)
2 cups frozen corn kernels ($1)
salt and pepper

In a medium saucepan, bring 2½ cups of water to a boil, add the brown rice, and bring back to a boil. Reduce the heat, cover, and simmer for 40 to 50 minutes. Fluff the rice with a fork before serving.

In a separate saucepan, bring 3 cups of water to a boil. Add the lentils. Return the water to a boil and cook the lentils for 20 to 30 minutes until tender. Drain excess water.

Combine the cooked rice and lentils in a large saucepan. Add tomato paste plus 2 tomato paste cans worth of water. Stir to combine. Add the onions, the taco seasoning or the ground cumin, chili powder, garlic powder, and onion powder. Let simmer about 10 minutes.

Spoon lentil-rice mixture into each corn or flour tortilla. Sprinkle shredded Cheddar cheese into each. Add salsa and/or sour cream into each burrito. Wrap up as a burrito.

Cook the frozen corn kernels according to the package instructions and season with salt and pepper to taste.

Serve Lentil Burritos with Corn.

Cost $4.54

FRUGAL FACT: *Corn tortillas are generally more inexpensive than wheat tortillas.*

Potato-Spinach Bake

....

6 large white potatoes ($.80)
½ cup milk ($.15)
2 to 3 tablespoons butter ($.25)
salt and pepper
1 teaspoon garlic powder ($.03)
1 box (10 ounces) frozen chopped
    spinach ($.50)

1 cup shredded sharp Cheddar cheese
    ($.75)
8 carrots ($.80)
1 tablespoon extra-virgin olive oil
    ($.10)
2 tablespoons honey ($.15)

Peel and quarter the potatoes. Boil them in water to cover for about 10 minutes, or until tender. Drain and return to the saucepan. Add the milk little by little, the butter, salt, and pepper and mash with a potato masher. (Add the milk 2 tablespoons at a time, until the potatoes reach the desired consistency.) Put mashed potatoes into a 8×8-inch glass baking dish. Preheat the oven to 350 degrees.

Cook the frozen spinach according to the package directions. Drain, squeeze, and pat dry with paper towels.

Distribute the cooked and drained spinach over the top of the potatoes in the baking dish. Sprinkle the cheese over the top of the spinach. Bake in the preheated oven for 20 minutes.

Peel and slice carrots into ⅛- to ¼-inch rounds. To a small saucepan, add ¼ cup water and the olive oil and honey. Add the carrot rounds to the saucepan. Cook 4 to 5 minutes until the carrots have softened slightly and are nicely glazed. Drain excess water.

Serve Potato-Spinach Bake with Honey-Glazed Carrots.

Cost $3.53

FRUGAL FACT: *Buy carrots that are not prepackaged or processed. If you worry about not using all the carrots before they go bad, you can peel them and place them in a plastic container with water to keep them fresh and crunchy.*

Potato-Vegetable Medley

12 small white potatoes ($1.25)
2 tablespoons extra-virgin olive oil
   ($.20)
3 carrots ($.30)
1 onion, quartered ($.30)
salt and pepper

½ cup water or homemade Chicken
   Stock (page 273)
2 small zucchini, diced ($1.58)
2 boxes (10 ounces each) frozen
   spinach ($1)

Preheat the oven to 350 degrees. Wash and scrub the potatoes. Peel, if you prefer peeled potatoes. Cut them into quarters and place in 9×13-inch glass baking dish.

Peel and cut the carrots into 1-inch pieces. Spread potatoes throughout the baking dish.

Peel and quarter the onion. Mix the onion quarters in with the potatoes and carrots. Sprinkle the olive oil over the vegetables. Pour the water or broth over the potatoes and veggies. Sprinkle with salt and pepper, and cover the dish with aluminum foil.

Bake in the preheated oven for 40 minutes. Remove from the oven, add the diced zucchini, return to the oven and bake, uncovered, for another 10 to 15 minutes.

Cook the frozen spinach according to the package directions. Season with salt and pepper to taste.

Serve Potato-Vegetable Medley with Spinach.

Cost $4.63

FRUGAL FACT: *Pair a coupon with a $1 sale price for the boxed spinach and pay $.50 or less per box.*

Sweet and Sour Lentils

....

1 cup green lentils ($.40)

1 teaspoon salt

¼ cup apple juice ($.15)

¼ cup cider vinegar ($.15)

¼ cup brown sugar ($.15)

1 garlic clove, crushed ($.05)

½ onion, chopped ($.15)

1 cup white rice ($.20)

1 zucchini ($.79)

1 tablespoon extra-virgin olive oil ($.10)

To a medium saucepan, add the green lentils and 3 cups water. Bring to boil, and reduce the heat to medium. Cover tightly and simmer for 30 minutes, or until the lentils are tender. Drain excess liquid.

Return the lentils to the saucepan and add the apple juice, vinegar, brown sugar, garlic, and finely chopped onion. Mix well and simmer for 8 to 10 minutes.

In a medium saucepan, bring 2½ cups of water to a boil, add the rice, and bring back to a boil. Reduce the heat, cover, and simmer for 20 minutes. Fluff the rice with a fork before serving.

Wash and slice the zucchini into ⅛-inch rounds. In a small skillet, sauté the zucchini in olive oil, and season with salt and pepper. Sauté for 3 to 4 minutes, turn the zucchini and sauté for another 3 to 4 minutes. The zucchini can also be steamed in the microwave. Place the zucchini rounds in microwave-safe dish with ½ cup of water and cook on high for 4 to 5 minutes, or until the zucchini are translucent.

Serve Sweet and Sour Lentils over Rice with Sautéed Zucchini.

Cost $2.14

FRUGAL FACT: *Not only are lentils an inexpensive source of protein, they are loaded with fiber, complex carbohydrates, folic acid, and other nutrients. They are low in calories, low in fat, and have no cholesterol!*

Twice-Baked Potatoes

6 large baking potatoes ($1.25)
2 tablespoons butter ($.20)
½ cup milk ($.10)
½ cup sour cream (free)
salt and pepper
¼ teaspoon garlic powder ($.03)

1 cup chopped scallions ($.50)
1 cup shredded Cheddar cheese ($.75)
2 heads broccoli ($.79)
homemade Honey Wheat Rolls
   (page 260) ($.50)

Prepare the dough for the rolls in a bread machine or in a mixing bowl.

Preheat the oven to 350 degrees. Scrub the potatoes and pat dry. Slit the potatoes lengthwise. Place them directly onto the oven rack. Bake for 50 to 60 minutes, until soft. Larger potatoes may take longer to cook through.

When the potatoes are cooked, remove them from the oven and let cool about 10 minutes. Cut them in half and scoop out the potato flesh. Set the skins aside for refilling later.

In a large mixing bowl, mash the potatoes and add the butter, milk, and sour cream. Mix with spoon or blend with a hand mixer. Season with salt, pepper, and the garlic powder, and stir through. (Other mix-ins could be chopped cooked bacon pieces, chopped chives, or diced ham for a small additional cost.)

Scoop the mashed potato pulp back into the reserved skins. Sprinkle each potato with half chopped scallions and the shredded Cheddar cheese.

Return the potatoes to the oven and bake at 350 degrees for 20 minutes, or until the cheese has melted.

Remove the stems from the broccoli and separate the broccoli into florets. Steam the florets in a stovetop steamer for 4 to 5 minutes, or microwave for 4 to 5 minutes in a microwave-safe bowl, covered with plastic wrap.

Finish preparing the bread as directed on page 260.

Serve Twice-Baked Potato with Steamed Broccoli and warm homemade Honey Wheat Rolls.

Cost $4.12

FRUGAL FACT: *Sour cream is often on sale for $1 or $1.50. If your grocery store doubles coupons, use the coupons when sour cream is on sale and the sour cream will be free, or just $.50!*

Vegetarian Chili

1 cup dried red kidney and black beans, mixed ($.40)

½ green bell pepper and ½ red bell pepper, stemmed, seeded, and chopped ($1)

1 onion, chopped ($.30)

1 can (15 ounces) crushed tomatoes ($.59)

1 can (8 ounces) tomato sauce ($.33)

2 garlic cloves, crushed ($.10)

3 tablespoons chili powder ($.30)

salt and pepper

1 zucchini ($.79)

2 tablespoons extra-virgin olive oil ($.10)

1 cup shredded Cheddar cheese ($.75)

Soak the beans in water overnight. Drain and rinse.

Place the soaked beans in a slow cooker with 2 cups of water. Add the chopped bell peppers, chopped onion, crushed tomatoes, tomato sauce, crushed garlic, and chili powder, and salt and pepper. Set the slow cooker on low and cook the chili for 8 hours.

Slice the zucchini into ⅛-inch rounds. In a skillet, sauté the zucchini in the olive oil for 5 to 6 minutes. Turn the zucchini over and sauté another 3 minutes, or until the zucchini becomes opaque.

Serve the chili in individual bowls, topped with the shredded Cheddar cheese.

Serve Vegetarian Chili with Sautéed Zucchini.

Cost $4.66

FRUGAL FACT: *Ask your local farmer if and how they sell produce that needs to be sold quickly. See if you can make an arrangement with them to sell you ripe or overly ripe produce for a discount; then use it quickly or chop and freeze it for meals like this one.*

Veggie Lasagna

½ box lasagna noodles, cooked ($.60)
2 cups homemade Spaghetti Sauce
   (page 275) ($.60)
1 large yellow summer squash ($.79)
1 large eggplant ($.99)

4 slices provolone cheese ($.75)
1 cup shredded Cheddar cheese ($.75)
homemade Honey Wheat Rolls
   (page 260) ($.50)

Prepare the dough for the homemade rolls in a bread machine or in a mixing bowl.

Cook the lasagna noodles according to the package directions. Preheat the oven to 350 degrees.

Slice the summer squash and eggplant lengthwise into ⅛-inch strips to layer into the lasagna.

Spread a few spoonfuls of spaghetti sauce on bottom of 9×13-inch glass baking dish. Place a layer of noodles on top of sauce. Place a layer of thin veggies on top, and place 4 provolone slices on top of the veggies. Spread more sauce over cheese. Repeat the layering. Top with the shredded Cheddar cheese. Bake the lasagna in the preheated oven for 30 minutes.

Finish preparing bread as directed in the recipe.

Serve Veggie Lasagna with Homemade Honey Wheat Rolls.

Cost $4.98

FRUGAL FACT: *Late summer would be the perfect time to get these vegetables from your farmers' market or, better yet, free from your own garden!*

Veggie Tacos with Spanish Rice

1 cup white rice ($.20)
½ can (6 ounces) tomato sauce ($.18)
½ to 1 teaspoon ground cumin ($.03)
dash of garlic powder ($.01)
salt and pepper
2 green bell peppers ($1.36)
4 mushrooms ($.50)

1 onion ($.40)
2 teaspoons olive oil ($.10)
8 taco-size corn tortillas ($.55)
1 cup shredded Monterey Jack cheese ($.75)
1 avocado ($.68)
1 teaspoon lemon juice ($.05)

In a medium saucepan, bring 2½ cups of water to a boil, add the rice, and bring back to a boil. Reduce the heat, cover, and simmer for 20 minutes. Fluff the rice with a fork before serving. While the rice is cooking, stir in ½ of a 6-ounce can of tomato paste, the ground cumin, and garlic powder, and season with salt and pepper to taste.

Preheat the oven to 350 degrees. Cut the bell peppers, onions, and mushrooms into strips and/or slices. Sauté in the olive oil until the vegetables are tender, stirring often.

Place the tortillas open on a baking sheet. Top with shredded Jack cheese. Bake in the preheated oven for 10 minutes, or until all the cheese has melted. Remove from the oven, top with the warm sautéed vegetables. Roll up the tortillas and serve.

Slice the avocado into wedges and sprinkle with lemon juice and salt.

Serve the Veggie Tacos with Spanish Rice and Avocado Wedges.

Cost $4.91

FRUGAL FACT: *To keep this dinner under $5, plan to make it during a week when both mushrooms and green peppers are on sale.*

ELEVEN

Homemade Recipes

Homemade Breads, Sauces, and Dressings

Cloverleaf Dinner Rolls

1 cup hot water

3 cups flour ($.42)

1 tablespoon active dry or packet
   yeast ($.25)

1 tablespoon sugar ($.05)

1 teaspoon salt

1 tablespoon oil ($.05)

2 tablespoons butter, melted ($.20)

BY HAND DIRECTIONS

In a mixing bowl, combine the hot water and 1 cup of the flour. Add the yeast, sugar, salt, and oil. Whisk together to make a "spongy" dough. Let sit for 10 to 15 minutes.

Add the remaining 2 cups of flour to the spongy dough and stir with a wooden spoon. When the dough becomes thick enough, knead it by hand for 6 to 8 minutes on a floured surface or in a floured bowl, until it reaches the consistency of soft baby skin. Place in a floured or greased bowl and let rise for 45 minutes to 1 hour.

Once the dough has risen and doubled in size, the dough is ready to be formed. Grease a 12-well muffin tin. Divide the dough ball into 4 smaller balls. Then divide each dough ball into small ½-inch mini balls.

Place three or four ½-inch balls into each greased well in the muffin tin. Once the muffin tin is filled with rolls, brush the tops with melted butter. Set aside and let rise for 20 minutes. Preheat the oven to 350 degrees.

Bake the rolls in the preheated oven for 10 to 15 minutes, or until golden brown on top. Remove the muffin tin from the oven and let the rolls cool on a rack. Serve warm.

BREAD MACHINE DIRECTIONS

Place the ingredients in the order listed, *except for the melted butter,* into the bread machine bowl. Set the machine to the dough cycle. Grease a 12-well muffin tin.

Once the dough cycle is completed, flour your fingers, remove the dough from the bread machine, and place on a floured surface. Knead, and divide the dough into 4 smaller balls. Then divide each dough ball into small ½-inch mini balls.

Place three or four ½-inch balls into each greased well in the muffin tin. Once the muffin tin is filled with rolls, brush the tops with melted butter. Set aside and let rise for 20 minutes. Preheat the oven to 350 degrees.

Bake the rolls in the preheated oven for 10 to 15 minutes, or until golden brown on top. Remove the muffin tin from the oven and let the rolls cool on a rack. Serve warm.

Cost $.97 for 12 rolls

FRUGAL FACT: *If you can comfortably touch the stream of hot water, then it is not too hot to kill the yeast. Water that is too hot can kill the yeast, thus "kill your rolls."*

Honey Wheat Rolls

1 cup hot water
2 cups white flour ($.28)
1 cup wheat flour ($.20)
2 tablespoons honey ($.15)
1 tablespoon or packet active dry yeast
  ($.25)

1 teaspoon sugar ($.02)
1 teaspoon salt
1 tablespoon oil ($.05)

BY HAND DIRECTIONS

In a mixing bowl, combine the hot water with 1 cup of the flour. Add the honey, yeast, sugar, salt, and oil. Whisk together to make a "spongy" dough. Let sit for 10 to 15 minutes. Grease a baking sheet.

Add the remaining 2 cups of flour to the spongy dough and stir with a wooden spoon. When the dough becomes thick enough, knead it by hand for 6 to 8 minutes on a floured surface or in a floured bowl.

Divide the dough ball in half, then again into thirds. Form 12 dough balls into rolls and place on a greased baking sheet. Set aside and let rise for at least 30 minutes in a warm place. Preheat the oven to 350 degrees

Bake the rolls in the preheated oven for 15 to 20 minutes, until golden brown on top. Remove from the oven and let cool on a rack.

Serve warm with butter and honey.

BREAD MACHINE DIRECTIONS

Place the ingredients in the order listed into a bread machine bowl. Set the machine to the dough cycle. Grease a baking sheet.

Once the dough cycle is completed, flour your fingers, remove the dough, and place on a floured surface. Knead the dough for 3 to 4 minutes. Divide the dough ball in half, then again into thirds. Form 12 dough balls into rolls and place on the greased baking sheet. Set aside and let rise for at least 30 minutes in a warm place. Preheat the oven to 350 degrees.

Bake the rolls in the preheated oven for 15 to 20 minutes, until golden brown on top. Remove from the oven and let cool on a rack.

Serve warm with butter and honey.

Cost $.95 for 12 rolls

FRUGAL FACT: *Purchase a large glass jar of yeast instead of the yeast packets for a lower "unit" price on yeast.*

Italian Breadsticks

1 cup plus 2 tablespoons hot water
1 cup whole wheat flour ($.20)
2 cups, white flour ($.28)
2 teaspoons ground flaxseed ($.10)
1 teaspoon salt
2 teaspoons olive oil ($.05)
2 teaspoons sugar ($.02)
1 tablespoon or packet active dry yeast ($.25)

2 teaspoons dried Italian seasoning ($.05)
2 tablespoons grated Parmesan cheese ($.10)
2 tablespoons olive oil for brushing the breadsticks ($.20)
pinches of salt, for sprinkling

BY HAND DIRECTIONS

In a mixing bowl, combine the hot water with 1 cup of the flour. Add the salt, olive oil, flaxseed, sugar, yeast, Italian seasonings, and Parmesan cheese. Whisk together to make "spongy" dough. Let sit for 10 to 15 minutes. Grease a baking sheet.

Add the remaining 2 cups of flour to the spongy dough and stir with wooden spoon. When dough becomes thick enough, knead it by hand for 6 to 8 minutes on a floured surface or in a floured bowl.

Divide the dough ball into 4 medium balls. Then divide each ball into muffin-size balls. With your hands, roll out the balls into skinny, long pieces. Twist 2 pieces together and place on the greased baking sheet. Once all dough has been formed into the twisted sticks, brush with olive oil and sprinkle salt over the top. Set aside and let dough rise for at least 30 minutes in a warm place. Preheat the oven to 350 degrees.

Bake the breadsticks in the preheated oven for 10 to 12 minutes. The baking time will depend on the thickness of your breadsticks. Once they begin to turn golden, they are done. Serve warm.

BREAD MACHINE DIRECTIONS

In a bread machine, add ingredients in the order listed above. Set the machine to dough cycle.

Once the dough cycle is completed, flour your hands and remove the dough from the machine. Place dough on a lightly floured surface. Knead in extra flour, 1 tablespoon at a time, if the dough is sticking to your fingers. Divide the dough into 4 medium balls. Then divide each ball into muffin-size balls. With your hands roll out the balls into skinny, long pieces. Twist 2 pieces together and place on the greased baking sheet. Once all dough has been formed into the twisted sticks, brush with olive oil and sprinkle salt over the tops. Set aside and let the dough rise for at least 30 minutes in a warm place.

Bake at 350 for 10 to 12 minutes. The baking time will depend on the thickness of your breadsticks. Once they begin to turn golden, they are finished. Serve warm.

Cost $1.25 for 10 breadsticks

FRUGAL FACT: *When making homemade fresh bread, use the bread for 2 meals. Eat again the following night or freeze leftovers for future meals.*

French Bread

1 cup hot water

3 cups flour ($.42)

1 tablespoon or packet active dry yeast ($.25)

1 tablespoon sugar ($.05)

1 teaspoon salt

1 tablespoon olive oil ($.10)

BY HAND DIRECTIONS

In a mixing bowl, combine the hot water with 1 cup of the flour. Add the yeast, sugar, salt, and oil. Whisk together to make a "spongy" dough. Let sit for 10 to 15 minutes. Grease a baking sheet.

Add another 1½ cups of flour to the spongy dough and stir with wooden spoon. Then, knead in 2 tablespoons of flour at a time, until the dough can be handled easily and kneaded into a long loaf. Place one long loaf (or 2 shorter loaves) on a greased baking sheet. Cut diagonal 1-inch-long slits along the top of the loaf. Set the loaf aside and let rise for 30 minutes to 1 hour in a warm place.

Preheat the oven to 350 degrees. Bake the loaf for 15 to 20 minutes, until golden brown on top. Remove from oven and let cool on a rack. Slice the loaf when it has partially cooled.

BREAD MACHINE DIRECTIONS

Place the ingredients in the order listed into a bread machine bowl. Set the machine to the dough cycle. Grease a baking sheet.

Once the dough cycle is completed, flour your fingers, remove dough, and place it on a floured surface. Knead in 2 tablespoons of flour at a time, until the dough can be handled easily and kneaded into a long loaf. Place one long loaf (or 2 shorter loaves) on the greased baking sheet. Cut diagonal 1-inch-long slits along the top of the loaf. Set the loaf aside and let rise for 30 minutes to an hour in a warm place.

Preheat the oven to 350 degrees. Bake the loaf for 15 to 20 minutes, until golden brown on top. Remove the loaf from the oven and let cool on a rack. Slice the loaf when it has partially cooled.

Cost $.82 for 1 large or 2 small loaves

FRUGAL FACT: *Use leftover slices for sandwiches or paninis for lunch the following day. Stale or three-day-old French bread can be brought back to life in an egg or breakfast casserole.*

Hamburger or Hot Dog Buns

1 cup hot water
2 cups white flour ($.28)
1 cup whole wheat flour ($.20)
1 tablespoon or package active dry
   yeast ($.25)

1 teaspoon sugar ($.02)
1 teaspoon salt
1 tablespoon canola oil ($.05)
1 tablespoon butter, melted ($.10)
2 tablespoons milk ($.02)

BY HAND DIRECTIONS

In a mixing bowl, combine the hot water with 1 cup of the white flour. Add the yeast, sugar, salt, and oil. Whisk together to make a "spongy" dough. Let sit for 10 to 15 minutes.

Add other 1 cup of white flour plus 1 cup of wheat flour to the spongy dough and stir with a wooden spoon. When the dough becomes thick enough, knead it for 6 to 8 minutes on a floured surface or in a floured bowl, until it reaches the consistency of soft baby skin. Place the dough in a floured or greased bowl and let rise for 45 minutes to 1 hour.

Once the dough has risen and doubled in size, the dough is ready to be formed. Grease a baking sheet. Divide the dough ball in half, and then divide the 2 dough balls into thirds. Form smaller dough balls into bun shapes. Remember the dough will rise again, so "flat" buns are okay. Place the buns on the greased baking sheet. Set aside and let the buns rise for at least 30 minutes in a warm place. Preheat the oven to 350 degrees.

Bake the buns in the preheated oven for 20 to 25 minutes, until slightly golden on top. Remove the buns from the oven, brush the tops with melted butter, and return to oven for 2 minutes. Remove and let cool on a rack. Cool slightly before slicing.

BREAD MACHINE DIRECTIONS

Place the ingredients in the order listed, *except for the melted butter*, into a bread machine bowl. Set the machine to the dough cycle.

Once the dough cycle is complete, flour your fingers, remove the dough and place it on a floured surface. Shape into hamburger or hot dog bun–sizes. Place the buns on the greased baking sheet. Set aside and let the buns rise for at least 30 minutes in a warm place. Preheat the oven to 350 degrees.

Bake the buns in the preheated oven for 20 to 25 minutes, until slightly golden on top. Remove the buns from the oven, brush the tops with melted butter, and return to the oven for 2 minutes. Remove and let cool on a rack. Cool slightly before slicing.

Cost $.92 for 8 to 10 buns

FRUGAL FACT: *Yeast can be stored for up to 1 year in the freezer.*

Zucchini-Pineapple Bread

3 eggs ($.30)
1 cup sugar ($.15)
1 cup applesauce ($.25)
2 teaspoons vanilla extract ($.10)
3 cups flour ($.42)
1 teaspoon baking powder ($.05)
1 teaspoon baking soda ($.05)

1 teaspoon salt
1 cup chopped walnuts ($.79)
2 cups shredded or diced zucchini
   ($.79)
8½ ounce (half a 15-ounce can)
   crushed pineapple, drained ($.49)

Preheat the oven to 350 degrees. Grease two 9×5-inch loaf pans or one 9×13-inch baking dish.

In a large bowl, cream together the eggs, sugar, applesauce, and vanilla. Add the flour, baking powder, baking soda, and salt. Mix well. Fold in the walnuts and the shredded or diced zucchini and drained crushed pineapple. Pour the batter into the prepared loaf pans.

Bake the bread for 50 to 60 minutes in the loaf pan, or for 25 to 30 minutes in the 9×13-inch baking dish, or until knife inserted in the center comes out clean. Cool the loaves on a rack. Serve warm or cold.

Cost $3.39 for 2 loaves

FRUGAL FACT: *Place diced zucchini pieces in freezer ziplock bags and freeze for use in future zucchini breads. To use the entire can of crushed pineapples, double the recipe and either freeze the extra loaves, or give them to a neighbor or friend in need, or share at a brunch or potluck.*

Fruit or Veggie Muffins

2 eggs ($.20)
3 tablespoons vegetable oil ($.15)
⅓ cup sugar ($.05)
1 cup mashed or grated fruit or veggie * ($.50)
½ cup whole wheat flour ($.20)
½ cup white flour ($.15)
½ teaspoon baking soda ($.02)
1 teaspoon baking powder ($.05)
1 teaspoon ground cinnamon ($.05)
½ cup chopped nuts (optional)

- *Mashed fruit and vegetable ideas: Butternut squash, sweet potatoes*

- *Grated fruit and vegetable ideas: Apples, pears, carrots, zucchinis*

- *Chopped fruit ideas: Strawberries, raspberries, blueberries, blackberries*

Preheat the oven to 350 degrees. Grease two 12-well mini muffin tins or one 12-well (or two 6-well) regular muffin tin.

In a bowl, combine the eggs, oil, sugar, and 1 cup mashed fruit or veggie. Whisk until creamy.

Add the flours, baking soda, baking powder, and cinnamon. Mix well until it forms a batter. Fold in the nuts, if using.

Using an ice cream scoop, fill the muffin tins with the batter. The ice cream scoop will help reduce the mess of batter often left on top of the pans.

For 24 mini muffins, bake for 8 to 10 minutes. For regular muffins, bake for 15 to 20 minutes, or until the tops are golden and toothpick inserted in the center comes out clean.

Cool the muffins on a rack, and then serve to hungry little people!

You can double the recipe and experiment with different combinations of fruits and vegetables. Carrot-Apple Muffins, Zucchini-Squash Muffins *(The kids will never know it!)*

Cost $1.37 for 24 mini muffins or 12 regular muffins

FRUGAL FACT: *These mini muffins freeze well. They thaw in just minutes on the counter, or seconds in the microwave! A tasty snack!*

Banana Bread

2 medium, ripe bananas ($.30)
½ cup sugar ($.10)
1 cup applesauce ($.25)
2 eggs ($.20)

1 cup whole wheat flour ($.28)
¾ cup white flour ($.15)
1 teaspoon baking soda ($.05)
½ teaspoon salt

Preheat the oven to 375 degrees. Grease a 9×5-inch loaf pan.

In a large mixing bowl or stand mixer, mix the bananas, sugar, applesauce, and eggs, until creamy. Add the flours, baking soda, and salt and mix until a batter forms.

Pour the batter into the prepared loaf pan and bake for 50 to 55 minutes, or until a knife inserted in the center comes out clean. Remove the bread from the oven and place on a cooling rack. Serve the bread warm with butter, or cold.

Cost $1.33 for 1 loaf

FRUGAL FACT: *Got brown bananas? Brown, overly ripe bananas make the best and most moist banana bread. If you can't use the brown bananas right away, peel them and freeze them. Thaw completely before adding to this recipe. Buy extra bananas when they are on sale for prices like $.30/pound. Peel the bananas and cut in half. Freeze the banana halves on a rimmed baking sheet and then transfer to freezer ziplock bags. Toss the frozen bananas into the blender for quick smoothies.*

Homemade Stock

Making your own stock ranges from $.10/cup to FREE! Even with using coupons and matching with sale prices, canned or boxed broth cannot be bought for cheaper than that. Plus, homemade stock is preservative-free!

Vegetable Stock

....

2 cups of leftover vegetables or
   peelings* ($.50)
6 cups water

2 teaspoons freshly ground black
   pepper
1 bay leaf ($.05)

Suggested vegetables and their peelings to use when making vegetable stock: Potatoes, sweet potatoes, onions, garlic, carrots, celery, peas, empty corn cobs, green beans, green onions, and herbs. Asparagus, tomatoes, broccoli, cauliflower tend to be overpowering flavors in the stock, but do not have to be avoided.

Wash and rinse all the vegetables, peelings, and any other vegetable parts. Add to a large saucepan and add water, black pepper, and a bay leaf.

Simmer the stock for 1 hour. Remove from heat and let cool. Strain out any vegetable pieces. Let the stock cool completely before freezing.

Freeze vegetable stock in freezer ziplock bags or small 1- or 2-cup portion plastic, freezer-safe containers. Leave some air space in the baggie or container, as the stock will expand as it freezes.

Cost $.55 for approximately 6 cups, or $.09/cup

FRUGAL FACT: *Making homemade vegetable stock is a great way to use up vegetable pieces or whole vegetables that otherwise might be thrown out.*

Chicken Stock

leftover whole chicken carcass or
    leftover chicken bones or other
    chicken parts, such as the neck
    or back
water

1 onion, chopped ($.30)
2 celery stalks, chopped ($.20)
2 garlic cloves ($.10)
fresh whole black peppercorns

Add the chicken carcass, pieces, and/or bones to a large saucepan with the chopped onion, celery, garlic, and peppercorns.

Cover with at least 1 inch of water. Bring to a boil, reduce the heat, cover, and simmer over low heat for 2 hours.

Remove the stock from the heat and let cool. Strain out the chicken pieces and bones. Let the stock cool completely before freezing.

Freeze the chicken stock in freezer ziplock bags or small 1- or 2-cup portion plastic, freezer-safe container. Leave some air space in the baggie or container, as the stock will expand as it freezes.

Cost $.60 for approximately 6 cups of stock, or $.10/cup

FRUGAL FACT: *Stock can be partially thawed in a bowl of water in the refrigerator, then added to a saucepan to finish thawing.*

Beef Broth

3 to 4 pounds bone-in, beef roast
2 cups water
2 potatoes, peeled and quartered ($.30)

1 onion, quartered ($.30)
2 carrots ($.20)

Add the beef roast and 2 cups of water to the insert of a slow cooker. Add the potatoes, carrots, and onions around the beef roast. Set the slow cooker on low, and cook the roast for 8 hours.

When the roast has finished cooking, remove the beef roast and serve as a meal with the potatoes, carrots, and onions.

Strain the juices from the slow cooker and let the broth cool completely before freezing.

Freeze the beef broth in freezer ziplock bags or small 1- or 2-cup portion plastic, freezer-safe containers. Leave some air space in the baggie or container, as the stock will expand as it freezes.

Since you use the beef and vegetables in other recipes or meals, I'm going to say that this broth is "free" since all you're adding is water.

Cost $ FREE

FRUGAL FACT: *If you want smaller portions than the recommended 1- or 2-cup portions, freeze the broth into ice cube trays, then transfer the cubes to freezer ziplock bags once they are frozen. The cubes yield 2 to 3 tablespoons of stock or broth.*

Homemade Spaghetti Sauce

....

1 can (28 ounces) crushed tomatoes ($.79)
2 garlic cloves, crushed ($.10)
1 tablespoon dried basil ($.10)
1 tablespoon dried oregano ($.10)

1 tablespoon dried rosemary ($.10)
1 tablespoon extra-virgin olive oil ($.10)
salt and pepper

To a medium saucepan, add the crushed tomatoes, crushed garlic, basil, oregano, rosemary, olive oil, and salt and pepper to taste.

Simmer the sauce for 15 minutes, to allow the herbs and flavors to infuse.

The sauce can be stored for a week in the refrigerator, 6 months in the freezer, or indefinitely if canned.

Cost $1.39 for 4 cups

FRUGAL FACT: *Grow one pot of "Spaghetti Sauce Herbs" with basil, oregano, and rosemary. Don't let extra herbs go to waste—make a large batch of sauce and freeze in 2- or 3-cup portions.*

Homemade Basic White Sauce

....

4 tablespoons butter ($.40)　　　**3 cups milk ($.30)**
6 tablespoons flour ($.10)　　　　**salt and pepper**

In a medium saucepan, melt the butter over medium heat. Add the flour and whisk with the melted butter until it forms a paste and bubbles.

Whisk in the milk (or other specified liquids). Whisk until flour and butter have dissolved into the milk.

Cook the sauce over medium heat for 5 to 6 minutes, stirring continuosly. The sauce will begin to thicken, as it bubbles and cooks. (To reach the desired consistency of the sauce you need for your meal, add the milk or flour, 1 tablespoon at a time. To make the sauce thicker, whisk in more flour. To make the sauce thinner, whisk in more milk. Once the sauce reaches the desired consistency, use it in the meal as directed.)

Variations:

Cream of Chicken: Use 2 cups of milk and 1 cup of chicken broth in place of the 3 cups of milk.

Cream of Mushroom: Add 1 can (6 ounces) chopped mushrooms to the basic white sauce.

Cream of Celery: Use 2 cups of milk, 1 cup of vegetable broth in place of the 3 cups milk, and add 1 cup of finely chopped celery.

Cost $.80 for 4 cups

FRUGAL FACT: *Making your own white sauce is not only cheaper than buying a prepared sauce, but also by making your own sauce you eliminate many of the preservatives and sodium found in the prepared products.*

Salsa Fresca (Fresh Salsa)

6 large tomatoes ($2)
2 serrano chiles ($.79)
3 garlic cloves, crushed ($.15)

½ onion, quartered ($.15)
2 teaspoons olive oil ($.05)

Quarter the tomatoes and place in a food processor or blender.

Cut the stems off the chiles. Remove some seeds if you prefer a milder salsa. Add chiles, crushed garlic, quartered onions, and olive oil to the food processor or blender.

Blend or puree until the salsa reaches the desired consistency.

Serve the salsa with chips, or use when cooking or in recipes that call for salsa, like Cheese Enchiladas (page 236) and Lentil Burritos (page 246).

Cost $3.04 for 2 to 3 cups of salsa

FRUGAL FACT: *If you don't have space for a garden, consider growing a hot pepper plant in a medium pot on an outdoor table.*

Salsa Verde (Green Salsa)

1 pound tomatillos ($1.99)

1 jalapeño pepper ($.79)

2 garlic cloves, crushed ($.10)

1 teaspoon lemon juice ($.05)

1 teaspoon sugar ($.02)

½ teaspoon salt

Preheat the oven to 450 degrees. Peel the dried skin off the tomatillos. Cut the tomatillos in half, place cut side down in a baking dish and roast for 10 to 15 minutes, until softened. Let cool 5 minutes.

Place the cooled, roasted tomatillos in a blender or food processor along with the jalapeño pepper, crushed garlic, lemon juice, sugar, and salt. Blend to the desired consistency.

Store the salsa in the refrigerator for 1 week or freeze in 1-cup portions.

Use Salsa Verde in Sour Cream Chicken Enchiladas (page 125) or Cowboy Beans and Rice (page 170).

Cost $2.95 for 2 to 3 cups

FRUGAL FACT: *Because tomatillos are expensive, ask a local farmers' market if they have any ripe or overly ripe tomatillos that they wish to sell at a reduced price.*

Guacamole

2 avocados ($1)

1 tomato, seeded and diced ($.39)

2 garlic cloves, crushed ($.10)

1 teaspoon ground cumin ($.05)

1 teaspoon lemon juice ($.05)

salt and pepper

Cut the avocado in half lengthwise. Use a spoon or knife to remove the pit. Remove any browned spots, if necessary. Then, scoop out the avocado flesh with spoon and mash well with fork.

Add the seeded and diced tomato, crushed garlic, ground cumin, lemon juice, and salt and pepper to taste.

Other mix-in ideas: 2 to 3 tablespoons sour cream, 1 to 2 tablespoons taco seasoning.

Cost $1.59 for 2 cups of guacamole

FRUGAL FACT: *When selecting an avocado, press the avocado gently. If your thumb can press into the flesh, then it will be ripe soon. Do not buy hard avocados. The softer the avocado, the riper the fruit, and it will be ready to eat right away. A great sale price for avocado is $.50 each.*

Homemade Dressings

Making your own dressing is just plain healthier than using store-bought dressings. Your own dressings are preservative-free and simply taste fresher. I bet you'd be surprised that you have most of the ingredients in your pantry or refrigerator already.

Basic Vinaigrette

¼ cup vinegar ($.20)
½ cup extra-virgin olive oil ($.75)
1 teaspoon lemon juice ($.05)
1 garlic clove, crushed ($.05)

1 teaspoon sugar ($.02)
1 teaspoon dried basil ($.03)
salt and pepper

In a small bottle or plastic container, shake the vinegar, olive oil, lemon juice, crushed garlic, sugar, basil, and salt and pepper to taste.

Cost $1.10

Balsamic Vinaigrette

4 tablespoons balsamic vinegar
   ($.25)
½ cup extra-virgin olive oil ($.75)

1 garlic clove, crushed ($.05)
salt and pepper

In a small bottle or plastic container, shake the balsamic vinegar, olive oil, crushed garlic, and salt and pepper to taste.

Cost $1.05

Dijon Vinaigrette

....

3 tablespoons vinegar ($.15)   2 tablespoons Dijon mustard ($.10)
½ cup extra-virgin olive oil ($.75)   salt and pepper

In a small bottle or plastic container, shake the vinegar, olive oil, Dijon mustard, and salt and pepper to taste.

Cost $1.00 for ¾ cup

Honey-Mustard Salad Dressing

....

1 teaspoon vinegar ($.05)   ½ cup honey ($.75)
¼ cup mustard or Dijon mustard ($.20)   salt and pepper

In a small bottle or plastic container, shake the vinegar, mustard, honey, and salt and pepper to taste.

Add 1 tablespoon of milk for creamier dressing.

Cost $1.00 for ¾ cup

Greek Salad Dressing

....

½ cup vinegar ($.25)   1 teaspoon onion powder ($.05)
¼ cup extra-virgin olive oil ($.38)   salt and pepper
1 teaspoon dried basil ($.05)   2 tablespoons feta cheese ($.50)
1 teaspoon garlic powder ($.05)

In a small bottle or plastic container, shake the vinegar, olive oil, basil, garlic powder, onion powder, and salt and pepper to taste. Add the feta cheese and shake for 10 to 15 more seconds.

Cost $1.28

Grill Marinades and Rubs

Marinades, rubs, and brines are designed to infuse flavor into meats and create a perfectly tender and tasty grilled meat for your dinner plate.

FISH
Ginger Salmon Marinade

3 tablespoons soy sauce ($.20)   2 tablespoons canola oil ($.10)
1 teaspoon ground ginger ($.05)   salt and pepper

In a small bottle or plastic container, shake the soy sauce, ground ginger, oil, and salt and pepper.

Pour over 4 salmon fillets. Let marinate for at least 30 minutes in the refrigerator before grilling.

Cost $.35

Shrimp Marinade

....

2 garlic cloves, crushed ($.10)   salt and pepper
3 tablespoons butter, melted ($.30)

In a small bowl, whisk the crushed garlic with the melted butter and season with salt and pepper to taste.

Brush the butter over the shrimp and let marinate at least 30 minutes in the refrigerator. Grill shrimp.

Cost $.40

CHICKEN
Rosemary Rub

....

1 teaspoon extra-virgin olive oil ($.03)   1 garlic clove, crushed ($.05)
1 tablespoon chopped, fresh   salt and pepper
   rosemary ($.10)

Combine all the ingredients in a small bowl.

Rub the marinade directly onto the chicken pieces. Marinate at least 30 minutes in the refrigerator before grilling.

Cost $0.18

Honey-Mustard Marinade

....

¼ cup honey ($.28)   ½ teaspoon vinegar ($.02)
3 tablespoons mustard ($.15)

In a small bowl, whisk together the honey, mustard, and vinegar. Brush onto the chicken pieces.

Let the chicken marinate for at least 30 minutes in the refrigerator before grilling.

Cost $.45 for ½ cup

Homemade BBQ Marinade

....

1 can (6 ounces) tomato paste ($.19)   1 tablespoon brown sugar ($.05)
1 teaspoon vinegar ($.05)   1 teaspoon black pepper
1 tablespoon mustard ($.05)

Place the tomato paste and ½ tomato paste can of water in a small bowl. Whisk together. Add the vinegar, mustard, brown sugar, and pepper. Mix well and pour over chicken pieces.

Let the chicken marinate for at least 30 minutes in the refrigerator before grilling.

Cost $.34

FRUGAL FACT: *Use a coupon when buying the tomato paste.*

BEEF
Basic Steak Marinade

....

½ cup red wine vinegar ($.20)   1 tablespoon kosher salt ($.05)
3 tablespoons extra-virgin olive oil ($.30) 1 teaspoon sugar ($.05)
2 garlic cloves, crushed ($.10)   1 teaspoon black pepper

In a small bottle, shake the vinegar, olive oil, crushed garlic, kosher salt, sugar, and pepper. Pour over the steaks.

Let the steaks marinate for at least 30 minutes in the refrigerator before grilling.

Cost $.70

Steak Rub

....

2 tablespoons kosher salt ($.10)
2 tablespoons freshly ground black
   pepper ($.10)

1 teaspoon paprika ($.05)
1 teaspoon garlic powder ($.05)
1 teaspoon onion powder ($.05)

In a plastic ziplock bag, toss all the ingredients together. Rub directly onto steaks and cover with aluminum foil.

Refrigerate the steaks overnight and grill the following afternoon.

Cost $.35

PORK
Spicy Ribs Rub

....

1 tablespoon cayenne pepper ($.10)
1 tablespoon brown sugar ($.10)
1 tablespoon garlic powder ($.10)

1 tablespoon chili powder ($.10)
1 tablespoon paprika ($.10)
salt and pepper

In a plastic ziplock bag, toss all the ingredients together. Rub over pork ribs and wrap the ribs in aluminum foil.

Refrigerate the ribs overnight and grill the following afternoon.

Cost $.50

Apple Juice Pork Chop Brine

1 cup water
1 cup apple juice ($.15)
2 tablespoons salt

In a bottle, combine the water, apple juice, and salt. Shake until the salt dissolves.

Place the pork chops in shallow baking dish just large enough to hold all the chops in one layer. Pour the apple juice brine over the chops.

Refrigerate the chops for at least 4 hours. Remove from the baking dish and rinse. Pat dry, and grill.

Cost $.15

APPENDIX A

Another aspect of saving money and time when planning and making meals is having an organized and fully stocked kitchen. By utilizing certain electronic kitchen appliances and kitchen gadgets, time will be saved and frustrations reduced. By having "the basic" ingredients in my stockpile, I don't find myself thinking *I just don't have anything to cook today, so I'll have to run out for takeout.*

Below are my recommendations for "must haves" in the kitchen drawers, cabinets, and cupboards.

Essential Kitchen Gadgets

Slow Cooker
Bread Machine
Blender or Food Processor
Mini Chopper
Stand or hand mixer

Mixing bowls
Measuring cups and spoons
Mixing and serving spoons
Spatulas
Plastic scrapers

Cookie sheets
Square and rectangular baking dishes
Muffin tins—miniature to jumbo
Pizza pan or baking stone
Dutch oven or stockpot
Small, medium, and large saucepans
Skillet or frying pan
Stovetop steamer

Cheese grater
Garlic press
Slotted serving spoons
Wooden spoons
Kitchen shears
Chef's knife (8 to 10 inches)
Paring knife
Plastic and wood cutting boards

Pantry Essentials

FREEZER

Chicken breasts
Ground beef
Ground turkey
(Any favorite meat cuts that are not
    to be used right away)
Frozen vegetables
Frozen fruit
Breads that are not to be used right away

Sandwich Spread
Vinegar—white, cider, balsamic
Natural peanut butter
Natural jelly
Pickles

BAKING

White flour
Whole wheat flour
Baking powder
Baking soda
Salt
Unsweetened cocoa
Granulated sugar
Brown sugar
Confectioners' sugar
Honey
Stevia
Shortening
Oil
Flavored extracts, including vanilla

REFRIGERATOR

Milk
Eggs
Cheese—sliced, bar, shredded, grated
Deli meats
Butter or margarine
Yogurt
Fresh fruits
Fresh vegetables
Ketchup
Mustard
Mayonnaise

PANTRY/CUPBOARD

Bread
Tortillas
Buns
Dried beans
Canned beans—No Salt Added
Canned tuna
Canned tomatoes
White rice
Brown rice
Pasta, a variety—white and
    whole wheat
Pasta sauces
Tomato sauce

Tomato paste
Salsa
Herbs and spices
Olive oil

OTHER COOKING SUPPLIES

Aluminum foil
Plastic wrap
Freezer ziplock bags
Napkins
Paper towels

APPENDIX B

Today there exist hundreds, if not thousands, of resources on the Internet that help consumers save money, including my Web site, $5 Dinners.com or www.5dollardinners.com. My site has current resources for meal planning, couponing, and grocery store coupon matchups.

Below is a list of Web sites where coupons can be printed directly from the site, as well as information on how to find a blogger in your area who posts coupon matchups for your store, plus where to find details on recommended daily food requirements.

COUPONING RESOURCES

www.coupons.com
www.smartsource.com
www.redplum.com
www.hotcouponworld.com
www.slickdeals.net
www.couponmom.com

Grocery Store Coupon Matchups

Also, hundreds of bloggers post coupon matchups each week for hundreds of different stores across the country. To find a blogger in your area who offers this free service, simply "Google" your city's name and the phrase "frugal blog" or "grocery store coupon matchups."

By taking the time to explore these great online resources and make grocery lists and meal plans based on the sale items and coupon matchups, you are sure to start reducing your weekly grocery bill.

PORTION SIZES AND RECOMMENDED DAILY FOOD REQUIREMENTS

http://www.mypyramid.gov/mypyramid/index.aspx

INDEX

AS SIDE DISH: Beef Burrito Skillet, 134; Beef Fajitas, 138; Beef Goulash, 56; Beef Tacos, 141; Cheese Enchiladas, 236–37; Chicken Potato Pie, 101; Chicken Quesadillas with Corn and Black Bean Salsa, 122–23; Chicken Succotash, 102; Chicken Tortilla Soup, 210; Chicken Verde and Spanish Rice, 108; Cowboy Beans and Rice, 170; Creamy Potato Soup, 228–29; Cuban Black Beans and Rice, 238–39; Grilled Margarita Chicken, 115; Grilled Pork Chops, 175; Jerk Turk–Island Turkey, 113; Lentil Burritos, 246; Meat and Potato Lasagna, 153; Mexican Bean Soup, 223; Mexican Rice Casserole, 156; Orange Beef and Broccoli Stir-Fry, 157; Pickapeppa Beef Stew, 226; Pork and Beans, 181–82; Roasted Bell Pepper Rotini, 61; Round Steak and Mashed Potatoes, 164; Simple Cheeseburgers, 143; Sour Cream Chicken Enchiladas, 125; Southwest Chicken Pasta Salad, 62–63; Spaghetti, 64; Tex-Mex Chicken, 128; Tex-Mex Chili, 163
cottage cheese, in Cauliflower Bake, 235
Coupon Mom, Stephanie Nelson, 17, 18, 21, 22–24, 25
coupons
    etiquette, 23–24
    finding, 18–20
    fine print on, 21–23
    as free-money equivalents, 16–17
    matching with sale prices, 8
    misconceptions about, 17–18
    organizing, 20–21
    stockpiling principles, 26–29
    store policies on, 24–26
couscous, to accompany Beef Curry with Raisins, 135
Cowboy Beans and Rice, 170
Cowboy's Pie, 148
Cranberry and Beef Stew, 215
Cranberry Pork Chops, 171
Cuban Black Beans and Rice, 238–39
Curried Pumpkin Soup, 212
Curried Split Peas, 240

Deep Dish Pizza Potpie, 81–82
Dijon Vinaigrette, 281
Dinner Rolls, Cloverleaf, 258–59
Dominican Rice and Beans, 241–42
dressings. *See* salad dressings

eggplant, in Veggie Lasagna, 255
Eggplant, Rotelle Pasta with, 73–74
Enchiladas, Beef, 136–37
Enchiladas, Cheese, 236–37

Fajitas, Beef, 138
Fajitas, Slow Cooker Chicken, 98
feta cheese
    Greek Pasta Salad, 60
    Greek Salad Dressing, 281–82
Fettuccine Alfredo, 59
fish and seafood. *See specific types*
French Bread, 264–65
Fruit or Veggie Muffins, 269–70

Garden Fresh Chili, 150
Garden Pasta Salad, Summer, 55
Garlic Pork Chops, 173
Ginger Chicken Stir-Fry, 106
Ginger–Sweet Potato Chicken Bake, 107
Gnocchi and Spinach Bake, 243
Grammy's Pasta Salad, 54
great northern beans, in White Chicken Chili, 130
Greek Pasta Salad, 60
Greek Salad Dressing, 281–82
green beans
    Hearty Beef Stew, 208
    AS SIDE DISH: Apple-Walnut Pork, 167; Bacon-Wrapped Apple Chicken, 92; Beef and Cranberry Stew, 215; Cajun-Seasoned Pork Chops, 183; Chicken and Sweet Potato Stew, 209; Chili-Cornbread Cups, 146–47; Curried Pumpkin Soup, 212; Garlic Pork Chops, 173; Ginger Chicken Stir-Fry, 106; Ginger–Sweet Potato Chicken Bake, 107; Lemon Chicken on Pasta, 114; Lentil-Mashed Potato Bake, 247; Mango Chicken, 116; Maple Chicken, 117; Peachy Pork Chops, 180;